CROSSCURRENTS *Modern Critiques*

CROSSCURRENTS *Modern Critiques*
Harry T. Moore, *General Editor*

*Siegfried Mandel*

# Rainer Maria Rilke
## THE POETIC INSTINCT

WITH A PREFACE BY

*Harry T. Moore*

Carbondale and Edwardsville

SOUTHERN ILLINOIS UNIVERSITY PRESS

For Dorothy, Elise and Theo

Copyright © 1965 by Southern Illinois University Press
All rights reserved
Library of Congress Catalog Card Number 65–12390
Printed in the United States of America
Designed by Andor Braun

# PREFACE

RAINER MARIA RILKE is one of the few great poets of our time, as this new book about him by Siegfried Mandel so convincingly demonstrates. But this is more than just another book emphasizing Rilke's importance: it takes the reader more intimately through the Rilkean experience than any volume I have seen in English (and as the editor of an Anchor Book of Selected Letters of Rainer Maria Rilke, mentioned in Mr. Mandel's bibliography, I have read a great deal about this poet). The present book is the kind which Southern Illinois University Press is delighted to add to its Crosscurrents / Modern Critiques series.

In Boulder, Colorado, in 1963 I had the pleasure of reading parts of this volume as it was being written, and several times at Mr. Mandel's home I saw the pages of its manuscript in his typewriter. The excitement of that early acquaintance with the book has been intensified by my latest reading of it, just now, in galley proof; and I look forward to going through it many times again and referring to it often.

I can't resist mentioning one recent incident that has nothing to do with this volume but is at least remotely concerned with Rilke. Several years ago, during one of the series of meetings held by the Modern Language Association, I was in a smoke-filled and noisy New York hotel room at one of the publishers' parties which enliven the M.L.A. evenings. While talking to Harold Humes, the novelist and Paris Review editor, I noticed a solitary figure standing alone at one side of the crowd, holding a drink. I said to Humes, "Doesn't that fellow over there look like Rilke?" Humes agreed—there were the oriental-looking eyes, the mandarin's moustache, the whole Rilkean face. Humes suggested, "Let's go over and tell him." Since everyone is excessively friendly at publishers' parties at M.L.A., we stepped across to the stranger and one of us said, "Pardon me, but do you know you look like Rilke?" The stranger seemed a little surprised, but said, "I knew him." This hardly seemed possible, for the man we were talking to in the late 1950s didn't look old enough to have known a man who had died in 1926. One of us said, "You knew him?" "Oh yes," the stranger said, "I was his lawyer." "His lawyer?" I said. "But Rilke wasn't the type to have a lawyer—he'd avoid lawsuits and lawcourts, and he had little or no practical business for anyone to watch over; it doesn't seem possible." "But I was his lawyer," the stranger insisted, firmly but affably. "I never thought I looked like him, though—I was his lawyer at the time he was defeated in the Wisconsin primary." A great light of understanding broke over Humes and me, and after a few more pleasantries we left the Rilke-like gentleman, who we subsequently learned was the publishing company's attorney. Humes and I a little later ran into the poet Elder Olson, who listened patiently to our laughing account of the episode, and when we had finished he commented, "The trouble with you two is that you don't know how to pronounce R-R-R-R-ilke"—he gutturally came out the most echt Deutsch utterance possible. Well, maybe—anyhow, perhaps there is now a legend to the effect that Rilke, who was horrified at the thought of America's noise and never visited this country, was a guest at one of the publishers' brouhaha parties at M.L.A.!

One more note of reminiscence, definitely connected with the present book, concerns Edith Hutton, mentioned in Mr. Mandel's Acknowledgments section as having lived in the same house in which Rilke occupied a flat in Munich at the time of World War I. Mr. Mandel met Mrs. Hutton in a place far removed from Munich: Taos,

New Mexico. In the spring of 1963, I went to Taos with Siegfried Mandel and his artist-wife Dorothy—they had never been there before—and we paid appropriate tribute to the memory of D. H. Lawrence, visiting his ranch, calling on his friend the Hon. Dorothy Brett, and going to see Saki Karavas's collection of paintings at the La Fonda hotel, just now the largest single group of Lawrence's pictures. Saki Karavas kindly took us to dine at La Doña Luz, which must certainly be one of the world's finest restaurants. It is owned by an immense Germanic figure, Theodor Hutton, reputed to be Baron von Hutton, but for some odd reason known in Taos as Frenchy (and his restaurant, once a favorite dining place of Frieda Lawrence's, is called Frenchy's). The genial Frenchy, his hugeness increased by the high chef's cap he wears, came to our table to meet the Mandels.

"What would you like?" Frenchy said. "Name anything you wish, and I'll get it for you."

"Professor Mandel is writing a book about Rilke," I said, "He'd probably like to know something more about Rilke."

"That will take just a moment," Frenchy said. "Excuse me—I'll be right back."

And it was only a moment before Frenchy returned with his petite wife, the Edith Hutton thanked in the Acknowledgments section.

"This is my wife," Frenchy said. "When she was a little girl in Munich, she knew Rilke . . ." And that's how it all began; the Mandels have made other trips to Taos, where Dorothy Mandel exhibits her woodcuts, and have often talked with Mrs. Hutton.

But enough of reminiscences and back to Siegfried Mandel's book. One of its great virtues, I think, is its clarity. Rilke is a profound and not always an easy poet, but Mr. Mandel has cut through surfaces of apparent obscurity to the heart of meanings. He understands Rilke and, in a paraphrase of some lines in King Henry IV, one might say that he will be the cause of an understanding of Rilke in others.

Further, Mr. Mandel displays an expert knowledge of the technical-expressional side of the poet, again and again pointing out certain usages, methods, and other marks of Rilke's craftsmanship, as well as the talismans of his genius. Mr. Mandel not only provides translations of Rilke—the best he could find, accompanied by numerous excellent renditions of his own—but he also does what everyone in a volume of this kind should do, and that is to supply the original texts. So the book is, at this level, doubly rich.

And Mr. Mandel fortunately gives us, en route, a substantial biography of Rilke, so necessary to the full comprehension of the writings. What Rilke was and how he became what he was, are extremely important considerations for the understanding of his work, more so than is usual in such cases. We see the small boy growing up in Prague and given too much mothering; then we follow him through the cruel years at the military school until his final escape, with the subsequent first love affair with the bluestocking Vally, a Bohemian in more than one sense of the word. Later, Mr. Mandel discusses the young Rilke's two trips to Tsarist Russia, his enigmatic relationship with Lou Andreas-Salomé, and his meetings with Tolstoy. Afterward there was the art colony of Worpswede where Rilke met his wife, Clara, with whom he didn't stay very long. He took to drifting across Europe, penniless except for an allowance from his publisher, Kippenberg, but always living fairly comfortably, always capable of finding a princess or a duchess who would turn over a city apartment or a country castle to him. As my Introduction to Selected Letters of Rainer Maria Rilke noted, "He has been frequently criticized for evading his responsibilities as husband, father, and lover—and for sliding away from military obligations, after a brief taste of them, in the First World War. Yet those who knew Rilke have never blamed him for following the necessities of his poetical nature: if he sometimes avoided everyday obvious reality, he constantly sought a deeper reality. Those who have criticized his conduct couldn't have written his poetry."

Mr. Mandel, who doesn't criticize Rilke's conduct and

who has so fine an insight into his poetry, links the events of Rilke's life to his poems and his "fiction" (quotation marks belong around that last word, for reasons which Mr. Mandel's examination of Rilke's work will show). Through all his various experiences, Rilke was writing his grand letters—he stands with Keats, D. H. Lawrence, and a very few others among the greatest of literary letter-writers. Mr. Mandel says in this book that Rilke wrote about 10,000 letters, only about a third of which have found their way into print: readers of the future have further treats in store for them.

But readers of today have an exhilarating experience awaiting them in Mr. Mandel's book. Another of its many virtues is that it deals extensively with the last four years of Rilke's life, the time following his completion of the Duino Elegies and his writing of the Sonnets to Orpheus (both in 1922). Rilke lived during those last years at the Château Muzot in Switzerland and traveled little. He was often ill, and this period has generally been assumed, by too many of us, to be a generally unproductive one. The contrary is true: Mr. Mandel speaks of "the many superlative poems" of Rilke's last years, poems which have been too little known. They express a new tranquillity and, toward the last, an acceptance of the approach of death. Mr. Mandel has greatly added to the value of this book by presenting the texts of a large number of these less-familiar poems; it helps him complete his picture of Rilke.

The reader who knows little of Rilke will find the present volume a first-rate introduction to the poet, while seasoned Rilkeans will be grateful for its insights. I hope that both types of reader will feel the kind of excitement I knew when I began going through parts of this book in its early stages, an excitement which, as I have said, has been intensified by later readings. All you have to do now is turn the page and start.

HARRY T. MOORE

Southern Illinois University
November 4, 1964

# ACKNOWLEDGMENTS

ALTHOUGH more than twenty years have passed since my contact with a remarkable and inspiring guide to the experience that is poetry, my gratitude remains undiminished for Dr. William R. Gaede and his encouragement of my interest in Rilke's work. The most useful, to me, of the mountainous critical and biographical sources sifted have been acknowledged in the book; ultimately, however, my interpretations rest on the "feel" for Rilke's poetry, which comes from having lived with it for a long time.

For verification of a number of impressions, mostly biographical, I am indebted to conversations with Ernst Křenek, the only composer asked by Rilke to put several poems to music; Edith Hutton who lived in the house in which Rilke occupied a flat during his World War I Munich-stay; and Eugene Salomé, the nephew of Lou Andreas-Salomé who played a major role in Rilke's life.

For courtesies shown me over an extended period at the Forty-second Street Library in New York City and for the opportunity to peruse the notable Rilke collection at Harvard University's Houghton Library, I am grateful. The indefatigable assistance of reference librarian Irving Adelman of East Meadow, N. Y., is recalled appreciatively.

When I asked a sensitive translator of Heine to try a few of Rilke's early lyrical poems, Aaron Kramer responded enthusiastically by translating most of the poems in Chapter 1, "Between Day and Dream." In the following chapters, poetry translations, other than my own, may be identified by the opening phrase: Chapter 2—"What will you do," "You, neighbor, God" (Babette Deutsch); Chapter 3—

"All will grow great" (Babette Deutsch); "Lord, it is time," "Make thou one lordly" (Ludwig Lewisohn); "Oh, the animals" (J. B. Leishman); "Like mirrored images" (C. F. MacIntyre); Chapter 4— "Carpenter, Haven't you," "But there" (Stephen Spender); "No, when longing," "Have you so fully," "On Attic stelês," "And he himself," "He, so new" (J. B. Leishman and Stephen Spender, italics mine); Chapter 6—"You, who have never" (M. D. Herter Norton whose exquisite rendering of Rilke's *Sonnets to Orpheus* would have made my other translations of some of these poems in this chapter superfluous were it not for the fact that I interpreted several lines differently); Chapter 7—"Were you the one" (N. K. Cruikshank); "they have finally" (J. B. Leishman and Stephen Spender, with minor changes).

I am grateful to the Insel-Verlag, publishers of *Rainer Maria Rilke: Sämtliche Werke* (referred to as SW in my book), for permission to quote from the original text and to provide translations of my own. Publishers' permission has been granted for quotes from the following books: *Letters of Rainer Maria Rilke*, translated by Jane Bannard Greene and M. D. Herter Norton, volumes I and II, 1945, 1947; *Letters to a Young Poet*, translated by M. D. Herter Norton, 1954 (copyright renewed in 1962); *The Journal of My Other Self*, translated by John Linton, 1930 (copyright renewed in 1958 by the Linton family); *Duino Elegies*, translated by J. B. Leishman and Stephen Spender, 1939; *Sonnets to Orpheus*, translated by M. D. Herter Norton, 1942; these titles are published by W. W. Norton & Co., Inc. *RMR: Selected Works*, volume I, translated by G. C. Houston and volume II, translated by J. B. Leishman, 1960, and *The Book of Hours*, translated by Babette Deutsch, 1941, are published in the United States by New Directions. *Rainer Maria Rilke: Correspondence in Verse with Erika Mitterer*, translated by N. K. Cruikshank, 1953, is published by the Hogarth Press, Ltd. *Letters to Merline*, translated by Violet M. MacDonald, 1951, is published by Methuen & Co., Ltd. *Rainer Maria Rilke: The Life of the Virgin Mary*, translated by Stephen Spender, 1951, is published by the Philosophical Library, Inc. *Rainer Maria Rilke: Fifty Selected Poems*, translated by C. F. MacIntyre, 1940, is published by the University of California Press.

S. M.

# CONTENTS

# INTRODUCTION

IN HIS POETRY, Rainer Maria Rilke (1875–1926) felt himself to be a power and a glory but outside of it "not even a little force." He experienced a reality in his creations that surmounted anything he encountered in life. As he noted, "In one of my poems that is successful, there is much more reality than in any relationship or affection that I feel; where I create, I am true." One reason he could be true to himself in his creations is the protective screen of metaphor and private references that often meant one thing to Rilke and another to the unprepared reader. During Rilke's lifetime it was impossible to ferret out the man hidden in the thickets of his poetry; for that we needed the posthumous publication of many poems, diaries, thinly-disguised fiction or self portraits, juvenilia, complemented by the body of letters; some poems did not reach print in their entirety until 1961. All of these writings make it increasingly possible to understand the close relation between Rilke's life and poetry.

Letters which Rilke distributed like confetti—possibly numbering 10,000, of which about a third are in print—were meticulously composed and are particularly valuable when they rehearse ideas for incipient poems, but are at their weakest in their explanation and commentary on the poetry because of his attempts to divert the reader and critic from the highly personal nature of the poetry. They hold another fascination. Since creation cannot precede experience, one being a distillation of the other, Rilke's letters mirror the richness and range of life to which he exposed himself and permit speculation on the process of transforming experience into poetic thought.

Rilke, like Yeats, is a poet's poet. Karl Shapiro recently discussed the standard to which he writes: "Would Rilke like this poem, I sometimes ask myself. Would Catullus?" Rilke almost invariably stood in the center of his own poetry, and so single-minded was his craft that the art of poetry became an equivalent for religion. Such self-centeredness causes Archibald MacLeish to fret that "even in Rilke there is something sealed and unventilated which sooner or later stifles the birds." Rilke chose to speak not for humanity but for himself; he left all pretensions to other poets. But he did ask haunting questions that apply to humanity as well, as for instance, "What keeps you from living your life like a painful and beautiful day in the history of the great gestation of God?"

In the extensive body of Rilke criticism there is a disturbing tendency to praise what is obscure in Rilke's poetry and to damn what is absolutely clear. It is not impossible to divorce idea—what is being said—from style—or the way something is said—but such attempts more often than not lead to futile disputations. Intuitive logic or subjective assumptions can neither prove nor invalidate Rilke's views on the reality of an inner world that encompasses all realms of being, his requirement of nonpossessiveness as a central attitude in love, his conception of one's "own" death, and the notion of a self-sustaining world of creation.

The persuasiveness of Rilke's ideas is effected by manner and method, which are traceable in his career. Stylized and often stereotyped neo-romanticism that opaquely reflects life experience through lyricism, a rich tonality and musical feeling are typical of his Prague days; the attempts at portrayal and resolution of ideas through poetry became a necessity in his newly-found independence beginning with the Munich years; poetry that is objective and "freed from all that is accidental, purely inspirational, cleared of all uncertainty, lifted out of time and set into space to become enduring and adapted to eternity" was Rilke's aim after Worpswede and work with Rodin. We might call the poems of those days primarily visual, exhibiting a finely-honed power of observation and structural discipline. After his 1912-stay in the castle of Duino, visionary poems with reflective and hymnical expression became dominant. Yet through the years there is a simultaneous proliferation of styles—neo-romanticism, brash and satiric expressionism, impressionism. Progressively, however, in whatever medium Rilke wrote—literary classifications meant nothing to him, we note a deepening of nuances and ambiguities, an increase in experimentation, a consistent mastering of the dynamics and infinite possibilities of language. The achievements during Rilke's mature years may be attributed to a remarkable tenacity of will and the physically consuming labor that are the marks of poetry created in loneliness, independent of contemporaneous literary activity.

SIEGFRIED MANDEL

University of Colorado
October 5, 1964

Rainer Maria Rilke
THE POETIC INSTINCT

SUFFERING THE LOSS of a baby girl in 1874, Sophie (Phia) Rilke prayed to the Virgin Mary for another girl and promised to dedicate her to a nun's life. The next year, after a seven-month pregnancy, the slender and vain woman gave birth to a boy who in the Catholic baptism was named René Karl Wilhelm Johann Josef Maria. Rather than accept the situation, she pretended that René was her girl, inflicting upon the boy emotional disorientation and feminine sensibilities that were to remain with him throughout life. Twenty-eight years later, the poet Rilke wrote to a correspondent about his early life, family origins, and his birthplace—the city of Prague in Czecho-Slovakia, which at the time was under Austro-Hungarian rule:

> Yes, my family is old. As early as 1276 it belonged to the ancient Carinthian nobility, later it emigrated (at least in part) to Saxony and Brandenburg, and in the seventeenth and in the first decades of the eighteenth century it blossoms richly into three powerful branches. Then comes the decline, lawsuits that wipe out the entire fortune and loss of all estates and lands and: poverty, almost obscurity. After almost a century, which passed in darkness, my great-grandfather again came into power. He was lord of Kamenitz an der Linde (a castle in Bohemia, whither the family had emigrated in the anxious transition period). He collected the old traditions, he rescued from oblivion what was on the point of dying away, the family's ancient name. But immediately behind him the depths close

again. My grandfather, who still spent his childhood at Kamenitz, was later steward of someone else's estate. My father began the career of officer (following a family tradition) but then switched over to that of official. He is a railroad official, holds a fairly high post in a private railroad, which he has earned with infinite conscientiousness. He lives in Prague. *There* I was born. . . . Of my mother's family I know nothing. Her father was a wealthy merchant whose fortune went to pieces on a prodigal son. My childhood home was a cramped, rented apartment in Prague; it was very sad. My parents' marriage was already faded when I was born. When I was nine years old, the discord broke out openly, and my mother left her husband. She was a very nervous, slender, dark woman, who wanted something indefinite of life. And so she continued. Actually these two people ought to have understood each other better, for they both attach an infinite amount of value to externals; our little household, which was in reality middle class, was supposed to deceive people, and certain lies passed as a matter of course. I don't know how it was with me. I had to wear very beautiful clothes and went about until school years like a little girl; I believe my mother played with me as with a big doll. For the rest, she was always proud when she was called "Miss." She wanted to pass for young, sickly, and unhappy. And unhappy she probably was too. I believe we all were. (Letter to Ellen Key, April 3, 1903)

The romantic picture of himself as last of a line of nobility of old Bohemian origin—closing the cycle from 1276–1875—started as a fantasy based on meager facts and continued with force throughout his life to serve the convenience of making himself confident and comfortable among a host of titled acquaintances; rather than being a pauper poet, his lineage made him an equal. Encouragement for ancestor hunting came from his uncle Jaroslav, a Prague lawyer, who was given the hereditary title of Rilke Ritter von Rüliken in 1873 by the Austrian Kaiser. Further, Rilke's great-grandfather Johann Josef used a seal that was transformed by his heirs from an official county seal into a personal seal of heraldry. The coat of arms pictured two crowned helmets and greyhounds rampant in fields of silver and black. Through relentless investigations, Rilke found a family of Rülko, Ruleke, also named Rulke, going back to the early sixteenth century, whose coat of arms contained greyhounds, a popular motif. This coincidence, both as to heraldry and name, was sufficient evidence for adopting the coat of arms and later using it as a seal for correspondence and for his own tombstone decoration. Rilke had little reservation about regaling people with these genealogical improvisations; but in his poetry there is a pleasantly contrasting humility. These imagined ancestors—aside from real ones with mental aberrations—became "contemporaries of his soul"; they gave him strength, standing, and began to exist silently within him.[1]

His father Josef was a frustrated civilian railroad inspector whose auspicious military career had been aborted by a throat ailment and economic circumstances. Willingness to pursue his lineage to past centuries was paralleled by a disinclination to trace members of his mother's side because her possible maternal Bohemian-Jewish ancestry would not yield titled forebears.[2]

Because of his mother's inclination for belles-lettres— she had been brought up in a cultural milieu in her parents' baroque mansion in Prague—René was trained to memorize, recite, copy poetry and paint, despite his father's objection to such unmasculine triflings. Phia's pretensions took such forms as dressing in the fashionable black of royal Hapsburg widows, vacationing in the vicinity of castles, teaching René French and discouraging contact with all things Czech, reflecting the social snobbery of the middle class Prague-German minority.

His feelings for her pursued every nuance of love and hate. Principally he rebelled against the exaggerated and bigoted display of religion by Phia who wanted the boy to kiss the wounds of Christ on the crucifix. Consequently, his poetry was to record a search for an ideal mother, a personal religion, antagonism toward Christ, and a fondness for the patriarchal God of the Old Testament. The emancipation from his mother's enveloping religious

mania was gradual but he retained an affection for the
baroque splendor of Prague's churches and castles and the
sensuous liturgical lyricism of Catholic expression.

Cramped tenement surroundings, participation in the
"society register" pretentions of both mother and father,
subjection to such parental hypochondria as the constant
pushing of a thermometer into René's mouth, enforced
girlish preoccupations, being treated like a doll, and being
stimulated erotically led to René's nervous debilitation.
Quite suddenly he was hurled into a sharply different
milieu:

> Soon after she left the house [Rilke's mother went to
> Vienna in 1884 to take part in the social whirl]—in the
> company of a cavalier—I was put in one of our big
> officers' training establishments. I (who had never known
> brothers, sisters, or playmates hitherto) found myself
> among fifty boys who all met me with the same scornful
> hostility. Noncommissioned officers trained us. What I
> suffered in those five years (for I remained that long in
> spite of sickness, in spite of opposition in the place) is a
> life in itself: a long difficult life. Even today (thirteen
> years later), my parents still suspect nothing of it. They
> could not understand it. When I came out and took off
> the uniform, I knew that they were quite remote from me.
> And that now manifested itself over and over again. They
> put me in a commercial school, in circumstances that
> nearly brought about my downfall, until a brother of my
> father (Jaroslav Rilke), had me take school studies pri-
> vately. By expending all my powers, I got over the eight
> classes in three years and passed the final examination.
> Then I was tired. (Letter to Ellen Key, April 3, 1903)

The change from an effeminate environment to a
coarsely masculine world came as a shock to René. Unlike
James Joyce, Thomas Mann, and Robert Musil (who
attended the same military academy René did at Mährisch-
Weisskirchen in Moravia and unburdened himself in the
novel *Young Törless*), Rilke was unable to exorcise his
childhood experiences. At the military school his emotions
were inflamed to the point where he wrote religious songs
which, as Rilke wryly put it later, "thanks to Providence

have all been lost." To escape, he projected himself into
the fantasy world of heroic characters who declaimed in
Friedrich Schiller's resounding rhetoric mingled with prayers for death. René's touching, brotherly affection for a
boy was dragged into the mud by comrades and the school
authorities. "My heart went on being orphaned," wrote
the youngster who promised "never again to attach it to
anyone." In a handful of the earliest boyish poetry released by Rilke's archivists, we can see the touching gesture of the nine-year-old as he plays the role of the Cartha-
ginian general Hannibal and addresses his parents on their
wedding anniversary:

> *Euer Leben sei nur Glück*
> *auf Unglück denket nie zurück*
>    *nie! nie! nie!*            (sw III,475)

> *Your life be only happiness*
> *never think back on unhappiness*
>    *never! never! never!*

Although the anniversary poem consists of conventional
greeting-card couplets designed to please both the father
whose bearing still reflected dreams of military glory and
his alternately indifferent and doting mother, the boy's
blessings and appeals show how deeply sensitive he was to
the parental rift. "In my childish mind I believed myself
through my patience near to the virtues of Jesus Christ,"
but all the response Rilke received from a few young,
unthinking tormentors at military school was derisive
laughter. More important, René learned that saintlike
sentiments and poses resulted in humiliation and frustra-
tion, and that neither Mary nor the conventional angels
answered his fierce prayers. Although he received kindness
and attention for his poetry, René preferred to act the
martyr and to call the academy (which he attended
tuition-free through his uncle's influence), a Dostoevskian
House of the Dead.

So rapidly did René's notebooks fill with verses that in
1891 he boasted to his mother that he was "a complete
*littérateur.*" Later that year, after having been removed

from the military academy, love triumphed over literature as he climaxed his education at the business school in Linz with an escapade involving an instructress. If nothing else, this episode showed that his male instincts had not been crushed by the morbid weight of the experiences he loved to unfold, and that he was willing to defy convention in order to please himself.

René's uncle and cousins subsidized his studies at the University of Prague, while he lived alone with an ailing aunt, and he was free to meet the coquettish Valéry von David-Rhonfeld. "Vally" became the first of a long line of mother figures who showered the poet with uncritical admiration and affection.[3] Although she was a literary "bohemian," her family boasted titled personages. To equalize their relation, René tried to impress her with the story of Prince Condé, a French forebear. With no economic worries, freedom to study as he pleased—changing from intended law courses to literature and art history—and the comforting adoration of Vally, who in 1894 financed the publication of his first volume of poetry, *Leben und Lieder* [*Life and Songs*], René aggressively followed his inner compulsion to authorship and to a poet's crown.

No poetic praise is spared by René in addressing his fiancée Vally as "a creature so magical / have I choice in naming you? / An Ideal!" Although he fervently promises to dedicate his life to her and be worthy of her, the opening poem, "Vorbei" ["Gone"], of *Leben und Lieder*, announces that even the most beautiful impulses, love and fidelity, grow tired and are gone, yet love's song remains quietly in one's heart. Rilke's formula in the declension of relationships is to remain constant: "Have loved, hoped, parted, bade farewell / that is the old, old song!"

The young René followed his every whim, and imitated with astonishing facility the tone and manner of poetry whether it was religious lyricism of the seventeenth-century baroque or the melody and color of the romanticists. The charm of the poetry and its musical softness are undeniable; its fluidity, its sound-play, is one step removed from sheer virtuosity. But, discipline, sensibility, and taste were as yet absent; that demonstration of superior talent as Goethe saw it "in wise self-restriction" came only with maturity.

In later years, all the first imitative poems were a source of embarrassment to Rilke and he was their harshest critic; yet they were indispensable to his progress. In *Leben und Lieder* are samples of abysmal bathos. Witness the ballad of the alms-begging invalid soldier who dies to the tune of the Radetzky-March and with his hand raised in salute cries out, "I come to you, my general." On the whole, however, the poetic tunes are muted, there is nothing strident; occasional mawkish portraits of loving mothers and dying children alternate with pleasantries and "gaieties—a kiss is not a sin . . . life is love." He thumbs his nose at carping critics and claims the whole province of life as a source for the poet's songs, but he takes a more serious view of the public that exacts its pound of entertainment from the artist, forcing the artist to don a mask to please.

Driven by a need for personal success and recognition by parents and relatives, the nineteen-year-old René flooded Prague with newspaper articles and reviews, rushed into print with poems, stories, and even stormed onto the stage. Every literary society, every writer with any sort of name, every publisher, every tendentious taste, was game for René. Spontaneity and superficiality went hand in hand as he tried to capture and captivate the public. Even though pretension exceeded fulfillment, the illusion of success helped to harden his ego and steel it for many of the ruthless and heartbreaking personal decisions he had to make later. With the same kind of self-assurance and deference with which young James Joyce greeted the old Henrik Ibsen, René hailed Maurice Maeterlinck and the deservedly popular Detlev von Liliencron. From Liliencron, René learned to absorb everyday, routine elements into poetry, to celebrate the ephemeralness of love, to poetize personal rootlessness, and to make ballads into acoustic structures where sound reverberates.

Determined to bring his poetry to the people, he literally made them a present of *Wegwarten* [*Wild Chicory*], a pamphlet collection of verse songs, distributing free copies in hospitals, street corners, at workers' meetings. He hoped that these poems would "wake to a higher life in the soul of the nation." While elevating the folk, René did not neglect to cultivate the titled, sending them poems and dedications and at one point styling himself as the castle poet—a Tarquatoo Tasso—of the Baroness Láska van Oestéren.[4]

In *Wegwarten*, René for the first time experiments with techniques which several decades later became the stock in trade of the German expressionists; René excoriates a society in which the artist must pull carts to earn his bread. Apparently, with the third—and last—October, 1896, issue of what was meant to be a continuing periodical, René had to discontinue his free poetic disbursements. Instead, three commercially procurable volumes of poetry that made rapid appearances between 1895 and 1897 had to suffice the curious. These so-called *Erste Gedichte* [*First Poems*], consist of *Larenopfer* [*An Offering to the Lares*], *Traumgekrönt* [*Crowned with Dreams*], and *Advent*.

In *Larenopfer*, its gauche dust jacket designed by Vally, René is our guide to the city of Prague as he impressionistically describes the green-domed St. Nicholas church, old steep-gabled houses with baroque friezes, the stone-bridge approach to the castle of the Hradschin wave-lapped by the Moldau, the mildewed air about St. Veit, toward which from a nearby house Gothic sculptured hands reach out in prayer amid erotic rococo ornamentations, the double towers of St. Mariens which, antenna-like, suck in the heaven's violet tints, the metal flowers and sabbath candlelight of St. Loretta and the young lovers who stand soulfully before an imitation Tintoretto. It is a love lyric to the city and its varied inhabitants—from Pater Guardian, a Capuchin who offers dark-red "cloister-schnaps" that can waken all the dead, to the tired children Ninka and Willy. René pays tribute to the nationalistic and cultural spirit of the Czech poet Julius Zeyer, Vally's

uncle, and despite a very limited knowledge of Czech
declares his affinity to the "böhmischen Volkes Weise,"
the songs of the Bohemian folk which creep into his heart.
Figures from Prague's history and rich legends—Kaiser
Rudolf, the wise Rabbi Löw, Jan Hus, episodes from the
Thirty Years War—crowd his poetry. René's emotional
identification with the Czech movement for liberation and
social sympathy for its lower classes vaguely lingered until
he found a substitute in the Russian peasantry. It is a
sympathy combined with a resentment of his own family
milieu which leads him to caricature with astonishing
ferocity the characteristics of his own middle class life
although he diplomatically dissociated himself from the
"Streitpoeten," the ultra radical poets.

Whether through natural affinity or desire to be *au
courant* with the naturalists who were pounding the boards
in Berlin, Vienna, and Prague, René joined the chorus
with an imitative one-act social and anti-capitalistic drama
entitled *Jetzt und in der Stunde unseres Absterbens* [*Now
and in the Hour of Our Dying*]. René published this
almost plagiarized drama in the second issue of *Wegwarten* and managed to have it produced on August, 1896,
at Prague's German Volkstheater. The drama features a
lecherous landlord who threatens a family with eviction
unless its daughter yields to his advances. She does, and we
learn the grim fact that the landlord is guilty of incest.

A year earlier René had spun out a similar naturalistic
theme in a three-act drama that has some interest because
it shows that he could muster a colloquial robustness—
despite a peculiar amalgam of Viennese and Prague
idioms—if he chose. The raw idiom, good characteriza-
tions, emotional roundness, and melodramatic intensity
are kin to qualities found in the early Gerhardt Hauptmann plays, but Rilke's dramas do not cling to memory.
Ever since Heinrich von Kleist's dramatic demonstration
of exquisite "tragic irony," there were attempts to imitate
the effects, but few equalled Kleist's perfect sense of
timing and dramatic appropriateness. Rilke's ironies are
not representations of life's bitter pills but the aspiring

playwright's sense of drama gone sadistic. Constantly implied is the dreariness of childhood and youth, the crushing effect of environment, the opportunism of those who have the upper hand, and a strong fatalism. Symbolically, an early frost can incapacitate one for love later in life; happiness or unhappiness is rooted in childhood.

A mood of languid self-absorption fluidly courses through the 1896 collection of poems, *Traumgekrönt*, only to be broken occasionally by such plaintive lines as, "Was haben sie mir statt der Wiege / nicht einen kleinen Sarg gemacht?" [Instead of a cradle, why did they not make a small coffin for me?] Deathly silences reign, roses proliferate the countryside, lovers' passions flare and subside, as the poet is more intent on retaining the innocence of maidens than are the maidens themselves. In all this misty realm, René wanders "earnest and lonely like a god" to escape the drone-like humdrum folk. René could have spun out such poetic exercises until the end of time and almost became a victim of his own brilliant verse-knitting techniques and flawless rhymes.

The Prague years certainly had been rewarding for René. He basked in the warmth of ego-ministration by Vally, the plaudits of the notable poet Detlev von Liliencron, the guidance of Professor August Sauer, the friendship of the artist Emil Orlik and minor talents like Hugo Salus and Alfred Klaar, the congeniality of editors and theatre directors—despite the mediocrity of his plays, everyone contributed understanding assistance. It was not ingratitude that decided René's move to Munich in the fall of 1896, but a realization that he had reached a dead end in the provincial atmosphere of Prague.

The transition to Munich was merely geographical; the emotional ties remained within, to appear again and again in his writings. In prose sketches, short stories, and dramas much of the material had centered on his milieu as in the Prague tales. His mother—the dark and slim lady—was the love object in such stories as "Pierre Dumont" and "Bonded" ["Einig"], disrupting love attachments he might forge with others, and inspiring a horror of sex as in the story "The Seamstress" ["Die Näherin"]. Also there was a proliferation of sad and sentimental death scenes in which children depart with the glow of fairy tale visions, as in the stories "The Christchild" ["Das Christkind"] and "The Golden Box" ["Die Goldene Kiste"].[5] These media were soon abandoned because Rilke found it more satisfying to explore and deepen their themes in poetry.

The Munich years were crucial in Rilke's life "since they determined his poetical course and implanted in his spirit the conception of a mission which was nothing less exacting than to found the religion of art." [6] These years constitute a cyclonic speeding up of personal growth and mark the beginning of a creative smithy that Rilke calls "Arbeit und Einsamkeit," work and solitude. From the descriptions given of René by people who remembered him from his Prague days contradictory portraits emerge. On the one hand, we see a vitally active and ambitious writer, a non-conformist who wishes to create under his aegis a literary society which he jokingly called "Bund Moderner Zopfverächter," an anti-mandarin group; on the other hand, we see a young man of calm, reverent, and ethereal demeanor. What lay beneath the activist and saintlike poses is told in *Ewald Tragy*,[7] which bridges his Prague and Munich days, an autobiographical novella written after leaving Prague but not published by Rilke because the autobiographical elements were too evident.

The second part of this autobiographical novella is of interest chiefly for his intimate details of living alone, his eccentricities, the self-exploring monologues, and the frightening intensity of his imagination. Real emotional stability is impossible for any length of time because René's alert senses are affected by every sight, sound, and smell and magnify things into grotesque proportions. He would sit before a window and "let it happen" that faces, faces, faces appear until one stares so closely that "the nose impressed itself on the panes and the features became something broad, vampirelike, greedy." Ewald follows the lines of the face until his glance suddenly falls into the abyss of the lurking, strange eyes. "No one can imagine how terrible this window is." Unseen presences of other inhabitants of the room spring alive in his mind. The nights bring terrors and the old, "old tortures that stem from the many fevernights of childhood," when a hand would suddenly appear through a wall. René remembers his military academy days and equates present and past feelings of fright, helplessness, and incapacity as if "some important organ" were missing without which there is no progressing. The basic source of his anguish finally is revealed when Ewald-René writes a letter to his mother, that slender, elegant lady who is proud to be addressed as Miss: "Take me, give me a shape, make me complete." It is a deeply elemental wish that can only be granted with emancipation from the mother, and to disguise it Ewald explains that it *really* is "a cry for motherliness, which goes far beyond a distinct female; it goes back to a first love." He veers from the specific to the vague, from his real mother to a concept of ideal motherliness. After expressing his torment, he burns the letter. Rilke's vocabulary begins to assume a specific shape, a code and a coda. "Life is so immense and yet there are only a few things (*Dinge*) in it, each an eternity (*Ewigkeit*). These transitions (*Übergänge*) make one anxious (*bange*) and tired (*müd*)." Life is a never-arriving but "in dreams everything is quite close—there is no fear (*Angst*)." All namable objects have a life of their own so that relationships become difficult and tiring. Rilke, for instance, always found it easier and less problematic to engage in love-relationships at a distance. Because in dreams there is an immediacy of contact and a vision that is not obscured by a censorious world, he willingly gives himself over to dreams and permits them to overwhelm him. All this is not untouched by astrological superstition as Ewald chides himself for having forgotten to dream on his arrival in Munich although he knew that first "dreams have particular significance."

During those brooding months, he started the poem cycle *Christus / Elf Visionen* [*Christ: Eleven Visions* or *Visions of Christ*], on which he worked sporadically from

October, 1896, to the middle of 1898. Only a few people were to see these poems because Rilke changed his mind about their publication: "I have many reasons to keep the Christ-Pictures secret—a long, long time. They are gestations which accompany me throughout life," calling them his "undatable works." [8] A less idealistic reason for withholding publication was his unwillingness to antagonize those who were supporting him. While writing the visions of Christ, he sent a letter to Karl Baron Du Prel, a spiritualistic philosopher who believed in one's "other self" which is in contact with the Beyond:

> Apart from the charm of the mysterious, the domains of spiritualism have for me an important power of attraction . . . I see the liberation of our remote descendants and believe that in particular every artist must struggle through the misty fumes of crass materialism to those spiritual intimations that build for him the golden bridge into shoreless eternities. . . . It will perhaps be vouchsafed me sometime to become with word and pen one of the adherents of the new faith that towers high above church-steeple crosses . . . it seems to me that in my "Visions of Christ" . . . I shall come a big step nearer to your group. (February 16, 1897)

Spiritualism—religion for those who find themselves outside of all religions—appealed to René because it views the material body as a manifestation of spirit, an absolute reality, close to the unseen, immortal world, and promises survival after death. Always open to new ideas and experiences, Rilke, when asked about the frauds of spiritualism, replied that an artificial flower does not disprove the genuineness of a natural rose. Rilke rarely made absolute commitments.

With an intensity that was rooted in emotional and intellectual antagonism, René worked on his visions of Christ, the childhood symbol of unanswered prayers, the interloper and intruder who denied life and mortal love and stood between himself and his mother. Christ, as his mother's other-directed love, and her spiritually gilded love—lavished on "poor, wooden saints"—was to Rilke a distortion. Unacceptable as were the concepts of martyrdom, resurrection, and sin, each man must experience religion as a private and not a public emotion, achieving a personal, "unmediated" vision. Rilke's idea of existence— life and death—centered on an "eternal present" in which all tenses combine; he needed to believe in a continuity of existence: "Immortality? I believe that nothing that is real can pass away." He saw the Christ figure as a captive of the bourgeois society which he despised, a pitiful, inconsolable figure who could help neither himself nor others, and a figure who pointed to the beyond instead of showing how life ought to be lived to the fullest. In retrospect, he associated Christ with the causes contributing to his real and imagined childhood sufferings. Still, René was not totally unsympathetic to the Christ figure—both have loneliness and homelessness in common—and he admires the strong-willed visionary, human Christ but quarrels with the presumptive divinity. Most of his scorn is directed against the "Pöbel," the mob, which has distorted the man into a god figure.

All of the eleven *Visions of Christ* poems have a narrative structure and form a composite inspired by a single point of view: Christ is not what Christianity has pictured him to be. "Die Waise" ["The Orphan"] is a tender portrait of a little girl who naively approaches a motionless, tired man in whose great and dark eye glows mourning, "like a dim candle of death." "Have you lost your mother too?" she asks consolingly. Immersed in thought, the stranger startles the child with his unresponsiveness and his failure to support her hope that she will see her mother again, in heaven. In "Der Narr" ["The Fool"] the eyes of Christ are not strange to young Anna, daughter of Magdalene, and when he asks her to repeat the word "Papa," a cry of jubilation breaks from him. But it turns into sadness, "I can give you nothing, little one / . . . I am poorer than you." Garbed like a beggar, proud in bearing like a king, and called a fool, Christ continues his journey. René then renders the Christ figure in radiant iconographical portraiture in the poem "Die Kinder"

["The Children"] as adoring multitudes crowd around
Christ whose sermon has the sound of New Testament
paradigms but carries René's reinterpretations:

> *Ihr wollt ins Leben, und das bin ich nicht,*
> *ihr müsst ins Dunkel, und ich bin das Licht,*
> *ihr hofft die Freude, ich bin der Verzicht,*
> *ihr sehnt das Glück und—ich bin das Gericht.*
>
> (SW III,137)

> *I am not life, and life's what you're after;*
> *The dark is your portion, and I illume;*
> *I bid you renounce—you love laughter;*
> *Good fortune you crave—and I am doom.*

Mirroring the conflict that rages in René between his
childhood faith and the harsh embarrassed hateful rejection of Christ in Munich is the poem "Der Maler" ["The
Painter"]. Christ remonstrates with the artist, René:
"Why do you paint me *thus?* Did I sit *thus* on your bed
when your fear screamed out childhood fevers . . . was
*this* the mien which lent you courage?" Despite feelings of
shame and guilt the artist bitterly rejects the Christ whose
meekness and poverty had been the original sources of
attraction and consolation.

At the annual October fair in Munich, a modern-
age version of Dionysic celebrations, the poet is drawn into
a wax exhibit of scenes from Christ's life. Outside, the
"Jahrmarkt" ["The Annual Fair"] is brilliantly evoked in
passages that remind one, in tempo, tune, and lifelikeness,
of Goethe's market scenes in "Faust"; inside of the exhibit
silence reigns as time drips through the wall clock, and the
yellow wax figure complains of being made impotent in
such profane exhibits just as in the sacred coldness of
churches. "One great revenge," however, is his: "My blood
flows externally from scars of nails, / and all believe my
blood is wine, / and drink the blood and passion."

Continuing with a satiric poem, "Die Nacht" ["The
Night"], René places Christ in an inn called "To the
Angels" and tempts him with a woman who boisterously
cries: "Come! Don't be a fool, I know something better

than gloomily dreaming life away." Christ compulsively tells her that the derision of the crowd and the tribunal judge goaded his vanity so that defiantly he screamed at them that he was God's Son: "To my Father's right is my throne!" Repentantly, however, he admits to the harlot: "Ich bin kein Gott!" ["I am no God!"] She readily agrees but ribaldly assures him that after a night with her he will be a king in the morning. Christ succumbs passionately and is crowned with a garland "and weeps, as from his brow / falls the last morningfaded rose: / 'We are the eternal, hereditary curse of this world: Eternal madness I—you the eternal hussy.'" René has dramatically projected the tormenting struggle between the ascetic and the sensual.

In a diary entry of this period, René expressed the idea that the oldest philosophy of Christianity was to transfigure the unbearable into consolation, whereas he wanted the raw experience of God's growth in man and not a watered-down sentiment. In these visions, Christ is a figure of lamentation and the God of naïve children as opposed to the personal God-father who could give sustenance and be life's guide. As man he would have retained godly greatness; as God he appears so humanly small. This is Rilke's main quarrel with Christ and, except for occasional outbursts later, he thoroughly worked the personal dispute out of his system by writing the *Visions*. Romano Guardini, a Catholic theologian, suggests that Rilke, like Hölderlin and Nietzsche, did not cull thoughts from his own center, but developed them in relation and in epiphenomenal opposition to Christian teachings; Rilke's thoughts are "an attempt to draw Christian existential elements into the purely secular." Eudo C. Mason speculates along the same lines that "Rilke, exactly like Nietzsche and so many other neo-heathen geniuses, inwardly possessed a secret Christian whom he constantly had to battle." [9] Whatever the case may be, Rilke was adamant in his rabid rejections of certain aspects of Christ and eclectic in his preservation of elements from the mystical and emotionally rich symbology of Catholic tradition. Esthetic appreciation and faith were separable entities for Rilke.

When René's future promised little but rudderless introspection, gloom, and imbalance, the remarkable story-teller Jakob Wasserman intervened by directing René toward the energetic Lou Andreas-Salomé who helped change René from a provincial talent to a cosmopolitan artist. Fifteen years older than René, and author of several works of fiction and philosophy, her fund of experience was richer but just as disturbed as René's. When René met her in May, 1897, she was married to a professor of Asiatic languages after having rejected the fierce wooing of Friedrich Nietzsche. Lou's marriage was one of appearance, but instead of divorce, Lou chose to keep up the illusion and attracted male companions to whose roster René was soon added.

An essay, "Jesus der Jude" ["Jesus the Jew"], which Lou had written for the April, 1896, issue of the *Neue Deutsche Rundschau*, broached the ideas that in the religious genius of Jesus is solved the contradiction of man who kneels before his man-created God; that early Christian theology, arising from a mighty yearning for a belief in the hereafter and possessing a new heaven-god, has no relation to the highest inner spirituality through which a single religious genius receives and preaches his God-revelation; only the "great solitary" like Jesus can reach the peak of religion and experience its fullest tragedy. In his first letter to Lou, René said ecstatically that she had masterfully expressed the very ideas of his "dream epics," the *Visions of Christ*. Both believed in religion without doctrine, in tradition only as a point of departure, in the translation of every life experience and contact into pure emotion, in the erasure of lines between the sacred and profane, and in the gesture that has no meaning other than its own emotion.

Rilke's strategy of courtship followed a line which was to become a habitual pattern: an opening request for an audience, thankful dedications inscribed in gift copies of his books, impetuous letters. Through sheer persistence, René succeeded in breaking through the worldly barrier to the feminine core of Lou and found a kindred soul. Love, to Lou, was to be a fulfillment and a proof of existence whose closest symbol is the sacrament; the lover, by the same token, is "a priest in sacred vestment who might only intuit what he is celebrating." Quite suitably, René's love expression took on an unmistakable religious tenor: "I have never desired you as other than having had to suffer for your sake. I have never yearned for you as other than that I might kneel before you." René's suit was not to be denied and for three years Lou and Rilke's association was companionable; they shared quarters in an apartment atop a farmer's barn and together enjoyed long journeys; until the fall of 1900 all of his love poems are directed to Lou.[10]

René's dedicatory and untitled poem for Lou, inscribed in a copy of *Traumgekrönt* [*Crowned with Dreams*] is consonant with the mood of the *Visions of Christ* poems in choice of subject matter and audacious end rhymes; it stands in stark contrast to the poems in *Traumgekrönt* written a few years earlier. The poem itself is no stranger than the ritualistic love which René and Lou were celebrating:

> *Das log das Mittelalter: dass den Nonnen,*
> *die sich in dumpfen Zellen eingesponnen,*
> *im tiefsten Taumel ihrer feigen Wonnen*
> *Wundspuren Christi an dem Leibe sonnen,*
> *in dem die Liebe krankt, wie jener Bronnen,*
> *draus nie ein Müder Mut und Kühle trank.*
> *Das log das Mittelalter. Doch im Zwang*
> *des Alltags schreiten sie durch alle Zeiten*
> *und was sie tun ist wie ein Vorbereiten—*
> *die Fremden, die dem Neuen Wege weiten,*
> *die durch die Kämpfe in den Frieden leiten*
> *und aus dem Sterben in die Ewigkeiten—*
> *Und diese Fremden tragen unbewusst*
> *an ihrem Leibe Jesu Wundenbrände:*
> *wegwunde Füsse, mühewehe Hände*
> *und jenes wilde Bluten in der Brust . . .*
>
> (sw III,566–67)

> *The Middle Ages had this lie to tell:*
> *that when each nun, self-immured in her dank cell,*
> *became intoxicated by her spell,*
> *the wounds of Christ on their own flesh fell,*

*their loveless, love-sick bodies—like that well*
*at which the tired have never slaked their thirst.*
*The Middle Ages lied. Yet from the first*
*they have been marching forth in stern formation,*
*and what they do is like a preparation—*
*novitiates who've chosen the new way*
*which leads from battle to the peace of prayer*
*and out of death into eternal day—*
*and on their bodies these novitiates bear*
*the wounds of Jesus, branded unaware:*
*path-wounded feet, worn hands that have no rest,*
*and that wild blood raging in the breast.*

Excessive rhyming pounds the ear, the metrics are labored
and the language gnarled, a characteristic of Rilke's poems
whenever a self-conscious idea is broached. Rilke seems to
be sympathizing with those who bear the legacy of Christ
on their bodies and in their deluded visions, without
realizing that Christ bore the same torment and raging in
his breast. Where Christ cannot help, the poet can. This
conceit, in which the nun by analogy is Lou, reappears
more clearly in another poem in the sequence for Lou, *Dir
zur Feier* [*In Your Honor*]:

> *Und lass zurück in deinen dunklen Schränken*
> *die schwarze Tracht. Die Kleider aus dem Gestern.*
> *Dein Leib soll nie mehr dieses Dunkel denken.*
>
> (sw III,195)

[And let remain, in your dark closets, / the black garbs.
The clothes of yesteryear. / Your body shall no longer
think about the darkness.] Pretentiously René vows a
soulful "sisterly" relationship and bodily release once the
nun's garb is put aside.

A sense of tidiness compelled René to finish what he
started, namely the *Visions of Christ* and *Advent*. Although he adjusted himself to the role of consort and poet
laureate to Lou, he did not neglect his mother, Christ, and
his own ego.

In *Advent* Rilke affirms his new-found intent:

> *Das ist mein Streit:*
> *Sehnsuchtgeweiht*
> *durch alle Tage schweifen.*

*Dann, stark und breit,*
*mit tausend Wurzelstreifen*
*tief in das Leben greifen—*
*und durch das Leid*
*weit aus dem Leben reifen,*
*weit aus der Zeit!*          (sw 1,103)

*This is my struggle:*
*consecrated to yearning*
*to roam through all the days.*
*Then strong and broad*
*with a thousand streaking roots*
*to reach deep into life—*
*and through suffering*
*to ripen far beyond life,*
*far beyond time!*

Noticeably the themes are more eclectic than in *Crowned with Dreams*, more ornamental and inflamed by imagination; yet his style becomes firmer and retains little of the naturalistic striations of his Prague poems. René's subjective impulse to overwhelm things strengthens, and the turn inward to vague contemplation becomes pronounced. "I love," says René, "the forgotten hallway-madonnas, dream-suffused blonde maidens at lonely fountains, the children in their astonished looking toward the stars." The bitter sting of memory forces the poet to recall his apartness from other children and from his mother:

*Kam meine Mutter im kühlem Kleid*
*abends mich küssen, Mein Danken und Denken*
*hätt ich wollen ⟨der⟩ Schönen schenken,*
*aber sie winkte und war so weit.*

*Und ich streckte die Arme aus.*
*Und mein Schatten wuchs an den Wänden,*
*und in den hilflosen Kinderhänden*
*welkte die Liebe wie ein Strauss.* (sw III, 586–87)

*Evenings, when Mother in cool array*
*came to kiss me, I wished I could share*
*thanks and thoughts with her who was fair;*
*but she would nod and seem far away.*

*And I held my arms out wide,*
*and my shadow grew on the wall,*
*and in the child's hands, helpless and small,*
*love, like a nosegay, withered and died.*

Rilke blamed his emotional deficiencies on his irremediable childhood experiences. Why was he a shy, self-dissatisfied child who could not love other children? His verse-answer to Lou is: "Because my devotion drove me to my mother / and because her bearing resisted my will, / so it was that love remained inside of me." So dominant were his childhood thoughts that on occasions he fashioned prenatal womb-tomb poetry, again exclusively for the eyes of Lou:

*. . . und endlich kauert, kalt und karg,*
*mit seinem Himmel in den Händen*
*das Wunder in des Weibes Wänden—*
*Und seine Mutter ist sein Sarg.*    (sw III,593–94)

*. . . and finally, within a womb*
*this wonder crouches, scant and cold;*
*a heaven all his the fingers hold—*
*and she who bears him is his tomb.*

He wanted Lou to play a redemptive role—as an acquiescent mother, a loved one, and as an object of prayer:

*Ich geh dir nach, wie aus des Fiebers Grauen*
*erschreckte Kinder gehn zu lichten Frauen,*
*die sie besänftigen und Furcht verstehn.*
                            (sw III,176)

*I call to you, as fever-frenzied children*
*call out to radiant women who can still them:*
*women who understand what terror means.*

Rilke's doctrine of "non-possessive" love is seen in germination:

*Unsere Liebe hat keine Gewalten.*
*So will uns unsere Liebe sehn:*
*dass wir uns bei den Händen halten*

> und durch Gesichte und Gestalten
> ihrem Garten entgegengehn.    (sw iii,180)

> There is no tyranny in our Love:
> Our Love desires to see us so:
> that hand in hand we two should rove
> and past all masks, all manners, go
> and solemnly approach her grove.

Love is an infinitely tender gesture of companionship
without domination. Love can be inspiring, but not in a
wildly romantic sense. To Rilke it is a formal preparation,
a ritual and ceremonious relationship:

> Sei du mir Omen und Orakel
> und führ mein Leben an zum Fest,
> wenn meine Seele, matt vom Makel
> die Flügel wieder fallen lässt.

> Gieb mir das Niebesessne wieder:
> das Glück der Tat, das Recht zu Ruhn,—
> mit einem Wiegen deiner Glieder,
> mit einem Blick für meine Lieder,
> mit einem Grüssen kannst du's tun.    (sw iii,181)

> Be oracle and mystic sign
> And lead my life to ritual's door,
> when, tired by sloth, this soul of mine
> allows its wings to droop once more.

> Give me back the neverpossessed:
> the joy of work, the right to rest,—
> a single motion of your limbs,
> a single glance at these my hymns,
> a single greeting, and I'm blest.

> Wenn eng mit Zeit und Stundenschlagen
> der Alltag ärmlich uns umspinnt,
> geschieht mir oft: ich muss dich fragen:
> Glaubst du, dass wir das selber sind?
>                                    (sw iii,183)

> When, hemmed in without hope or rescue,
> we feel the hours beat down our flame,

*it often strikes me: I must ask you:*
*Do you believe we are the same?*

In rhetorical form, Rilke's questions about existence, reality, and identity persist until the end of his life; they become his criteria for sorting the essentials from trivia. By simplifying everyday life and keeping his distance from time-consuming responsibilities, Rilke hoarded his time for writing.

All gamuts of love are touched by the poet. From the plea for the loved one to rock and cradle his soul to the jubilant outcry, "Now it rustles in her womb / like the fullness of plowing, and you need bread. / She will bear you MY son, / and him you must teach life." And from agricultural to horticultural love-euphemisms is but a small step as lovers entwine and sway like tree branches and gates open in the wooded grove. Half of the hundred poems in honor of Lou were too earthy and were destroyed by mutual consent. Those that survived are, in the main, gentle and lyrical expression of personal delight:

> *Das Land ist licht und dunkel ist die Laube,*
> *und du sprichst leise und ein Wunder naht.*
> *Und jedes deiner Worte stellt mein Glaube*
> *als Betbild auf an meinem stillen Pfad.*

> *Ich liebe dich. Du liegst im Gartenstuhle,*
> *und deine Hände schlafen weiss im Schooss.*
> *Mein Leben ruht wie eine Silberspule*
> *in ihrer Macht, Lös meinen Faden los.*    (sw III,177)

> *The land is bright, and shaded is the bower;*
> *you murmur, and wonder's soon to be.*
> *Illumining my pathway with its power,*
> *each word of yours becomes a shrine to me.*

> *I love you. In the garden-seat you're nesting;*
> *asleep your hands lie white: the lap's their bed.*
> *My life is like a spool of silver, resting*
> *within their sovereignty. Unwind my thread.*

Probably at Lou's suggestion, René changed his name to Rainer. Like Japanese artists who change their names with each new stage of creative life, Rilke sensed somewhat the same need. His mother, however, would persist in calling him René and invoke the blessings of the Madonna on "my baby-boy (Bubi), my little treasure," even when Rainer reached the age of fifty.[11] Paradoxically, he was to revert to signing his name René at a period of his greatest fulfillment.

The first volume of poetry to appear under his new name, assertively called *Mir zur Feier* [*In My Honor*], expansively deals with the motif "Ich bin zuhause zwischen Tag und Traum" [I am at home between day and dream]. Although many of Rilke's final and major themes are previewed here, their limpid musicality and undiluted sentimentality rob them of power. The "existence" thoughts raised by Rainer needed the rhetorical massivity of later days. For the time being, these thoughts were softly and lyrically sounded as in the "motto" poem of *Mir zur Feier*:

> Das ist die Sehnsucht: wohnen im Gewoge
> und keine Heimat haben in der Zeit.
> Und das sind Wünsche: leise Dialoge
> der armen Stunden mit der Ewigkeit.
>
> Und das ist Leben. Bis aus einem Gestern
> die einsamste von allen Stunden steigt,
> die, anders lächelnd wie die andern Schwestern,
> dem Ewigen entgegenschweigt.          (sw III,204)
>
> This is yearning: to toss upon the sea
> and within Time to have no habitation.
> And these are wishes: quiet conversation
> between the poor hours and eternity.
>
> And this is life. Till of one day that's done
> an hour returns—the very loneliest,
> which, smiling differently from all the rest,
> meets the Eternal: not a word, not one.

With some editing to produce a sharper image-focus, substituting "weightier" words, and changing punctuation to create longer and smoother sentences, these poems were republished by Rilke about nine years later (1908–1909) under the title of *Die Frühen Gedichte* [*Early Poems*]. Offsetting his feeling of homelessness is the comforting affinity with the world of words. It is a possessive affinity, to be sure, for it is the poet who has the power to give words new dress and infuse them with new emotions.

> *Die armen Worte, die im Alltag darben,*
> *die zagen, blassen Worte, lieb ich so.*
> *Aus meinen Festen schenk ich ihnen Farben,*
> *da lächeln sie und werden langsam froh.* (sw iii,207)

> *The words I'm fondest of, are the most lowly:*
> *the pale, scared words that starve to death each day.*
> *Out of my feasts I fetch them color: slowly*
> *their smile revives, and slowly they grow gay.*

As Lou remarked, she learned from Rainer that poetry was "Nicht werkhaft, sondern leibhaft," a physical experience which, however, she could hardly share. How tentacular Rilke's attachments were to the living past and the deceased may be gauged in a simple, observational poem:

> *Und da weiss ich, dass nichts vergeht,*
> *keine Geste und kein Gebet,—*
> *dazu sind die Dinge zu schwer,—*
> *meine ganze Kindheit steht*
> *immer um mich her.*
> *Niemals bin ich allein.*
> *Viele, die vor mir lebten*
> *und fort von mir strebten,*
> *webten,*
> *webten*
> *an meinem Sein.* (sw iii,262)

> *And I know that nothing perishes,*
> *no gesture and no prayer*
> *for that things have too great a weight,*
> *my entire childhood stands*
> *ever around me.*
> *Never am I alone.*
> *Many who lived before me*

> and strove forth away from me,
> wove,
> wove
> at my being.

Aphoristic elements abound in *Mir zur Feier:* "You must not seek to understand life, / then will it become like a feast," "All fear is only an earliest beginning," "Anxiousness is only gesture, / and yearning its deepest meaning," "All who walk in beauty will be resurrected in beauty, And beauty is modesty," "Where fears end and God begins there perhaps are we."

In some of the poems—that seem like postscripts to the Renaissance paintings of Botticelli which he had admired in Florence—there is an aching tenderness, a feminine fragility, but suddenly a nameless fear intrudes to break the spell of what had seemed description of nature for art's sake as in "Prima-Vera":

> *Erste Rosen erwachen,*
> *und ihr Duften ist zag*
> *wie ein leisleises Lachen:*
> *flüchtig mit schwalbenflachen*
> *Flügeln streift es den Tag.*

> *Und wohin du langst,*
> *da ist Alles noch Angst.*                    (sw III,223)

> *Early roses have stirred,*
> *and as hushed is their sweetness*
> *as a laugh scarcely heard:*
> *brushing the day like a bird,*
> *swallow-winged in fleetness.*

> *And where you alight*
> *All is yet fright.*

A knot of fear, a vague anxiety, colors his idealizations of maidens, mothers, and matrons; but as yet, these themes are tentatively sounded with more melody than meaning. Rainer's purely poetic identification with these figures as well as with objects in nature, "Am I not a wave that lives in the lake?" slowly turns into more complex psychological relations.

While Rilke's poetry at the time reflected an intuitive direction, permitting expression and imagery to rise from feeling, he also attempted to clarify his aims intellectually. As a result there is a contrast between the introspective humility and softness of his poetry and the egocentric hardness of views expressed in prose. Attempting to prove himself to Lou, as he had tried earlier to impress his parents, relatives and denizens of Prague, he kept a record known as the *Tuscan Diary*, making such typical and dogmatic entries as:

> Know, then, that Art is this: the means by which the lonely and solitary fulfill themselves. What Napoleon was outwardly, every artist is inwardly. . . . Know, then, that the artist creates for himself, and for himself alone.[12]

When it came to his work, Rilke protected it with a Napoleonic ruthlessness and arrogance. He saw the artist as one "who builds dwellings nowhere" but lives in Art, the eternal, which reaches "beyond the roofs of centuries." The poet is apart from nothing: everything flows together within him: "trees, mountains, clouds, and waves are only symbols of those realities which *he* finds within himself." Rilke sensed the breath of eternity flow through him. "Durchwehen" for Rilke means an attitude of pure receptiveness and submission to impression, an attitude or state before the long struggle of creation that takes something out of one's self, like flinging words into infinity. The artist is a creator—like the sculptor—whose emotional experiences resembles female gestation and giving birth. Rilke's empathy for women coincides with envy for their unique experience which he can only simulate by way of poetic creativity.

The end poem of *Mir zur Feier*—aside from its new, vigorous tone and structure—also marks the serious beginning of his search for a God who can fill the void of a lost childhood religion. This God was no venerative symbol or a tutelary deity for the artist but an *essentia* to be deeply and personally experienced.

> *Du darfst nicht warten, bis Gott zu dir geht*
> *und sagt: ich bin.*
> *Ein Gott, der seine Stärke eingesteht,*
> *hat keinen Sinn.*
> *Da musst du wissen, dass dich Gott durchweht*
> *seit Anbeginn,*
> *und wenn dein Herz Ihn heimlich dir verrät,*
> *dann schafft Er drin.*          (sw III,263)

> You must not wait until God comes to you
> and says: I am.
> A god who confesses his strength,
> has no meaning.
> You must know that God breathes through you
> since the origin of time,
> and when your heart secretly reveals him to you,
> then He creates inside it.

God is visualized as the creative power, synonymous with art—badly preserved, the oldest work of art—an élan vital—an immanent force, a passion—to be sought within and not outside. A conviction such as this—and soon to be diluted with romantic pantheism—could not be compatible with orthodox revelation and institutional faith. The moment of epiphany for Rilke was not to be found in the church mass but in the broad spectrum of an "ever present" life-eternity.

Lou's companionship made up for the cold shoulder Rainer received from Germany's most élite corps of poets dominated by the prophet Stefan George whose pedagogic, law-giving verses were the scriptures for a revival of the cult of Greek beauty and severity. Rainer had no appetite for despotic spiritual reformism and would have been an unhappy disciple among the elders in the Olympian altitude of the George circle, nor was Rainer ready to reject the father image of "the God of yore," as did George, in favor of a neo-paganistic Nietzschean god. George's holy mission was directed to the conversion of a nation while Rainer's mission was to be purely personal. Although Rainer had won physical emancipation from his Prague environment and clung stubbornly to a poet's vocation, he had not as yet, like George, experienced the all-consuming demonology of creativity. The aristocratic bearing of the poet George and the ascetic earnestness of his work made an impression on Rainer who still had to become more worldly and sophisticated before he could shed his adolescent lyricism. Perhaps his failure to succeed as a playwright and to storm the important cultural circles that would have given him a false and immediate status was all to the good; it forced Rainer—as it did the frustrated playwright Henry James—to avoid the internecine activities of ingrown literary circles. As a poet, Rilke was truly to be alone.

IN PREPARING for two trips to Lou's native land, Russia, trips that were to total some six months during 1899 and 1900, Rilke studied Russian language and literature and learned frugal domesticity—cooking Russian groats and borsch, chopping wood, drying dishes, and wearing a blue Russian shirt. In Moscow, Lou and Rainer listened to Count Leo Tolstoy's tirade against the mystic and superstitious display of the Moscow Easter celebrants; nonetheless they joined the Easter Eve throng at the Kremlin. On another occasion when Lou and Rainer dropped in uninvited on the 71-year-old world-famous theistic moralist, they shared the embarrassment of overhearing one of the perennial and pitched verbal battles between the count and countess. Irritatedly, Tolstoy took his company for a quick stroll around his Yasnaya Polyana gardens, oblivious to whom he was entertaining, and treated them like the disciples who flocked to his mecca to hear the master's expositions on the ethics of the Gospels, his Rousseauistic condemnation of private property, the morally bad art of Homer and Shakespeare and the highest form of art, as exhibited by such writers as Harriet Beecher Stowe, inspired by love for God and man. Rilke—during two interviews—did not understand much of what Tolstoy said in Russian, but later he rebuked Tolstoy's views expressed in the tract *What is Art?* Rilke had shed the idea that art must communicate with all readers and instead began to see art as a reflection of private experience.

Rilke was emotionally overpowered by the elemental

and passionate devotion of the patiently enduring Russian peasant, "his singing heart," his primitive frugality, and the simplicity of his needs. If Rilke's view was a symptom "of decadence seeking its cure," as E. M. Butler notes,[1] or simply a longing for what seemed an uncomplicated existence far removed from his own tortuous quest for identity and stability, in either case Rilke ignored social realities and brutal aspects of peasant life by blithely spiritualizing it. About Russia, to which he came fully prepared to be overwhelmed, he wrote that it seemed "as if I had witnessed creation itself" amid a landscape that meant "home and heaven." The gigantic forests and immense rivers and plains—a far cry from Prague's placid parks—made the ancient towns with their churches and cloisters appear dwarfish and heightened the sensation of an otherworldly dimension. Although he called Russia his spiritual home, he never returned after his two trips, sensing that the personal myth he created might be destroyed by closer contact and knowing that he could not submit and surrender himself either to fate or God as did the peasants. Of Rilke's initially enormous enthusiasm to mine the riches of Russian folklore and literature, little remained after he had creditably translated into German the Russian epic *The Lay of the Band of Igor*, some poems by the noted peasant poet Spiridin Droshin, whom he befriended, and some by Lermontov and Fofanov.

From his hotel window in Moscow, Rilke was stirred by the devoutness of groups of pilgrims waiting for the opening of the silver doors of the chapel at the foot of the Kremlin. A similar urgency to give expression to his meditations brought words to his lips in the silence of mornings and evenings. As he recited words they became "Gebete," prayers; as he put them to paper through "inner dictation" they became art. Rilke's prayers were purely personal creations of objectless "delight and vanity" that distinguish them from any formal theological expression.[2] As a result, in *Das Buch vom mönchischen Leben* [*The Book of the Monastic Life*] a mood of romantic religiosity triumphs over religious meaning.

Rilke intended *Die Gebete* to be as organically structured as a veined leaf, but they bear greater resemblance to tiled mosaics of different colors, sizes, and shapes. Each prayer-poem is a colloquy with God and each has a hue different from the others, as perennially changing similes and metaphors appear to match Rilke's concept of God as something revealed in eternal metamorphoses. God is hidden in at least a hundred distinct similes and metaphors, appearing as the limitless present, a mountain, firebrand, earth, strength, a young bird, song, semen, forest, tree, comet, king of roses, an ancient tower, great homesickness, the dark unknown, a forest of contradiction, battle, evening hours, a venerable father with white hair, a ball, a peasant with a beard, a neighbor. "I find Thee in all these things," says the monk-poet, "You thing of things" ["Du Ding der Dinge"].

Logic and reason yield to intuitive perception as Rilke's God becomes both an immanent spirit and a transcendent being, a creator as well as the created. Six years later, in the 1905 edition of *Das Stunden-Buch* [*The Book of Hours*],[3] Rilke drops the venerative capitalization of personal pronouns and address and omits interpolative descriptions of the monk in order to place himself closer to his subject, the God who is a "becoming." "You see that I am a seeker," says the poet, and in his dream to fulfill himself by "completing" God, he admonishes himself to be a stranger to no emotion and be receptive to everything: beauty and terror, "Schönheit and Schrecken;" "Go to the boundary (Rand) of your yearning." Gone is Rilke's Nietzschean "Apostle" who proclaimed in a story written in 1896 that only the strong have a right to live and build the kingdom of the future on the bones of the weak. Instead, Rilke's new "Apostol" is an humble and ecstatically devout monk. In the intervening years, too, there has been progression from intellectual dilettantism and superficial estheticism to uniquely personal ethics.

In *Die Gebete,* art is synonymous with devotion and worship. Devotion without institutional dogma becomes religiosity, a reverence for his own art and by this token a narcissistic experience. "Know then," Rilke had the courage to declare, "the artist creates for himself—only for himself." Art is not to be pursued for the sake of art, but for the sake of devotional self-fulfillment and to close the void left by traditions abandoned. Meditation becomes the visionary state out of which grow poems that are festive and ceremonious in tone, abounding with reference to gestures that are infinitely tender and humble. The sixty-six prayer-poems—speedily composed from September 20 to October 14—represent a private poetic act and were not committed to print until six years after their original composition.

In some lines Rilke is indifferent to the existence of God, but then, without bothering to reconcile the contradiction, Rilke conceives the *imago dei* of his monk in a personalized vision of ecstasy similar to that of Angelus Silesius' *Cherubinic Wanderer*. In 1657 the baroque mystic Silesius wrote:

> *Ich weiss, dass ohne mich Gott nicht ein*
> *Nu kann leben;*
> *Werd ich zunicht, er muss vor Not den*
> *Geist aufgeben.*

> *I know that without me God cannot*
> *live one moment,*
> *Were I to become nought, he must perforce*
> *give up the ghost.*

Rilke's monk, too, speaks of the inseparability of man and God:

> *Was wirst Du tun, Gott, wenn ich sterbe?*
> *Ich bin Dein Krug,—wenn ich zerscherbe?*
> *Ich bin Dein Trank,—wenn ich verderbe?*
> *Bin Dein Gewand und Dein Gewerbe,*
> *mit mir verlierst Du Deinen Sinn.*    (sw III,334)

> *What will you do, God, when I die?*
> *When I, your pitcher, shattered lie?*
> *When I, your drink, go stale or dry?*
> *I am your garb, the trade you ply,*
> *you lose your meaning, losing me.*

Even closer is the monk's vocabulary and sentiment to Silesius' wanderer:

> *Gott liebet mich allein, nach*
> *mir ist ihm so bange,*
> *Dass er auch stirbt vor Angst,*
> *weil ich ihm nicht anhange.*

> *God loves me alone, for me*
> *he is so anxious*
> *That he also dies of fear*
> *because I do not cleave to him.*

Rilke's monk echoes this feeling: "and I feel your heart and mine beating—/ and both with fear." Baroque mysticism and Rilke's religiosity coincide in terminology: *Nu, Angst, bange, Dinge* (the eternal moment, fear, anxiousness, things). For Rilke the dimensions of time are experienced through the sensation of the moment, nameless fear—akin to Coleridge's "holy dread"—becomes the common denominator of experience for all creatures and anxiety creates a state of tension.

A mystic's vision generally roosts in a pantheistic fusion of feeling and being as suggested in a baroque couplet:

> *Mensch, allererst, wenn du bist alle Dinge worden,*
> *So stehst du in dem Wort und in der Götter Orden.*

> *Man, when you have become all things, primarily,*
> *Then you stand in the gods' word and hierarchy.*

Like the mystic, Rilke was able to obscure generic differences between objects and self. Lou tells of an afternoon walk with Rainer and his sudden insistence that he could not pass a certain locust tree. His emotional identification with the tree was so persuasive that Lou herself had the startling sensation of seeing the tree take on a ghostly appearance. Such projections into objects fortunately were sporadic and never reached the point of no-return for Rilke as it did for Silesius who weeks before his death refused all visitors so that he could be in undisturbed communion with the Divine Countenance.

God is the partner of the poet-monk's solitude, a state of revelation. The eye of God becomes synonymous with the monk's. All of the artist's creations, arising from the center of his solitude, are given a sanctity through the presence of God's eye (which "watches over my shoulder, from infinity to infinity"). Rilke's visionary experience is similar to that of such German mystics as Johann Eckhart (1260–1327) who wrote: "The eye by which I see God is the same as the eye by which God sees me. My eye and God's eye are one and the same—one in seeing, one in knowing, and one in loving." [4] Rilke's mystique though by no means makes him a mystic.

Physicality—eye, ear, hand, mouth ("You force yourself darkly into mouths"), hair ("His rootlike hair through all things grew")—is tightly linked to abstractions like "I was song, and God, the rime, still rustles in my ear." Through a complement of all senses, the monk's hymns reach "the highest thralldom of his soul." His expectancy is feminine in the "deep and awesome bridal night of all inner pictures and all anxious gestures . . ." that evoke childhood, the angels, the "princely rescuers" and inhabitants of regions in whose heights light dissolves into nothingness and who stand in contrast to the dark power that eternally constitutes God's depth. Rilke tentatively outlines psychic-mystical regions that eventually become more fully populated.

The flood of synonyms which Rilke uses for God obliterates any conventional or metaphysical kernels we may wish to discover as his poetry reversibly veers from immanence to transcendence and from the anthropomorphic to the abstract; the poet's desire for union with all things alternates with the most strenuous attempts at self-identification—to prove, as it were, his existence by apartness from other elements in the universe. Where angels, the madonna, Christ, dolls, and other things had been his childhood confidantes, he now broaches the possibility that God "in whom all is communion and brotherliness" will take their place. "I lived long on my knees in the anteroom of his name," says Rilke in reflecting on the monastic period, and some of the poems seem almost apologetically insistent that God become aware of the existence of the poet-monk: "I am, you timid one. Do you not hear me / surge against you with all my senses? My feelings, finding wings, / whitely encircle your countenance," "I am a new beginning for you."

> Du, Nachbar Gott, wenn ich dich manchesmal
> in langer Nacht mit hartem Klopfen störe,—
> so ists, weil ich dich selten atmen höre
> und weiss: Du bist allein im Saal.
> Und wenn du etwas brauchsts, ist keiner da,
> um deinem Tasten einen Trank zu reichen:
> Ich horche immer. Gieb ein kleines Zeichen.
> Ich bin ganz nah.                    (sw 1,255)

> You, neighbor God, if sometimes in the night
> I rouse you with loud knocking, I do so
> Only because I seldom hear you breathe;
> I know: you are alone.
> And should you need a drink, no one is there
> to reach it to you, groping in the dark.
> Always I hearken. Give but a small sign.
> I am quite near.

However, there is no sign of recognition so that the poet's exhausted senses must "go their homeless way." Knowledge of God is only "in my inmost soul"; the ascent of God is out of the poet's breathing heart and prayer. "Workmen are we—apprentice, journeyman, master, building you, you towering nave," who can only discern the contours of God in a vague and growing shape. Is it we who have created God or are we God's dream, asks Rilke. "If you are the dreamer, I am your dream."

> Ich kreise um Gott, um den uralten Turm,
> und ich kreise jahrtausendelang;
> und ich weiss noch nicht: bin ich ein Falke, ein Sturm
> oder ein grosser Gesang.               (sw 1,253)

> I gyre around God, around the ancient tower,
> and I have gyred for centuries;

*and still I do not know: am I a falcon, a storm*
*or a mighty song.*

"Yet, when I incline into myself: *my* God is dark . . . /
Only that I ascend out of *his* warmth / that is all I
know. . . ." Introspective descent and exultant ascent as
well as the gyring about God and the living of life in
expanding circles symbolize the spatial dimensions of
Rilke's speculative thoughts about God and existence. The
tranquillity which overmists the prayer-poem stems from
assumed, submissive naiveté, while the boldness of address
simulates that of children before they are intimidated by
the adult world. At this point the triad of his emotional
concern—life, death, being—receive optimistic accents:
"You said 'life' loudly and 'die' quietly, / and constantly
repeated 'be.' " Lou herself calls attention to one of the
"monk's pilgrimage" poems, later incorporated in *Das
Stunden-Buch,* as having been specifically addressed to
her:

*Lösch mir die Augen aus: ich kann dich sehn,*
*wirf mir die Ohren zu: ich kann dich hören,*
*und ohne Füsse kann ich zu dir gehn,*
*und ohne Mund noch kann ich dich beschwören.*
*Brich mir die Arme ab, ich fasse dich*
*mit meinem Herzen wie mit einer Hand,*
*halt mir das Herz zu, und mein Hirn wird schlagen,*
*und wirfst du in mein Hirn den Brand,*
*so werd ich dich auf meinem Blute tragen.*   (sw 1,313)

*Extinguish my eyes: I can see you,*
*close my ears: I can hear you,*
*and without feet I can draw near you,*
*and even without mouth can I implore you.*
*Break my arms, I grasp you*
*with my heart as with hand,*
*arrest my heart and my brain will beat,*
*and if you cast a firebrand into my brain,*
*I will carry you in my blood's stream.*

Unlike the early lyrics to which Lou admitted that she
"brought no understanding despite their musicality," Lou

responded to this poem as a celebration of their experience
which reached into "the rootground of physicality." Rilke
powerfully fused the language of mysticism and eroticism.
Rilke's childhood God, a product of a peculiar blend of his
mother's orthodoxy and spiritualism, was resisted briefly in
adolescence by rebellious atheism, reshaped into the
mythological god of Rilke's early diaries, sought as a
pantheistic immanence in the monk's prayers, viewed in
Rilke's *Stories of the dear God* anthropomorphically as a
doddering old man and animistically as a spirit or emotion,
metamorphosed into the Angels of the *Duino Elegies*, and
finally lost in a host of vague synonyms in Rilke's last years.
That there was a more tumultuous side to Rilke than the
ascetic, meditative monk Apostol is emphasized by a
militant ancestor he created one stormy autumn night in
1899, *Die Weise von Liebe und Tod des Cornets Chris-
toph Rilke* [*The Lay of the Love and Death of Cornet
Christopher Rilke*], inspired by a reading of family docu-
ment fascicles—one dated 1663—assiduously collected by
Uncle Jaroslav. Rilke wrote while the night wind fluttered
two candles and the clouds moved across the moon. From
all sides associations streamed into brilliantly rhythmic,
sketchlike sequences of the mongrelistic prose-poem, indebted in some ways to Liliencron's martial and lyric
balladry.

Essentially Rilke's *Cornet* tells about the campaign of
an Austrian regiment commanded by Baron von Pirovano
against the Turks who invaded Hungary during the early
seventeenth century and the heroic fall of his 18-year-
old "ancestor" Christopher Rilke, a cavalry officer privi-
leged to carry the company regimental flag. From the very
start there is a headlong pace interrupted sporadically by
stretches of exhaustion: "Riding, riding, riding through
the day, through the night, through the day. Riding,
riding, riding. And courage has become so tired and
yearning so great." The landscape reels by impressionistically and the conversation of the saddle companions—
and later brothers-in-arms—is fragmentary, as if torn apart
by the wind. Their mood reflects melancholy yearning and
homesickness, symbolized by images of mother, maidens

singing in the fields at harvest time, roses, and the Madonna. In the heat of war and to the beat of drums, "wine and blood" become one heady emotion. Like the chivalric St. George, Rilke's hero rescues a brown, nude maiden tied to a tree. In the first version, Rilke is content to be rather general in the description of this scene, but in revising it he accents its sensuality by making the maiden a young woman, "bloody and nude," with eyes of passion and teeth that bite. Even the ropes which bind her are hot from body contact. A shudder seizes the Cornet as he jumps to saddle, rides into the night over the bodies of slain peasants, and hears the howling chorus of bereaved dogs. Before his death, one night of love is granted him, naturally in a castle and naturally with a countess—no plebeian maidens for Christopher. In bed "prayers are shorter but more devout" is a masculine aphorism addressed to God that would have appalled the monk Apostol. "Like children who have fear," they seek one another desperately and playfully and the "dark womb of their yearning" becomes an image of a door (in the revised version) that opens to intimacy and oblivion of yesterday and tomorrow. They ask no questions but give each other new names out of memories of "stories, dreams, and in a hundred languages." She removes the cloak of his childhood innocence so that the Cornet stands "naked like a holy man." Symbolically attending their love and pleasure is the "dark and slim" flag, as if it were "an unconscious woman"—leaning against the window-*cross*. Again love is surrounded by a visualistic religiosity that also refracts the mother image. And, as "behind a hundred doors is this (great) sleep which two beings have in common as they have *one* mother or *one* death." Just as he had given himself to love, the Cornet now gives himself joyfully and festively to death, with a hopeful question on his lips, "Is this *the* Life?"

Only the first version of the *Cornet* contains a wishful ending:

A gigantic armor-clad cavalryman (he fell later at St. Gotthardt) carried the countess out of the burning castle. The escape was like a miracle. But no one knew her name nor the name of the son to whom she soon gave birth in other peaceful lands.[5]

What impelled Rainer to abandon Christopher's heir is not clear, except possibly that his own sensibilities had a saturation point. Some critics have regarded this mellifluous libretto a little masterpiece of episodic richness and stinging freshness; others have scored it as a self-indulgent bravura exercise in sentimentality. That there is more artifice than art in the *Cornet* and more ebullient fantasy than esthetic constraint was evident to Rilke himself who in later conversation demoted the Cornet to a corporal seized by hysteria. When the *Cornet* was written, it failed to roost with any publisher. A Prague periodical, however, printed the slightly revised version in 1904, and two years later it made an unimpressive debut in book form; but, republished in 1912, it was carried upward by a ground-swell of readers. During the war it became grist for a veritable orgy of patriotic sentimentality, becoming an indispensable part of public readings and trench literature. Since then music has been composed for it, something which Rilke resented and graphically called a bastardization of art forms, a film has been made, and copies of the little book—in the original and translation—have made their way into the hands of millions of readers.

After three years of intimacy, the relation of Lou and Rainer was beginning to take a downturn in August, 1900, toward the conclusion of their second visit to Russia. An immediate cause was a letter which Rilke had sent to Lou begging for a quick return to his side after she had left him alone while visiting some of her Russian relatives. His plea was so self-derogatory and pathological, expressing a wish again to become a child and a devoted "squirrel," that it raised Lou's hackles. His fears, childlike expression of dependence, and possessive insistences had led to an "Ineinanderleben," a symbiotic entwining of their lives, becoming unbearable to Lou. As long as Rilke maintained what Lou called his *Traumsicherheit*, the ability to bridge with ease and dreamlike self-confidence the inner world of the poet and the outerworld of man, there was no danger. However, periodically, the swamplike fixations of his inner world threatened to suck him under. From the start, Rilke had fastened onto Lou in the hope of finding release from his childhood fears and gaining an approving mother-mistress, undeterred by Lou's initial displeasure at the excessiveness (*Überschwenglichkeit*) in "your letters which follow me daily." What did attract her was the similarity of their psychological experiences, but finally she realized that the problems which attracted her to Rilke were precisely the ones that would tear her away from him.

Almost immediately after his trip to Russia, Rilke decided to accept a long-standing invitation to join the painter Heinrich Vogeler at Worpswede, the artists' colony located near Hamburg. Through Rilke's diary, letters, and poems we know that during these summer months he felt himself to be living as if in a fairy tale, primarily through the charm of "two maidens in white," the expressionistic painter Paula Becker and the sculptor Rodin's pupil Clara Westhoff. Their attentiveness was a balm. The quiescent and changing landscape so different from the massively static Russian, musicales that featured Strauss, Schubert, and Beethoven Lieder, conversations joined by the playwright Carl Hauptmann and Hermann Büttner, a compiler of baroque mystical writings, dances—which the uninitiated Rainer could well have done without—poetry and verse readings, all contributed to Rilke's new-found delight. Ideas took shape and images were formed: "Every moment something is held in the sounding air—a tree, a house, a mill which turns slowly, a man with black shoulders, a large cow, or a sharp-edged jagged goat pointing into the heavens. There are conversations in which only the landscape takes part, from all sides and with a hundred voices." In such diary entries, he not only sketched what he saw but with a sense of isolation he again stressed that all "Dinge" (things) have a life of their own—as is the inexorable fate of humans. If the meaning of existence was driven home to him by the indifference and hostility of nature and God, the rebuffs were gradually accepted as indicating that life's essence was in non-relationships or in severely conditional relations. Occasionally a cloud crossed his vision and his keen sensitivity to changes in seasons—the cycle of growth and decay—asserted itself: "Autumn—everything green vanishes. Only the deep brown of the moorland remains, as if shaded by great invisible things. . . . Death in the moor. How easy it must be to meet him here." [6] Death is a hard-shouldered figure with heavy-hanging, grasping hands. There is no escape from this figure, no battling the blind figure's inexorable and indifferent advance.

Aside from learning to view things through the painter's eyes—significant detail, color, and isolated forms in space—it was a brief recuperative and gestative period for him: "Here I have no memories." The floodgates of memory were temporarily closed and as a result there were no inspirational fits to drive him to poetize; his prose and verse entries in the diaries show a calm control over stormy fantasies.

Rilke deliberately searched for words and images that would be equivalents for his emotions. In his diary he writes: "Ich ruhe nicht, bis ich das eine erreicht: / Bilder zu finden für meine Verwandlungen" ["I rest not, until I have achieved one thing: to find images for my transformations"]. The idea of *transformation* is to undergo changes in meaning for Rilke. It embodies at different times an acute consciousness of his own evolution as a person, his changing perception of people and landscape, the translation of the vague emotion within to the reality of an independently existing poem, and the ability of the poetic thought to persuade and transform the reader. Most deeply rooted, however, is Rilke's almost obstinate psychological attempt to absorb things—objects in nature as well as persons living or dead—and to compel their transformation quite literally within his own being. This pathology of the poetic spirit, a fearful urge to dominate memory and the material, is given free rein. As a result, many of Rilke's stories and poems have a macabre atonality. Perhaps the climax of his preoccupation with transformation is reached, many years after Worpswede, in the ninth of the

*Duino Elegies:* "Earth, is it not this you wish: an invisible / re-arising in us. . . . What, if not *transformation*, is your urgent command?" Existence is a self-centered all-absorbing act, and for Rilke a transvaluation of values, a spiritualization of the material, a crowning iteration of the belief that reality is only within himself or in a poem. This absolute emotional and intellectual formulation was almost inevitable; it became his personal solution to the existential question.

In September, 1900, Rilke quite suddenly changed his residence to Berlin, but he still kept up an assiduous correspondence with the "two sisters of my soul," Paula and Clara. To each he responded in a special way. Intriguingly, some of his poems show that the transition from prose-thought to verse-thought was frequently only a matter of mechanics. In mood and predisposition he was ready, for instance, for a letter from Clara which he paraphrased in his diary:

Clara W. writes today about a black ivy-wreath—this heavy black wreath which she took unsuspectingly from the gable of her house out of the gray November air and then became so monstrously earnest in the room, a thing in itself, a thing more suddenly, which seemed to become constantly heavier, drinking in the sorrowing in the air of the room and the early dawn. And all this shall then lie on the thin wood-coffin of the poor girl who had died in the South. . . . The black wreath will, perhaps, impress itself on the coffin and its long roots will crawl up the white shroud and entwine with the folded hands and become engrown with the never-loved hair and engrown with the heart which, full of clogged blood, has also become black and flat and, in the twilight of the dead one, will be hardly distinguishable from the heartlike leaves of the ivy. . . . And through the empty halls of the blood will go the ivy, leaf upon leaf on its long roots, like nuns who lead each other with a single rope and who pilgrimage to the deceased heart whose doors are lightly ajar.

As a postscript to this diary entry, Rilke notes: "I would like to write a requiem around this image." And he did, shocking prose into verse through devices of prosody:

*Sieh her,*
*Dieser Kranz ist so schwer,*
*und sie werden ihn auf dich legen,*
*diesen schweren Kranz.*
*Kann's dein Sarg aushalten?*
*Wenn er bricht*
*unter dem schwarzen Gewicht,*
*kriecht in die Falten*
*von deinem Kleid:*
*Efeu.*
*Weit rankt er hinauf,*
*rings rankt er dich um,*
*und der Saft, der sich in seinen Ranken bewegt,*
*regt dich auf mit seinem Geräusch.*
*So keusch bist du.*
*Aber du bist nicht mehr zu,*
*langgedehnt bist du und lass.*
*Deines Leibes Türen sind angelehnt,*
*und nass tritt der Efeu ein,*
*wie Reihn*
*von Nonnen*
*die sich führen*
*am schwarzen Seil,*
*weil es dunkel ist in dir, du Bronnen.*[7]

*Look here.*
*This wreath is so heavy,*
*and they will place it upon you,*
*this heavy wreath.*
*Can your coffin bear it?*
*When it breaks*
*under the dark heavy weight*
*there crawls in the folds*
*of your shroud:*
*ivy.*
*High uprears himself,*
*encircling uprears himself around you,*
*and the juice, which stirs in his roots,*
*excites you with his commotion.*
*So virginal are you.*
*But you are no longer closed,*
*long distended and weary are you.*

*Your body's doors are ajar,*
*and wet the ivy enters,*
*like rows*
*of nuns*
*who lead each other*
*along a black rope,*
*because it is dark in you, you well.*

Dedicated to Clara, this requiem is long, twining, and rambling, textually and typographically, in approximation of the ivy that is the central image. While the death and defloration fantasy, the erotic attraction to corpses, and the Freudian symbols without benefit of Freud are set off by the stimulus of Clara's letter, pathology also merges with a philosophy of the animistic relation of man and nature. The human heart and the ivy's heartlike leaves are equated: "And my strength / circulates in the wreath." In the midst of the impromptu requiem, an extravagant necrophilic hymn, there arise some splendid spiritualistic lines:

*Und du lebtest in Ungeduld,*
*denn du wusstest: Das ist nicht das Ganze.*
*Leben ist nur ein Teil . . . , wovon?*
*Leben ist nur ein Ton . . . , worin?*
*Leben hat Sinn nur verbunden mit vielen*
*Ereignissen des unendlichen Raumes,*
*Leben ist nur der Traum eines Traumes,—*
*und das Wachsein ist anderswo.*

*For you lived with impatience,*
*for you knew: That is not the whole.*
*Life is only a part . . . of what?*
*Life is only a tone . . . in what?*
*Life makes sense only if tied to many*
*events of the unending space,*
*Life is only the dream of a dream,—*
*and wakefulness is elsewhere.*

Most of the poetry of the Worpswede and the earlier Munich period was collected in *Das Buch der Bilder* [*The Book of Images*], whose poems centered largely around the thoughts provoked by certain pictures or images. Many of the poems he wrote at Worpswede have a simplicity and symmetry that are breathtaking. Most often, he composed at night, solemn and alone:

### ERNSTE STUNDE

*Wer jetzt weint irgendwo in der Welt,*
  *ohne Grund weint in der Welt,*
  *weint über mich.*

*Wer jetzt lacht irgendwo in der Nacht,*
  *ohne Grund lacht in der Nacht,*
  *lacht mich aus.*

*Wer jetzt geht irgendwo in der Welt,*
  *ohne Grund geht in der Welt,*
  *geht zu mir.*

*Wer jetzt stirbt irgendwo in der Welt,*
  *ohne Grund stirbt in der Welt:*
  *sieht mich an.*                    (SW 1,405–6)

### SOLEMN HOUR

*Who cries now anywhere in the world,*
*without cause in the world,*
*cries over me.*

*Who laughs now anywhere in the night,*
*without cause laughs in the night,*
*laughs at me.*

*Who goes now anywhere in the world,*
*without cause journeys in the world,*
*comes to me.*

*Who dies now anywhere in the world,*
*without cause dies in the world,*
*looks at me.*

The thought that gave birth to the poem, we find in a diary entry: " . . . the world is no laughing matter, but [laughter] is the loudest communal expression. In the midst of life we harbor a weeping death within and are his laughing mouth." [8] For the solitary and the serious, laughter seems a disturbing expression of enmity by the masses. A need for communality in seriousness, rather than in laughter, is what Rilke suggested in a conversation with Carl Hauptmann at Worpswede. Yet, Rilke found his strongest identity in a detachment from others so that the world of reality often became a strange place with strange shapes while his interior and transcendent world assumed an absolute reality for him. Many of the poems in *The Book of Images* were composed at night, and in his own description he gives himself over to waking dreams that unroll like picture-strips, images, when viewed through the slits of his eyelids. As these endless strips fuse episodically, the poet becomes so enmeshed that he cannot extricate himself but allows himself to passively experience whatever comes. At those moments he actually lived in a deeper dimension of consciousness from which memories arose that were cast into poetic form. Reminiscently he says:

> *In solchen Nächten wächst mein Schwesterlein,*
> *das vor mir war und vor mir starb, ganz klein.*
> *Viel solche Nächte waren schon seither:*
> *Sie muss schon schön sein. Bald wird irgendwer*
> *　　sie frein.*　　　　　　　　　　　　(sw 1,464)

> *During such nights, grows my little sister,*
> *who lived before me and died before me, quite small.*
> *Many such nights have existed since then:*
> *She must be beautiful by now. Soon someone*
> *　　will woo her.*

Plainly, this memory-poem is autobiographical in bitter retrospect of the years when he was put into the deceased's clothing to perform as a substitute for his mother's loss. The childhood episodes return with explosive psychological force, suggesting that out of them grew his songs to maidenhood, the lamentations for the young-deceased, his necrophilia, the interior absorption of all deceased acquaintances—their subjugation and their new existence as contemporaries. Two words in the poem are ambiguous and allow multiple meanings: *frein* and *wächst*. "Frein" or *freien* can signify to free, to release, or to woo. All have validity. Rilke implies that eventually his deceased sister will be free of his rancor; he sadly refers to her premature death and personal unfulfillment that would be remedied if someone would woo her (as the ivy symbol, death, and the living poet had wooed the unknown girl in the coffin). Nostalgic sentiments blend the accusing and the forgiving, offering a release for both poet and sister.

*Wächst* (grows) has abstract and specific meanings. In one sense his sister still looms ominously large in his dreams and memories; in another sense, her existence and development continue either in Rilke's memory-interior—which he referred to as the dark side of one's personality—or in the spiritualistic afterlife. Rilke persistently clung to the concept of immortality, which he grounded in the belief that nothing real can ever be extinguished. The same thought is expressed aphoristically: "Every day is the beginning of life. Every life is the beginning of immortality." [9]

Rilke realized the danger of consorting with such unanswerable questions about life and death, so that he pauses amid the diary outpourings of despair to remind himself that madhouses are filled with people who have not returned from the *Zwischenland*, the borderland which he was exploring. However far sensation-seeking took Rilke into dark speculations, it was an iron will that saved his mind from collapse. Rilke knew from the disastrous examples of Hölderlin, Kleist, and Nietzsche—who were similarly possessed and tormented by the daimonic—that the abyss of mental disorder was all too ready to engulf the artist. Yet he clung to the idea that "Whoever rightly understands and celebrates death, he at the same time makes life great."

In January and February, 1901, Paula and Clara visited Rilke in Berlin. Paula had already become betrothed to the artist Otto Modersohn, leaving Clara as the only sister-soul in his care. In considerable turmoil, Rainer turned to Lou for advice and got more than he bargained for. Lou recalled that years ago she had come to him like a mother and that once again she would assume her duty by telling him that as long as he did not bind himself to anyone else, he would be responsible only to himself. She pointed to what both called the "other self" in Rainer— the dark side, the easily depressed and excited, the all-too-fearful and lacerated—which could lead to insanity and suicide. Accept, she said, life's "great plan" and grow, "go along the same path to your dark God" who can bless you. In short, Lou was against Rainer's self-burial in the Worpswede moorland and thoughts of marriage, closing her letter with the implication that Rainer was not to contact her again except in the hour of direst need.[10]

In March, 1901, after a brief illness caused by agitation, Rilke married Clara Westhoff and took abode in a farmhouse at Westerwede, not far from Worpswede.

COMPARED WITH the poems that Rilke had written for Lou, those composed for Clara lack fire. To his betrothed he spoke almost pitiably of his inability to "carry quietly my dark burdens to the shore of each night." Once she has consented to marriage and the sharing of the poet's loneliness, he writes gratefully: "and now we are alone, a pair, in the world / and the world is stirring like the ocean. / And we stand in mutual supporting / and hands rest recuperating in one another; / we have long yearned for heart and home." [1] The idyl soon was disrupted by economic pressures, Rilke's incapacity to assume the weight of daily responsibilities, and his temperamental inability to submit to a lasting marital relationship. What he needed was female friendship unencumbered by the material demands of a household. Their only child Ruth was born to them in December, 1901, amid jubilation, but soon she seemed like a stranger and eventually she was handed to the care of Clara's parents. "A joint life for two people is an impossibility" because it robs both partners of their fullest freedom and development, Rilke confided in a letter to an acquaintance. He had failed to realize the goals which he had set for an ideal marriage pair: to appoint one another the guardian of each other's solitude and to love the distance between each other. In a didactic poem "Ehe" ["Wedlock"] the husband Rilke insisted, "We do not wish to submit to one another." The wife in the poem accepts the necessity for merely living *nebeneinander*, side-by-side, as self-dependent solitaries. She appears resigned, if not grateful, for her spouse's sage declaration that every being bears his own torments and that not even "our child" is a unifier.

Charges of insincerity leveled at Rilke must cope with the fact that Rilke for a time tried strenuously to keep "heart and home" united, but that his desire for companionship and the simultaneous need for stringent solitude were irreconcilable and at tragic odds. Working against marriage was the fact that once he gained an objective—poetic or human—his interest could fade with astonishing rapidity. Subconsciously he perpetuated his mother's indifference, so that, ironically, his own child was to suffer from the same parental abdication he had experienced. Almost in premonition, Rilke wrote in his diary a year earlier that we invite guilt if we attach humans or even animals to us because our abilities are too limited to allow sharing and helping in an absolute sense. He mitigated his cavalier relations to wife and child by periodic and sentimental promises—through the media of correspondence and poems—for a better future.

During the early months of marriage, Rilke's poetry reveals that the past was still with him in all its dark aspects. The down-to-earth marriage seemed pale compared with the poet and painter's "reality." Art is eternal, nature ephemeral is one of the recurrent motifs in *Das Buch von der Pilgerschaft* [*The Book of Pilgrimage*], the second part of *Das Stunden-Buch* which he composed within a single week in September, 1901. Rilke's search for similes and images to picture the existential relation of "I" and "God" led him to return to the earlier "gyrations" of the monks and his prayers to God. "I am yet the same who knelt / before you in monk's garb: the deep, serving Levite / whom you fulfilled, who invented you." God appears to man in whatever image his conception can conjure up: anthropomorphically as an old man, as a son, or as an essence that in changing forms courses through all life as the inmost and unyieldingly secret meaning within all things, and that which shows itself "as haven to the ship and as ship to the land." Identities are lost, rather than gained, in similes and are as impervious to examination as a drop of water in one's palm. Relativity became a poetic certainty for Rilke and instability or change a condition of existence.

In a section, close to the ballad form, he describes the morning of a pilgrimage and the spectacular transformations of the monk, amid imagery of sensuousness and surrealistic brilliance. We feel the monk's illusory transposition into a soaring bird, his body hanging like a distorted marionette between small, meager arms; his abrupt turning into a fish to swim in the deep, green ocean of his torment; then changing his habitat to land where he is made bridegroom of a deceased "so that no strange and unespoused maid will tread the meadows of Paradise." On the meadows the monk is drawn into a dance, almost forgetting that it is time for prayer. All this transformational whirligig has made no impression on God, the half-asleep "Old Man," so that the monk, sick and distressed, does violence to himself until "der Alte" soothes him like a child and puts him under his chin as he would a violin. Symbols and cyphers are woven into this allegory, and if it is not quite clear, neither is an uninhibited dream or intuitive phantasmagoria.

Turning to a dominant theme, namely "the capacity to love," Rilke noted almost brutally that this dimension may not be within the reach of lovers and some die uncomprehending like animals, surrendering their love potential like green, unripe fruit that God inherits; misled by the material and the voluptuousness of sensations, others become possessive:

> Sie sagen mein und nennen das Besitz,
> wenn jedes Ding sich schliesst, dem sie sich nahn,
> so wie ein abgeschmackter Charlatan
> vielleicht die Sonne sein nennt und den Blitz.
> So sagen sie: mein Leben, meine Frau,
> mein Hund, mein Kind, und wissen doch genau,
> das alles: Leben, Frau und Hund und Kind
> fremde Gebilde sind, daran sie blind
> mit ihren ausgestreckten Händen stossen.    (sw 1,338)

*They still say "mine," and claim possession, though*
*each thing, as they approach, withdraws and closes;*
*a silly charlatan perhaps thus poses*
*as owner of the lightning and the sun.*
*And so they say: my life, my wife, my child,*
*my dog, well knowing all that they have styled*
*their own: life, wife, child, dog remain*
*shapes alien and unknown,*
*that blindly groping they must stumble on.*

Rilke's wish to lead so frighteningly a detached existence, abjuring the possessive, was an *idée fixe* as unnatural in its conception as it became natural by almost life-long practice.

Since the present held so little to celebrate, what of the future? And here Rilke unfurls a panorama, quite similar—but more stately and hymnic—in view and tone to the "Venedig" poem in the *Visions of Christ* cycle, of a pastoral society with a simplicity of living that is derived not from church institutions and materialistic technology but from a totally self-dependent way of life free from the fear of death:

*Alles wird wieder gross sein und gewaltig.*
*Die Lande einfach und die Wasser faltig,*
*die Bäume riesig und sehr klein die Mauern;*
*und in den Tälern, stark und vielgestaltig,*
*ein Volk von Hirten und von Ackerbauern.*

*Und keine Kirchen, welche Gott umklammern*
*wie einen Flüchtling und ihn dann bejammern*
*wie ein gefangenes und wundes Tier,—*
*die Häuser gastlich allen Einlassklopfern*
*und ein Gefühl von unbegrenztem Opfern*
*in allem Handeln und in dir und mir.*

*Kein Jenseitswarten und kein Schaun nach drüben,*
*nur Sehnsucht, auch den Tod nicht zu entweihn*
*und dienend sich am irdischen zu üben,*
*um seinen Händen nicht mehr neu zu sein.*    (sw 1,329–30)

*All will grow great and powerful again:*
*the seas be wrinkled and the land be plain,*
*the trees gigantic and the walls be low;*

*and in the valleys, strong and multiform,*
*a race of herdsmen and of farmers grow.*

*No churches to encircle God as though*
*he were a fugitive, and then bewail him*
*as if he were a captured wounded creature,—*
*all houses will prove friendly, there will be*
*a sense of boundless sacrifice prevailing*
*in dealings between men, in you, in me.*

*No waiting the beyond, no peering toward it,*
*but longing to degrade not even death;*
*we shall learn earthliness, and serve its ends,*
*to feel its hands about us like a friend's.*

Visions, similes, and paradoxes abound in the *Pilgrimage* cycle. Only through nonpossessiveness, implies Rilke, can we experience true possession; only by not loving in a human way can we achieve love; only by grasping spirituality without dogma can we experience religion; only through art can we experience reality. For Rilke both the act of loving and the act of creating transcend the object and become the sensation that *is* life. So radical a view can be supported only by a narcissistic idealist who puts art as a way of life above everything else.

With the end of the subsidy from home, the slim economic margin for the survival of Rilke's marriage was gone and he was forced to make a choice. For himself it was quite possible to subsist on vegetables and oat cereal from California, culinary preferences that brought him "close to what is simple . . . life intensified by nothing that is foreign," like meat and alcohol; but Rilke's frugalities would hardly be sufficient for wife, child and the upkeep of a home. Journalism, which he regarded as "a trade in the midst of time" rather than art that "looks to eternity," was too demanding an occupation, while the prospects of an office job held out by his father in Prague gave Rilke the chilling vision of "a new military school," a new prison, a form of suicide, a sedentary death. Instead, he chose to wander and find bed and board wherever proffered so that he could continue to devote himself to

art. For the next twenty-five years of his life he was to
change his residences at least fifty times, with mainstays in
France, Italy, Germany, and Switzerland; a well-paged
*Baedeker* was his most constant companion. For Clara,
there also followed years of wandering and working: Paris,
Rome, Berlin, Munich. Until close to the end, their paths
occasionally crossed and on the surface their relationship
remained friendly.

In 1902, Rilke took the time, encouraged by commis-
sions, to reflect and write about the artist and his relation
to his craft and sources. *Von der Landschaft* [*Concerning
Landscape*], *Worpswede*, and *Auguste Rodin* [2] (which
brought him to Paris and into fateful contact with the
great sculptor) are essayistic monographs whose impressionistic style verges on prose-poetry, expressing a highly
personal form of art appreciation and distinctively Rilkean
concepts. Central to Rilke's thinking was the idea that
art:

> is the medium in which man and landscape, form and
> world, meet and find one another. . . . The theme and
> purpose of all art would seem to lie in the reconciliation of
> the Individual and the All, and the moment of exaltation,
> the artistically important Moment, would seem to be that
> in which the two scales of the balance counterpoise one
> another. . . .

The hostility Rilke envisioned in nature, the opposition
of his father to the poet's vocation, the laughter of the
cadre at the military school—which rang in his ears deep
into his mature years—nourished his art. For Rilke, beauty
lay in the sublime loftiness of nature and its indifference
that "fill all her movements," and only solitary children are
in innocent harmony with them. To the adult the landscape is foreign:

> . . . we are fearfully alone amongst trees which blossom
> and by streams which flow. Alone with the dead one is not
> nearly so defenseless as when alone with trees. For, however
> mysterious death may be, life that is not our life is far
> more mysterious, life that is not concerned with us, and
> which, without seeing us, celebrates its festivals, as it were,

at which we look on with a certain embarrassment, like chance guests who speak another language.

In the presence of the 62-year-old Rodin at Meudon near Paris, Rilke felt the dynamic creativity of a craftsman at the height of his power. Although the sculptor's creativity through constant, disciplined activity—without waiting for inspiration—was alien to Rilke, he was soon to experiment with it in his *Neue Gedichte*, with dazzling effects, but then give it up by reverting to his own stylistic and creative temperament.

The technical and esthetic insights which Rilke gained from a close view of Rodin's work were invaluable. By permitting the viewer to see the work of art as a self-contained object in spatial freedom, sculpture reinforced Rilke's sense of the isolation of things. He described Rodin's work subjectively: "I am no critic . . . I measure a work of art by the happiness it gives me." In the essays on Rodin, then, one is prepared to learn as much about Rilke's creativity as about Rodin's. The inordinate purple patches may have something to do with a translation of Walter Pater's *Renaissance* which he absorbed and reviewed. In talking about Rodin's "Man with the Broken Nose," Rilke wrote:

> . . . the head of an aging and ugly man, whose broken nose only tends to accentuate the tormented expression of the face; it was the immense concentration of life in these features; the fact that there was no symmetry in the planes of his face, no repetition, no part empty, uncommunicative or neutral. Life had not simply touched this face, it had wrought it through and through, like some inexorable hand thrusting it into destiny and holding it there as in the rush of swirling, cleansing waters.

Pure lyrical art appreciation cascades through *The Rodin Book* and Rodin's figures in the *Gate of Hell* and the *Burghers of Calais* groups seem to live and pulsate under the urgings of Rilke's prose.

Despite the nearness of Rodin and Clara—she had returned to her studies with Rodin and explored the art treasures of Paris with Rainer—nothing could dispel the gloom that gradually settled over Rilke. Scenes from childhood emerged again in his poetry, especially recall of his early and persistent differentiation from others—"in a small child's dress then," estranged from companions, and a similar loneliness now.

Consonant with his dark mood (and autobiographical reflection) is the majestic poem "Herbsttag" ["Autumn Day"] with its gustlike rhythm, mounting internal alliterations, and changing rhyme pattern:

> *Herr: es ist Zeit. Der Sommer war sehr gross.*
> *Leg deinen Schatten auf die Sonnenuhren,*
> *und auf den Fluren lass die Winde los.*
>
> *Befiehl den letzten Früchten voll zu sein;*
> *gib ihnen noch zwei südlichere Tage,*
> *dränge sie zur Vollendung hin und jage*
> *die letzte Süsse in den schweren Wein.*
>
> *Wer jetzt kein Haus hat, baut sich keines mehr.*
> *Wer jetzt allein ist, wird es lange bleiben,*
> *wird wachen, lesen, lange Briefe schreiben*
> *und wird in den Alleen hin und her*
> *unruhig wandern, wenn die Blätter treiben.*   (sw 1,398)

> *Lord, it is time. The summer was quite great.*
> *Lay now your shadow over the sun dial faces,*
> *and on the level places let the wind grate.*
>
> *Command the last fruits to be ripe;*
> *give them yet two southerly days,*
> *force them to completion and chase*
> *the last sweetness into the heavy wine.*
>
> *Who now has no home, will never again build one,*
> *Who now is alone, will long so remain,*
> *will waken, read, write long letters*
> *and in the will be driven to and fro in wide streets*
> *to wander restlessly when leaves propel.*

The last stanza speaks of resignation to the state of affairs and the wandering, reading, and writing that lie ahead.

To escape the overwhelming effect of Rodin and the oppressively teeming humanity of Paris, Rilke went briefly to Italy's Viareggio—to the roaring, great, lonely sea—where the third part of *Das Stunden-Buch* was completed during April 13–20, 1903. Rilke called this part *Das Buch von der Armut und vom Tode* [*The Book of Poverty and of Death*], in which the figure of the itinerant monk very nearly disappears and that of the poet disquietingly rises amid the milling mass of Parisians: ". . . is this the fear in which I am encapsuled? / The deep fear of the overgreat cities / in which you have placed me up to my chin?" "There live people, live poorly and heavily, / in deep rooms, anxious of gesture, / more fearful than a yearling herd; / and outside wakes and breathes your earth; / they exist but no longer know it." This refrain embodies the revulsion of the intellectual to the mass living of the cities, but like Balzac, Baudelaire, Verlaine, and Mallarmé, Rilke was magnetized by the terror embodied in the scene. Death, life, and love are the central images of the poem cycle:

> O Herr, gieb jedem seinen eignen Tod.
> Das Sterben, das aus jenem Leben geht,
> darin er Liebe hatte, Sinn und Not.   (sw 1,347)

> O Lord, grant each his own death,
> the dying which out of that same life evolves,
> wherein he once had love, sense, and need.

The sheer centrifugal force of language gives these images a semblance of complete relatedness, but Rilke instinctively knew that improvisation necessarily sacrifices precise direction. The ideas here are quite chaotic.

In the writings of the Danish poet-novelist Jens Peter Jacobsen—devoured by Rilke since the Munich stay—appear such clichés as "everyone lives his own life and dies his own death." In Rilke's poetry they became rhapsodic revelations: "For we are only the skin and the leaf. / The great death, which everyone has within, / that is the fruit around which everything revolves." Rilke draws distinctions between the great death, one's own death—the destiny and result of rare personal fulfillment—as against the small death that waits in beleaguered hospitals of cities or the impersonal death of the young or that of the unfulfilled masses with their stereotyped and soulless existence. Death is the "other side" of life, an ever-present reality. The unique reciprocity which Rilke envisioned was the subordination to life of "even what was dead" and death as a possible world where the soul will be confronted by new challenges. An urge to see existence sustained through life *and* death was the eternity or immortality wish that lurked in Rilke's writing.

Intoxicated with the idea of the entwining relationship of life and death, he apotheosizes the procreative force and its hermaphroditic aspects:

*Mach Einen herrlich, Herr, mach Einen gross,*
*bau seinem Leben einen schönen Schooss,*
*und seine Scham errichte wie ein Tor*
*in einem blonden Wald von jungen Haaren,*
*und ziehe durch das Glied des Unsagbaren*
*den Reisigen, den weissen Heeresscharen,*
*den tausend Samen, die sich sammeln, vor.*    (sw 1,349)

*Make thou one lordly, Lord, and make him great,*
*give him a womb as wondrous as his fate.*
*And let his phallus like a gate of awe*
*by a blond forest of young hair protected,*
*through strength of the ineffable elected*
*for silver armies under flags collected,*
*the thousand seeds of consecration draw.*

Not without grotesqueness, overstatement, and a tendency drawn from mystical traditions, Rilke's biological hymnology and sexual symbolism envision God and Death as attributes of life. Like Milton, he has the power to instill terror in such abstractions as death: In the past, "With eternity we have played the whore, / and when the time for delivery has come, the dead abortion of our death is born, / that twisted, pathetic embryo. . . ." In the future, we must look to the death-bearing man (*Tod-Gebärer*), presumably the artist rather than the god-bearing virgin, to bring the redeemer into the world. And, it is the coming of the new Messiah that Rilke is willing to celebrate with a dedication that recalls the fervor of John the Baptist.

If it was poverty that he would be fated to endure, Rilke was determined that it would not be that of the quietly desperate masses but that of St. Francis of Assisi, Il Poverello—the lover of nature and the poor: "For poverty is a great glow from within." Poverty, Rilke rationalized, for all its distress, keeps the superficialities of life away from the poet, forcing him to rely on his inner resources. In the representations of poverty it was God, "the eternal metamorphosis," who manifested himself in various guises—as the beggar, the homeless, the likeness and strength of an unwanted seed within a pregnant girl, the leper, and as the symbolic "rose of poverty," the subjects of a many-hued, fuguelike sequence of poems. Rilke's pantheistic fantasy envisions the song of a St. Francis-like poet, a Christly Orpheus, whose pollen will bring fertility to women, beasts; nature and cherubs will be the messengers of annunciations. All this amounts to a refiguration by Rilke of traditional Christian belief, emphasizing aspects of poverty at the heart of early Christian teaching, eliminating the Christ figure that, according to Rilke, devalues the life of the here-and-now, extolling the virtues of poverty borne with joy and matureness, and introducing as a counterpoise to the God-within (*entheos*), the death-within (*enmori*), who will become the great, personal death through the proper shaping of one's life. Outer and inner necessity had molded Rilke's vision, discernible in all his future work. The abstractions, life, love, death, God, longing, that were rapidly and fluidly improvised in the *Stunden-Buch*, now becomes specific images and objects with contours.

At the beginning of *The Book of Poverty and of Death*, Rilke implored the Lord, ". . . make yourself heavy, break in / so that your entire hand becomes my experience / and my experience becomes yours with my complete outcry." For twelve years he made Paris the hub of his universe from which radiated short, periodic wanderings to Italy, Sweden, Belgium. He chose to stay *because* of the anguish that the city caused him and because its frightening reality excited all his senses to a pitch of complete aliveness; it was a flagellant's dream. He needed this stimulus for his work. The years 1902–1910 mark the most stable period in Rilke's life and art; he achieved a workable balance between the two. Accordingly, the end of 1910 saw the completion of the *Book of Images, Neue Gedichte* [*New Poems*], *Die Aufzeichnungen Malte Laurids Brigge, The Journal of My Other Self* (a semi-autobiographical novel), and a revision of *Die Weisse Fürstin* [*The White Princess*]. Wishful critical attempts to simplify the creative exponent in Rilke's work to a linear development — from youthful ego-lyrics to a new objectivity — flounder on Rilke's variety of poetic and prose writings and the profusion of subjects and contrasting styles during his Paris days.

Rarely has programmatic theory and the excitement of working out a technical problem paid off in so startling a poetic innovation as Rilke's so-called *Ding-Gedicht* (thing or object poem), "adding a new type of lyrical expression to German verse," [3] or at the very least contributing the finest models of intensely disciplined compression into the simplest poetic format of three or four short stanzas. Rilke's art criticism helped him to see objects as focused entities; contact with the craft of Rodin and the pellucid perfection of Baudelaire's poetry showed him the need for projecting a concentrated emotion into a clear image; and the art of Cézanne taught him the importance of motif. Only in a limited sense can this be termed a new objectivity for Rilke, for although the poet is not the exclusive subject of the poem, feeling is still the focal point, and the projection of his personal problems is only slightly less acute than in the *Stunden-Buch*. What Rilke sought and felt he had achieved was a "more detached mastery of reality." Some of the "thing" poems required much more revision than the so-called inspiration poems and frequently tend to *Kunstübung*, a deliberate exercise in artistic handling of conventional metrics and ingeniously improvising multiple end-rhymes and simultaneous *enjambments* with cunning internal balance and over-all symmetry. In the "thing" poems there is no diffusion or proliferation of similes, metaphors, or symbols; instead, a single figure of speech is extended into a conceit, the details accrete around the feeling, and from faintly etched planes and surfaces of the object poetized the reader is led inward. As F. W. Belmore notes, "the character of Rilke's '*Dinggedichte*' is not that they treat of things, but rather that they deal with all subjects, including persons as if they were things." [4] Rilke gives things a psychological and physical animation in a relativistic setting: to the viewer, the object is in motion, while to the object, its surroundings are in motion.

In preparation for one of the earliest of the "Ding" poems, he closely observed a small bronze of a tiger sculptured by Rodin and then went to Paris' Jardin des Plantes to watch the measured pacing of a panther in a cage. Out of his hands, as it were, emerges the poem "Der Panther," not a sculpturesque but an animated figure whose concentric motion terminates in the psychological terror of absolute inward stillness. Although the boundary between the viewer and the object abruptly vanishes, the poet or viewer detachedly and completely understands the animal and its routine existence. Long-drawn vowels, contrasts that create motion (soft walk of supple strong steps), and synonymous recurrence (walk, step, dance) create a visual surface for the poem:

> *Sein Blick ist vom Vorübergehn der Stäbe*
> *so müd geworden, dass er nichts mehr hält.*
> *Ihm ist, als ob es tausend Stäbe gäbe*
> *und hinter tausend Stäben keine Welt.*
>
> *Der weiche Gang geschmeidig starker Schritte,*
> *der sich im allerkleinsten Kreise dreht,*
> *ist wie ein Tanz von Kraft um eine Mitte,*
> *in der betäubt ein grosser Wille steht.*
>
> *Nur manchmal schiebt der Vorhang der Pupille*
> *sich lautlos auf—. Dann geht ein Bild hinein,*

geht durch der Glieder angespannte Stille—
und hört im Herzen auf zu sein.     (sw 1,505)

So wearied by the passing of the bars,
his gaze no longer steady holds.
To him they seem like thousand bars—
behind the thousand bars no world.

The lissom stride of supple-strong steps,
which turns within the ever-smallest circle,
is like a dance of strength around a center
in which a mighty will stands numb.

Only sometimes the curtain of the pupil
silently shutters open. An image enters,
then glides through the tense silence of limbs,
and ceases to exist in the heart.

The automatic motion of the animal, unconscious of its power, and its mechanical acceptance of images show a brute perception that gazes open beyond this world. Its elemental stare and close affinity with nature give the creature, and later the angels of the *Duino Elegies*, intuitive intimations of a greater reality not shared by humans. The poet has taken us into the innermost core of creatures and things where the image petrifies. As for humans, the image enters "into our heart's inmost chamber" and thence into the blood causing us to change; only a vague and passing sadness informs us of the inner flux and transition. Rilke's metaphysical biology, a poetic conception of human growth and "destiny" which subsequently "goes forth out of us to others," resembles the metaphoric "great chain of being," which horizontally unites all generations of mankind and vertically stretches from the throne of God to the lowliest insect. Rilke stresses, however, that awareness of isolation in the universe belongs only to humans.

Closely related in time (1902/03) and substance to the "Ding" poem "The Panther," "Die Aschanti" typifies opposite techniques—fluidity of image, tone and commentary—of many poems that were brought into the 1906 collection of *Das Buch der Bilder*.

> *O wie sind die Tiere so viel treuer,*
> *die in Gittern auf und niedergehn,*
> *ohne Eintracht mit dem Treiben neuer*
> *fremder Dinge, die sie nicht verstehn;*
> *und sie brennen wie ein stilles Feuer*
> *leise aus und sinken in sich ein,*
> *teilnahmslos dem neuen Abenteuer*
> *und mit ihrem grossen Blut allein.*    (sw 1,395)

> *Oh, the animals are so much truer,*
> *pacing in a cage from end to end,*
> *unconforming to the drift of newer,*
> *foreign things they do not comprehend;*
> *burning quietly out like silent fire*
> *into their own embers, they disown*
> *all the new adventure and retire*
> *into their own mighty blood, alone.*

The poet's almost melancholy envy of the animal's self-sufficiency is undisguised and no attempt is made in the image poem as in the "Ding" poem, to coolly objectify emotions.

From late 1902 until mid-1908, *Ding* poems would come into being through "enormous concentration," as Rilke said, and were collected as part of the *Neue Gedichte* and *Der Neuen Gedichte anderer Teil*, poems that like "Der Panther" were lean, symmetrical, and empathically "objective," while others like the "Egyptian Maria," "Judgment Day," and "Crucifixion" are decidedly expressionistic in tone and tempo. The act of vicarious transformation, an almost casual transition, is most evident in "Leda." The Greek legend of the Zeus-swan and Leda has intrigued poets from Homer to Yeats, but Rilke's "Leda" is almost single-mindedly concerned with the psychology of transformation: how Zeus feels in unaccustomed surroundings within the swan and during the moment of violation, the swift moment of his absolute, metamorphosed existence. The objectification of emotion is the uniqueness of Rilke's *Ding-Gedicht.* "I have intended not to form emotions but things which I have felt," Rilke explained. There are no ornamental Spenserian settings to soften Leda's fall, no Yeatsian intimations of historical significance superimposed on male-female sexuality, or amused Goethean tolerance of a male daydream, rather the momentary feeling as it might be crystallized in stone is Rilke's focus. Projected, too, is Rilke's personal association of love and fright. Although the "Ding" poems "Der Panther" and "Leda" are five years apart in composition, technically they have much in common. We might say that the "Ding" poems form a poetic enclave apart from the other poems in both the *New Poems* and *The Book of Images.* Almost invariably they speak of a search for the essence-characteristic of the object and its inner rhythm, the discovery of "die Mitte" or center, and concentrate on moments that verge on release of tension or moments of ecstatic resolution. The word "weight" and its verbal and suggestive corollaries such as hold (*halten*), carry (*tragen*) signify a taking of the true measure of the object. To achieve his aim, Rilke artfully extends figures of speech into lyrical conceits.

In the *Ding* poems Rilke seems to measure his powers of evocation against that of painters, from Dürer to Fragonard, sculptors from the Greeks to Rodin, and against musicians, though his raw materials were but "poor words." Rilke was able to re-create sound through word melody, visual images through metaphors, perspective through the illusion of motion, psychological effects through an inward pulling of the reader to the object-essence. Rilke's "Leda" is as erotic as Michelangelo's; his "Flamingos" is as delicately lustrous as Fragonard's:

> *In Spiegelbildern wie von Fragonard*
> *ist doch von ihrem Weiss und ihrer Röte*
> *nicht mehr gegeben, als dir einer böte,*
> *wenn er von seiner Freundin sagt: sie war*
>
> *noch sanft von Schlaf. Dann steigen sie ins Grüne*
> *und stehn, auf rosa Stielen leicht gedreht,*

*beisammen, blühend, wie in einem Beet,*
*verführen sie verführender als Phryne*

*sich selber; bis sie ihres Auges Bleiche*
*hinhalsend bergen in der eignen Weiche,*
*in welcher Schwarz und Fruchtrot sich versteckt.*

*Auf einmal kreischt ein Neid durch die Volière;*
*sie aber haben sich erstaunt gestreckt*
*und schreiten einzeln ins Imaginäre*    (sw 1,629–30)

*Like mirrored images by Fragonard,*
*so little of their red and white is shown,*
*and delicately, as if one came alone*
*and whispered of his mistress in your ear:*

*She lay there, flushed with sleep. . . . Above the green*
*reeds they rise and on their rose-stilts turn,*
*blooming together, as if on a parterre,*
*seducing (more seductive than Phryne)*

*themselves; and in the softness where the black*
*and apple-red are veiled they sink their necks,*
*hiding the pallid circles of their eyes,*

*till through their wire cage swift envy shrieks;*
*they waken in astonishment and stretch*
*themselves and soar imaginary skies.*

Through alliterative softness and pastel word-shadings, Rilke has reproduced the seductive features which the painter Fragonard saw in the model; at the same time symbol, simile, analogy, and expressive personification rapidly and lightly are linked to one another.

Not all the animals of the *Ding* poems have the quietude of the gazelle or the solitary flamingos. In the "Schwarze Katze" ["The Black Cat"] as the poet's eye suddenly confronts the animal's, we sense an unbridgeable distance: "you meet your gaze unexpectedly again / in the yellow amber of her round eye-stones: / locked-in like a long-dead insect race." Rilke can, when he wishes, match the massiveness of the sculptor's stone and give it motion and meaning as in "Archäischer Torso Apollos" ["Archaic Torso of Apollo"]. The poem as a mastered art form has assumed the same significant and creative existence as a painting and a sculpture. If Rilke assigns to poetry a role that transcends the other arts as well as nature, he may be justified by the fact that particularly through the poet's perception one experiences a new dimension: Nature is what the poet shows it to be.

The last *Ding* poem to appear in the *New Poems* was "Buddha in der Glorie," for which Rodin's statue and one in the Völkerkunde Museum of Berlin served as models. All the essential features of the *Ding* poem are here. The Buddha—in his glory—is the center of centers, the symbol of isolation—a kernel within fruit-flesh, and characterizes the immortality of an object of art. It has androgynous life, is sensuously narcissistic, aloof in its responsibility to others, and contains an essence that will survive the suns of the universe.

That this culture object should personify the personal ideals of the poet is a chilling thought. But unlike the Buddha Gotama, Rilke needed human contact. Again he wrote to Lou who permitted a resumption of correspondence, assuring him that her husband would not intrude on their epistolary privacy. When in her distress Clara engaged Lou's sympathy, Lou tried to persuade Rainer to resume his husbandly duties. He answered with casuistic adroitness, pleading poetically with Clara for postponement, "Is there not a house about us, a real one, for which only a visible sign is lacking. . . . Will we not step out of this affectionate house into the garden?" [5] Another pacifier was Rainer's "Liebes-Lied" ["Lovesong"] for Clara, a poem that spoke of a spiritual togetherness in their apartness. What marked this sentiment as sheer subterfuge at the time was the romantic passion which he lavished on a lovely girl, Signorina Romanelli, while staying in a Venetian pension. Mimi slowly learned about Rilke's doctrine of nonpossessive love when his inflamed declarations of love signed "R. Maria" cooled, after awhile, into epistles of friendship signed formally "R. M. Rilke."

The tension between devotion to life and art played havoc on his nerves; he never had the courage to make an absolute choice or admit the impossibility of making one. Instead, he hid from himself the fact that he used his relations with women to stimulate his work. He miscalculated the effect he had on women and then declined to deal with the upheaval of emotions he had aroused. Hypnotized by his own mythology of love, he found support for his imposition of selflessness on women in ancient legends such as the sacrifice of Alcestis, the unrequited love of the Biblical Mary Magdalen, or in more modern sources such as the life of the 17th century Franciscan nun Marianna Alcoforado. Sternly he told the importuning Mimi, "I *beg* of those that love me to love my solitude in which I must hide myself from their eyes and from their arms, like a savage animal hides itself during the pursuit by its enemies." [6] The psychology of the narcissist prohibits the love of another to interfere with love of self; that is why perhaps most of Rilke's poems are mirrors of his own soul rather than examples of pure objectivity.

In 1908, a year after the death of Paula Becker-Modersohn, Rilke wrote the "Requiem für eine Freundin" ["Requiem to a Friend"]. Of all the dead who are "at home in being dead," poetized Rilke, "You [Paula] alone return . . . you are mistaken if you are disturbed into a homesick yearning for something here . . . It is not here, we transmute it all and reflect it from ourselves as soon as we perceive it." Since she ate the unripe, green seeds of death, she has herself to blame for an unseasoned experience. At the close of the requiem, he bids Paula's poltergeist to return to the occupied dead, "But help me . . . as the most distant sometimes helps: in me." This explicit invitation to join Rilke's well-populated interior graveyard, the inward room of memory and timelessness, was later supplemented by the remark that she was the heaviest to bear of all the dead. It was not until his eyes were opened by Cézanne's work that he appreciated her unique powers as a painter. Of the portraits for which Rilke sat, hers was the only one of which he said, "this *is*."

Rilke was more charitable in his "Requiem für Wolf Graf von Kalckreuth," 1908, because the young poet was no intimate like Paula, who had the benefit of his existence gospel. Kalckreuth was chided for being too impatient to meet death, although it promised an existence where commendably no one places value on possessions. In life, sermonized Rilke, one is close enough to death so that there is no need to hurry that experience before one has fully tasted life, difficult as it may be. It is the ancient curse of poets to feel sorry for themselves and to pass judgment on their feelings instead of shaping them with the raw materials of words into celebrative poems just as "cathedral carvers transform themselves doggedly into a stone's indifference." The poet finds his salvation by unburdening his pains, putting them into verse. Of our life, "Wer spricht von Siegen? Überstehn ist alles" ["Who speaks of victory? To survive is all"].[7] To endure to the end ("What really is end?") was Rilke's admonition to would-be suicides, especially the predisposed among artists.

With advice to young women and artists, Rilke was generous, possibly because it gave him an opportunity for putting his thinking into periodic manifestoes. Some five years earlier, in 1903, he began a series of ten epistolary essays in reply to a fledgling poet, Franz X. Kappus, a nineteen-year-old boy in an Austrian military school. From these *Letters to a Young Poet* we might extract some significant kernels that retain in many ways the dicta of the earlier diaries, without the Nietzschean thunder, and that define the special meanings which Rilke's key words— especially beauty, solitude, motion, destiny, God, love, existence, bearing—assume in his work.

Art is only a way of living.

Ask yourself in the stillest hour of your night: must I write? . . . And if this should be affirmative . . . then build your life according to this necessity; your life, even in its most indifferent and slightest hour, must be a sign of this urgency and a testimony to it.

A work of art is good if it has sprung from necessity. You cannot disturb your development more rudely than by looking outward and expecting from outside replies to questions that only your inmost feeling in your quietest hours can perhaps answer.

Works of art are of an infinite loneliness.

*Everything* is gestation and then bringing forth.

I learn it daily, learn it with pain to which I am grateful: *patience* is everything!

Artistic experience lies so incredibly close to that of sex, to its pain and its desire, that the two manifestations are indeed but different forms of one and the same yearning and delight.

Physical pleasure is a sensual experience no different from pure seeing or the pure sensation with which a fine fruit fills the tongue; it is a great unending experience that is given to us, a knowing of the world, the fullness and the glory of knowing.

In one creative thought a thousand forgotten nights of love revive and fill it with sublimity and exaltation.

All beauty in animals and plants is a quiet, enduring form of love and desire. . . .

The beauty of the virgin . . . is motherhood that begins to sense itself and to prepare; it is fearful and desirous. And the mother's beauty is ministering motherhood, and in the old woman it is a great remembering. And even in the man there is motherhood . . . bodily and mental; his procreating is also a kind of bearing, and bearing it is when he creates out of his inmost fullness.

Solitude: Going-into oneself and for hours meeting no one—this one must be able to attain.

God: the coming one, imminent from all eternity, the future one, the final fruit of a tree whose leaves we are. . . . Everything that happens is always beginning again, and could it not be *his* beginning. . . . As the bees bring in honey, so do we fetch the sweetest out of everything and build him.

Human love consists of this: that two solitudes protect and touch and greet each other.

Sorrows are the moments when something new has entered into us, something unknown, and stands silent in the midst of our mute feelings.

Sadnesses are moments of tension that we find paralyzing because we no longer hear our estranged feelings living.

We have already had to re-think many of our conceptions of motion; we will also gradually learn to realize that which we call destiny goes forth from within people and not from without into them.

The future enters into us in order to transform itself long before it happens and becomes destiny. Through attentiveness and receptiveness does this destiny become absorbed and transmuted before it leaves to enter others.

The blood of ancestors ceaselessly stirs and mingles with our own into that unique and unrepeatable being which we are at every turning of our life.

The future stands firm, but we move in infinite space.

We *are* solitary. We may delude ourselves and act as if this were not so.

We must assume our existence broadly . . . to have courage that is demanded of us for the most extraordinary and the most inexplicable that we may encounter. That mankind has in this sense been cowardly has done life endless harm; the experiences that are called "appearances," the so-called "spirit-world," death, all those things that are so closely akin to us, have been by daily parrying so driven out of life that the senses with which we could have grasped them are crippled.

When we hold still we are, through a happy mimicry, scarcely to be distinguished from all that is around us.[8]

These reflections sustained Rilke; they were organic and not quilted from philosophic texts or borrowed from the artistic creed of others. For Rilke, attempts at disciplined studies led to bewilderment rather than clarification, to static rather than dynamic experience, as he found out through weeks of futile sitting and reading at the Bibliothèque Nationale in Paris. Like Pascal, Rilke allowed his heart to have its reasons and did his thinking mainly with his heart, building a structured and impregnable rationale. "Let life happen to you," said Rilke. And this is what he permitted life to do, transmuting his experiences into a fullness of poetry and poetic prose at every turn during the 1902–1910 period.

Of grousing there was never an end, but it was invariably submerged by exaltation. Rome at first seemed "for the most part a bad museum . . . of senseless statues"; however, the Borghese Gardens with delightful fountains balanced his distemper as did the Villa Strohl-Fern area where he took pleasure in "the great wide open nights with the sound of animals that move, fruits that fall, winds that stir." And the same intoxication stirred him at Capri where he described the reckless blossoming of nature: "If it were voices instead of colors, there would be an unbelievable shrieking into the heart of night. But in spite of the days with much rain, the air keeps letting the scent fall as if its hands were still too cold for it." Or, "all the hard trees, prepared for sea wind, became audible again in all their hardness as their leaves turned and struck against each other." Almost physically attuned to the sounds, color, and rhythm in nature, Rilke, without missing a beat, directly transposed his feelings into the lyrical cadence of numerous poems like the "Lied vom Meer" ["Song of the Sea"]:

> *Uraltes Wehn vom Meer,*
> *Meerwind bei Nacht:*

*du kommst zu keinem her;*
*wenn einer wacht*
*so muss er sehn, wie er*
*dich übersteht:*
    *uraltes Wehn vom Meer,*
*welches weht*
*nur wie für Ur-Gestein,*
*lauter Raum*
*reissend von weit herein* . . .


    *O wie fühlt dich ein*
*treibender Feigenbaum*
*oben im Mondschein.*          (sw 1,600–601)


*Primeval breath of the sea,*
*sea-wind by night:*
    *you come to no one;*
*when someone wakes*
*he must see, how he*
*transcends you:*
    *primeval breath from sea*
*which breathes*
*only as if for primal stone,*
*pure space*
*rushing in from afar* . . .


    *Oh how you are sensed*
*by a ripening fig tree*
*yonder in moonlight.*

Splendid impressionistic imagery sparks poems like "Spätherbst in Venedig" ["Late Autumn in Venice"] which begins with, "Nun treibt die Stadt schon nicht mehr wie ein Köder, / der alle aufgetauchten Tage fängt." ["Now drifts the city no longer like a bait / which catches all the days that to the surface rise."] In the *New Poems* conventionally unpoetic objects like "bait" are transformed into poetic metaphors. Rilke, like Eliot with his coffee spoon and the etherized patient in *Prufrock,* learned much from Baudelaire's elevation of the commonplace and the emotive juxtaposition of the ordinary and the sublime, techniques that revolutionized modern poetry.

Just as nature inspired him so did almost everything else that came into his ken, particularly architecture and sculpture. The Greek bas-relief of Orpheus in the Louvre and the Museo Nazionale in Naples, antique sarcophogi, and antique ruins spontaneously became models for such powerful poems in blank verse as "Hetären-Gräber" ["Graves of the Hetaerae"], "Orpheus. Euridyke. Hermes," "Geburt der Venus" ["Birth of Venus"]. Gloriously descriptive, they also begin to show his modernization and personalization of Greek myth as in the portrayal of Eurydice in "Orpheus. Euridyke. Hermes":

> Sie war in sich. Und ihr Gestorbensein
> erfüllte sie wie Fülle.
> Wie eine Frucht von Süssigkeit und Dunkel,
> so war sie voll von ihrem grossen Tode,
> der also neu war, dass sie nichts begriff.
>
> Sie war in einem neuen Mädchentum
> und unberührbar; ihr Geschlecht war zu
> wie eine junge Blume gegen Abend,
> und ihre Hände waren der Vermählung
> so sehr entwöhnt, dass selbst des leichten Gottes
> unendlich leise, leitende Berührung
> sie kränkte wie zu sehr Vertraulichkeit.
>
> (sw 1,544–45)

> She was within herself. And her being dead
> ripened her like fullness.
> Like a fruit of sweetness and darkness,
> so was she filled by her great death,
> a newness she did not comprehend.
>
> She was in her maidenhood
> and untouchable; her sex was closed
> like a young flower toward evening,
> and her hands were so weaned from marriage
> that even the infinitely light, leading touch
> of the god offended her as too much intimacy.

Rilke's old wine, we see, has been poured into new bottles; the great death-god of the *Stunden-Buch* has been resurrected, and the Orpheus-Eurydice theme begins its eighteen-year-long gestation that is to flower into the sonnet cycle to Orpheus. But whenever Rilke talked of death, he also balanced it with life so that the descent of Eurydice to the "eversweet land of the shades" was followed by the *Birth of Venus*, a hymn that scintillates with a sensuous iridescence of metaphors drawn from his anatomy clinic; both Eurydice and Venus mirror Rilke's creative transformation.

BEFORE HIS ardent admirer Ellen Key, the suffragette and
writer, extended an invitation to visit Sweden in 1904,
Rilke had already decided to put his novel-in-progress, the
diary-like *Malte Laurids Brigge*, in a Scandinavian setting,
where the supernatural and the traditional fused. Rilke
also had learned Danish in order to be able to read
Jacobsen and, like Miguel de Unamuno, he was rewarded
by discovering Kierkegaard's interpretation of Christianity,
which exerted a powerful grip on minds like Nietzsche's.
Many of Kierkegaard's ideas supported the beliefs already
cherished by Rilke: inwardness is truth; subjectivity is
reality. They shared a certain amount of nostalgia for
antiquity when society was dominated by individuals
rather than the leveling public.

In Kierkegaard's *Postscript* is a statement on the relationship and reversibility of immanence and transcendence that illuminates the entire frame of Rilke's *Stunden-
Buch*: "Within the individual man there is a potentiality
(man is potentially spirit) which is awakened in inwardness to become a God-relationship, and then it becomes
possible to see God everywhere." Though in many ways
intellectually reassuring, Kierkegaard faded into the back-
ground when Rilke returned to Paris to don a hairshirt and
to acquire Baudelaire as his guide. In the public gardens,
forty years earlier, Baudelaire saw "cheated souls . . .
trysting places of the cripples of life"; Rilke saw them
again. Although Rilke's focus on the same figures is as

sharp as Baudelaire's, his prose is distinguishably softer.
We listen to Rilke's Malte:

> This city is full of those who slowly glide downward. Most
> of them resist at first; but then there are those blanched,
> aging girls who constantly without resistance let themselves
> be carried across, terribly unused inwardly, never having
> been loved.[1]

Rilke admired the master craftsman in Baudelaire, as
strong as Rodin in his medium and métier. Of Baudelaire,
the American critic James Huneker said that he "carved
rather than sang; the plastic arts spoke to his soul," and
this is one good reason why Rodin was attracted to
Baudelaire. And to close the circle, one contemporaneous
French writer who did not know of the Rodin-Rilke
relationship was impelled to say on reading Rilke's *Neue
Gedichte*, "I see the marble poems of Rodin."

Many of the figures in Baudelaire's *Parisian Scenes*—
"Les sept vieillards," "La mort des pauvres," "Les petites
Vieilles"—rise like "Voices" in Rilke's cycle "Die Stimmen"; yet, the poems bear the stamp of his own inspiration. These poems, Rilke noted self-consciously, "can no
longer be regarded as mere estheticism." In the prefatory
poem, Rilke makes it clear that the good "songs" of the
beggar, the blind, the drunk, the suicide, the widow, the
idiot, the waif, the dwarf, and the leper are passed by like
unnoticed "things," although they have a quality that
stems from necessity. "People," Rilke comments ironically, "are strange; they listen / preferably to the castrated
in boy-choirs." Rilke prefers to listen to the voices and
songs of those who are branded by *life*. All speak in the
first person; all recount the woes that have set them apart
from the rest of society. Although one feels Rilke's compassionate identification, the voices are more pitiable than
poetic. These, and similar "social" poems in *Das Buch der
Bilder*, are rather mechanical both in metrics and expression; the poet and his anguish are not at the center of the
poem. When these same desolate figures, however, appear
in Rilke's prose, especially in *Malte*, they are superbly
rendered.

From Baudelaire Rilke gleaned a greater appreciation of form wedded to content, techniques of exteriorization, and symbolic expression of anguish. Some of Baudelaire's poems—like those about cats which became prototypes for Rilke's own "Schwarze Katze" and "Les vieux Saltimbanques" who also were memorialized in the *Elegies*—stayed with Rilke as examples of incomparable craft, work, and observation. For Rilke, poetry "must come before everything else: before my hunger, before my pleasure, before my mother." (He liked to echo the story about Cézanne's refusal to attend his mother's funeral because it would have cost him a day's work.) The dedication and compulsion to art was the same for Baudelaire and Rilke, creating through art a reality in the center of which they could find fulfillment. In other respects, however, they parted ways. To Baudelaire art is man's great, though futile, gesture of rebellion against God; to Rilke art is a means of loving reconciliation with God, destiny, nature. To Baudelaire, nature was a symbol; to Rilke it was an object, a thing.

From February, 1904, until March, 1910, great spurts of effort went into the shaping of the book, a continuation of *Ewald Tragy*; but, the more Rilke put into it, the more shapeless it became. One might call the journal a confessional into which were poured paraphrases of *The Book of Hours*, *The Book of Images*, and the *New Poems*, large extracts from letters sent and received, short stories, vignettes, fictionalized or factual reminiscences, prose poems, esthetic credoes, excerpts from readings, philosophical monologues, occult fantasies, impressionistic art-critiques, and travelogues. At first, Rilke thought of modeling his *Malte* on the young-deceased Norwegian novelist Sigbjörn Obstfelder, author of *The Diary of a Priest*, who went mad in his search for God. Gradually, however, Obstfelder became to Rilke's *Malte* what the character Jerusalem had been to Goethe's *Werther* and *André Walter* to Gide, a vague prototype, a sacrificial scapegoat. Years later, he called himself Malte's survivor.

What narrative levels we can discern consist of an

immediate present in the city-Gehenna of Paris, associative flashbacks to Rilke-Malte childhood experiences in Prague-Denmark, and ruminations in past and present literatures concentrating on figures that are willed into lifelike dimensions. The dominant subjects sounded in extended monologues are already familiar: art, fear, love, God, childhood, death. No new overtones occur in the iterated themes, except perhaps a greater determination to take hold of his fears and anxieties and to make objects out of them instead of recoiling from them. Yet "I prayed for my childhood and it has come back to me," says Malte, "and I feel that it is just as burdensome as it was before, and that I have grown older to no purpose." Paris was as oppressive to Malte as Munich had been to Ewald, a prefiguration of the monumental *Leidstadt*, the symbol of the city of pain that appears in the *Elegies*. "People come here (to Paris) to live? I should rather have thought that they came here to die." Almost neurasthenically, Rilke exaggerated his surroundings into a plethora of miseries, a noisy, odiferous, turmoil-ridden world; however, "The chief thing is to keep on living." As an artist and a human being Rilke wanted to penetrate deeply into the life of things around him and to find a meaningful continuity from the past to the present. All realities, he felt, are nothing; people's lives, entwined with nothing, merely run out like a clock standing in an empty room. It dawned on Malte-Rilke that creation begins anew with every writer, that each is thrown upon his own resources, that, as in E. M. Forster's provocative thought, "History develops, art stands still." In this sense Rilke considered himself a beginner at each significant turn of his life.

Some writers, like Proust, find salvation in the complete and deliberate recapture of time past; Rilke, however, was never quite sure as to how he might find release from the barnacles of the past—the maladies that tenaciously clung to every present and conscious moment:

   . . . this malady, which has always affected me so strangely. . . . This disease has no particular characteristics; it takes on those of the person it attacks. With a somnambulistic assurance it drags from the profoundest depths of each one's being a danger that seemed past, and sets it before him again, quite near, imminent. Men, who once in their schooldays attempted the helpless vice that had for its duped partner the poor, hard hands of boys, find themselves tempted afresh by it; or an illness they had conquered in childhood recurs in them; or a lost habit reappears, a certain hesitating turn of the head that had been peculiar to them years before. And with whatever comes, there rises a whole medley of confused memories, which hangs about it like wet seaweed on something long sunk in the sea. Lives of which one never knew mount to the surface and mingle with what has actually been, and obliterate past things that one had thought to know: for in that which ascends is a fresh, rested strength, but that which has always been there is wearied by too much remembrance.

These generalizations rise from private experiences so prolific that they overwhelm and confuse rather than calm his mind. All details have an elephantine and equal weight. Poverty is as great a fear as that the little button on his nightshirt may become bigger than his head or that a falling crumb of bread may shatter to pieces like glass and break everything apart forever. Nameless and general anxieties (*Angst*) are as great as specific fears (*Furcht*), although he is beginning to recognize the need for separating the two. He feared personal regression, masturbatory hands which he visualized as detaching themselves from him—a hallucination which he had not dared to share with his mother or little boy-cousin—and the encroachment of other lives or deaths upon his own existence. Hands, for example, have a shifting significance in Rilke's poetry: the independently willful and quarrelsome hands of God, the creative means of the sculptor, the bearers of the infinitely tender gesture, the expressive intermediaries between lovers, the narcissistically soothing hands. The variety of roles played by hands is symptomatic of Rilke's personality. Often he reaches the point where his identity is no longer clear to himself except by contrast, where interior reality and exterior pose clash so that he feels himself neither "a being nor an actor."

Throughout his life, Rilke had an affinity for costuming. In childhood he donned dresses to please his mother, in adolescence his suits were cut to please his clothes-conscious father, from Russia he derived the peasant blouses he liked to wear while writing, and equally well-known are the dandyish-aristocratic apparel of his later years. These clothes fetishes Malte shares, submitting to the influence that emanates from particular costumes. How deeply Rilke's philosophic concept of transformation is rooted in fetish can be seen in Malte's reminiscences:

> These disguises never, indeed, went so far as to make me feel a stranger to myself: on the contrary, the more varied my transformations, the more assured I was of my own identity.

These costume-disguises and masks encouraged unrestricted and endlessly varied existence-sensations, "I might be a slave girl about to be sold, or Joan of Arc, or an old king, or a wizard." Emboldened by his previous ability to retain his identity in the midst of costuming, he once succumbed to the temptation of pushing his security too far. Standing before a mirror, he had forgotten what he had intended to represent and no amount of exorcistic gesturing could bring his identity back:

> Hot and angry, I rushed to the mirror and watched with difficulty through the mask the working of my hands. But just for this the mirror had been waiting. Its moment of revenge had come. While I strove with measurelessly increasing anguish to tear myself somehow out of my disguise, it forced me, by what means I know not, to lift my eyes, and impose on me an image, nay, a reality, an alien, unbelievable, monstrous reality, with which, against my will, I became permeated: for now it was the stronger, and it was I who was the mirror. I stared at this great, terrifying, unknown personage before me, and it seemed appalling to me that I should be alone with him. But at the very moment I thought thus, the worst befell: I lost all knowledge of myself, I simply ceased to exist. For one second I had an unutterable, sad, and futile longing for myself, then there was only he—there was nothing but he.

Like Dostoevsky's Yakov Petrovich Golyadkin, Malte feels himself usurped by a double who reduces him to a heap of clothes. No interpretation need rest there, because suggestive too is Malte's fear of death as an emasculator of identity. This passage also is highly revealing in that it traces Rilke's narcissism, the "longing for myself," not to egocentric-love or self-veneration but to fears of identity loss and efforts at identity retention. It explains his complex relations with people, animals and things. Like himself, they have masks, disguises, and experience transformation, making it, in his mind, impossible to confront one reality with another.

In *Malte* the most intimate scenes of childhood are filtered through the adult mind. And what stands out is the closeness between mother and son and the aura of feminine sentimentality that enveloped and emotionally debilitated Rilke-Malte. Love, Rilke well understood, requires responsibility, meticulous cultivation, and draining reciprocity. These he was unwilling to endure, and toward the end of *Malte* he took drastic measures to indicate his withdrawal by retelling the New Testament parable of the Prodigal Son, the sinner who repents, returns to his family and is forgiven as well as showered with love. The text by Saint Luke had for some time been a favorite with Rilke and letters tell of his reading from it to Clara. It was as if he were culling from it in self-justification. "Let the dead bury their dead: but go thou and preach the kingdom of God," was to Rilke an apostolic injunction not to assume responsibilities for others but to single-mindedly follow his art. Not only did he wish to abjure responsibility, but also he went further by trying to eliminate conditions that might give rise to it: Rilke's Prodigal Son is the legend of one who did not want to be loved, imploring others not to love him. In the margin of the *Malte* manuscript, Rilke wrote: "To be loved means to be consumed. To love means to radiate with inexhaustible light. To be loved is to pass away, to love is to endure." What he cherished was the passion and the trembling anticipation more than the fulfillment, the sensation of the pure effort, the striving more than the goal—a dedication to the ideal that marks the romantic attitude from Socrates to Goethe. Dostoevsky's prodigal son, Raskolnikov, had plaintively cried out, "Oh, if only I were alone and no one loved me and I, too, had never loved anyone!" From Dostoevsky and André Gide's *Retour de l'Enfant Prodigue* (1907) Rilke had taken a cue in making the Prodigal Son a rebel against family and conventions; yet one senses something here beyond Saint Luke, Dostoevsky, or Gide, namely the feeling of fear. In the "Requiem on the Death of a Boy," composed years later in 1914, Rilke said, "I loved no one. The act of loving is, after all, fear." Nameless fears pursue him like a band of Furies, and attempts have been made to trace them to specific root-experiences. Whatever the facts may have been, the really important point is that—real or imagined—they were his creative stimuli. Rilke himself characterized his life as an alternation between "terror and pretense." How much of this is self-induced can be gauged by Malte's cryptic declaration: "Life is difficult because of its simplicity."

Exhausted by his *Malte* efforts, Rilke craved human contact, and in 1909 welcomed a December invitation to visit Princess Marie von Thurn und Taxis Hohenlohe, a continental *grande Dame* and scion of the old Austrian nobility. Her generosity and kind but deflating humor was to have an enormously sobering and protective influence on Rilke almost down to his last days. From the first misspelled salutation, "Herr Rielke," she quickly progressed to a fond characterization of Rilke as "Dottor Serafico," a title he himself had ingratiatingly suggested.[2] The lifetime of correspondence and contact between "Serafico carissimo" and "My dearest Princess" shows an exceptional candor. On a footing of cordiality and confidence, Rilke wrote to her:

> Perhaps I may now learn to be a little human: up to now my art could only be achieved at the price of concentrating on *things*—that was a kind of stubbornness, and I am afraid arrogance too—dear Lord, and it must have been an

immense covetousness. It makes me shudder a little when I think of all the violence I exercised in *Malte Laurids*, how, with him, in consequential despair, I reached beyond everything, so to say even beyond death, so that everything became impossible, even to die. I believe nobody has ever experienced more clearly how fundamentally opposed art is to nature; it is the most passionate inversion in the world, the road back from the infinite. (Letter, August 30, 1910)

When Rilke began regurgitating the terrors of Malte, Marie was capable of gentle chiding, ". . . now stop thinking of Malte Laurids. I am beginning to get cross with him." By calling Malte "him," the other self, she was entering into Rilke's world, taking the place of Mama who used to talk to her son in girl's clothing about that bad boy "René." After her initial shock, Marie tried to mitigate Rilke's "terrible attacks of deepest melancholia and despondency," conditions of mind that were cyclical and symptomatic of the eerie "inner dare-deviltry" that led him to seek experiences beyond the pale of norms, making it easy for him eventually to join—with reservations—the spiritualistic parlor games of his new-found friends.

From the "passionate inversion" called art, Rilke turned to more prosaic things for the better part of the next two years but left the door open for a return to Paris, "the exacting Paradise of my work." In a whirl of activity, he made contact with his public through lectures and readings, making the same memorable impression he had created in Vienna in 1907. (The famous poet and host Hugo von Hofmannsthal offered to continue for Rilke after he was seized by a violent nosebleed.) Then followed a short stay in Leipzig with the Kippenbergs, his publishers who brought stability into his financial affairs, then on to Berlin for a brief reunion with Clara Rilke and Ruth, a first encounter with Marie's fateful Duino castle on the Adriatic sea, a recuperative spell in Marie's Bohemian retreat, and finally several months (1910/11) in Africa. Once the gates of memory were opened, it seemed that renewed creativity was inevitable. A short poem was inscribed in a copy of *The Confessions of Saint Augustine*,

"To my dear Mamma, this glorious book in memory of the hours spent over it together. René." At the same time, he wrote three poems for Lou, filled with private allusions to vastation, defloration, his skipped youth, and his ripening in her arms, poems seemingly diverse in substance as those about the Egyptian god Horus, the "Pietà in the Cathedral at Aquileja," and two translated sonnets from the 16th century work of an eccentric French beauty who sought adventure in male disguise among the troops of Francis I. Whenever Rilke translated, it was material to which he himself was inclined. In the Labé sonnets, there is an intense mystical and sensual yearning for something vaguely denied and an expression of contradictory states of feeling: "I suffer scorching heat but feel as though immersed in ice."

He also translated a 17th century French sermon *L'Amour de Madeleine* that spoke of the unrequited passion of Mary Magdalene and the need for renunciation. The figures in these translations and poems make for a mixed company: Pan, Horus, Christ, Orpheus, Mary, Mary Magdalene. Like Yeats, Rilke commingled the deities, legends, and re-interpreted the beliefs of the ancient Greeks and Christians. He strongly preferred the pantheistic fate to which Greek vision had resigned Linos and Orpheus as against the cruel destiny of martyrdom and eternal resurrection he felt Christians had imposed on Christ.

By September, 1911, his letters to Princess Marie had become so chaotic that worriedly she summoned him to Castle Duino to help sort out his ideas. Together they began to translate Dante's *Vita Nuova*, nothing of which has been preserved, and he enjoyed a brief calm before the squall. He had written to Marie, "I long to feel so magnificently endangered inwardly as in days gone by, at the time of the *Studen-Buch*." In the middle of December when she left him to his "divinely ordained solitude," the elixir that drives disease to the surface, Rilke again began to court the demon: "I creep around in the thickets of my life all day long, shouting like a savage and clapping my hands. You would hardly believe what horrible creatures fly up." He felt the need "to plunge into the funnel of solitude once more to see if I strike bottom."

What prompted immediate action—between January 15 and 23, 1912—on a cycle called "Das Marien-Leben" ["The Life of the Virgin Mary"] was the news that Heinrich Vogeler intended to illustrate and publish a book of Mary poems which Rilke had written in Vogeler's guest book [3] during the Westerwede days. Despite their long-standing friendship, Rilke was able to see objectively that Vogeler in respect to religious art was no Dürer but a person "daintily entangled in his reveries." It was true that the tone of Rilke's Mary poems in Vogeler's guest book also had been conducive to reverie; now it was something he shunned. Rilke's personalized approach was quite different from the poetic Mariolatry in old German legends and songs like,

> Maria, you gentle one,
> You are a rose garden
> Graced by God himself . . . ;
>
> Ave Maria, a rose without any thorns
> . . . Ave Maria! Through your child's death
> Which hung before you red with blood.
> Help, that I receive the angels' bread
> Contritely in the hour of death.[4]

Rilke's new version departs from traditions and approaches a serious religious subject without solemnity or mystical symbolism as the fierceness of the *Visions of Christ* give way to gentle irony and deflation that put everything on a human footing.

However, Rilke's playful treatment of a traditionally devotional subject more often than not becomes somewhat ponderous. Rich tonal lines end in horrid false rhymes, colloquialisms jostle pompous words, ingenuity of rhyme overwhelms the directness of the ideas, changes of tempo and line lengths from section to section give the poem cycle an imbalance and inconsistency.[5] Parodistic, autobiographical, and mythical elements, as well as special Rilkean terminology, lend the Mary cycle greater interest than the intrinsic poetry. That Rilke seemed intent on psychological rather than portraitistic views is evident in his Greek inscription to this cycle—ζάλην ἔνδοθεν ἔχων —which refers to "Joseph's Suspicion," part of the early Byzantine Akathistos hymn.

In the Gospel according to St. Matthew, the angel of the Lord appears in Joseph's sleep to tell him that what is conceived in Mary is of the Holy Ghost. Matthew's Joseph accepts with docility, but Rilke's Joseph is a peasant who balls his fist and must be bludgeoned with a hyperbole before he shifts a thick cap off his head in respect, as the angel cries out: "Carpenter, / haven't you noticed this is the Lord's dealing? / In your pride, because you saw up boards, / would you really call upon him to explain, / who modestly from out of the same woods / makes leaves thrust and buds swell each year again?"

As for the annunciation to Mary, Rilke ascribes no more shock to her than to others "when sunbeam or moon bustle about their room." Like the God-visited women of the Greek and Egyptian legends, Mary did not "care now to be indignant." Again, Rilke resorts to hyperbole, explaining the purity of Mary to be so great that when her gaze intermingled with that of a hind it gave birth to a unicorn, one of the favorite medieval symbols of virginity. If this were so, then the ensuing union "nowhere but" through the "eye and eye's delight" of Mary and the angel-youth is even less susceptible to doubt. The act of penetrative gazing, inseeing, is Rilke's physical equivalent for procreation. Yet to Rilke, eyes were always frightening, and thus terror comes to the angel and Mary at the height of their ocular experience. In one stanza Rilke overplays the assurance that the union is mystical rather than physical; in another he recapitulates the Zeus-Leda relation as "God feels himself into a virgin's womb."

Of the Marriage at Cana the verses in St. John read: "And when they wanted wine, the mother of Jesus saith unto him, They have no wine. Jesus saith unto her, Woman, what have I to do with thee? mine hour is not yet come." Then Jesus turned the water in the six stone pots into wine: "This beginning of miracles did Jesus in

Cana of Galilee, and manifested forth his glory; and his disciples believed in him." Rilke's version of the incident takes an editorial departure:

> *Aber da bei jenem Hochzeitsfeste,*
> *als es unversehns an Wein gebrach,—*
> *sah sie hin und bat um eine Geste*
> *und begriff nicht, dass er widersprach.*

> *Und dann tat er's. Sie verstand es später,*
> *wie sie ihn in seinen Weg gedrängt:*
> *denn jetzt war er wirklich Wundertäter,*
> *und das ganze Opfer war verhängt,*

> *unaufhaltsam. Ja, es stand geschrieben.*
> *Aber war es damals schon bereit?*
> *Sie: sie hatte es herbeigetrieben*
> *in der Blindheit ihrer Eitelkeit.*

> *An dem Tisch voll Früchten und Gemüsen*
> *freute sie sich mit und sah nicht ein,*
> *dass das Wasser ihrer Tränendrüsen*
> *Blut geworden war mit diesem Wein.*    (sw 1,675–76)

> But there on that day at the wedding feast
> when, unexpectedly, more wine was needed,
> she looked, and begged a gesture at the least
> and did not understand when he protested.

> Then he did it. And she saw much later
> how she had thrust him then upon his way.
> Now he'd become a real miracle maker,
> and in this act unalterably there lay

> the sacrifice. Yes, written and decreed,
> Then on that day, was it prepared already?
> She; it was she had driven on the dead
> in the blindness of her vanity.

> At the table, heaped with vegetables and fruits,
> she shared the joy, and never understood
> that the water from her own tear-ducts,
> with this wine, had been transformed to blood.

Being irritably conscious of his mother's vanity and how she thrust him almost as a babe in the direction of poetry, Rilke apparently saw a parallel in the Jesus-Mary relationship. Once the miracle of the wine and the miracle of the poetry had been wrought, Jesus' and Rilke's followers "believed"; but they did not know the men behind the wine and the poetry, nor did they know the anguished sense of mission that overshadowed their yearning for the common destiny of man. Particularly, in regard to Christ, Rilke felt that the assigned and involuntary mission was too great: "Men should quarry saviors from the mountains / where one hews the hard out of the hard."

With the completion of the Mary cycle, which was published a year later in 1913, Rilke permitted no new work to be put in print until 1922, the year of the final elegies. During that decade his poetry was a private affair, and his reputation among contemporaries rested only on what he had already accomplished.

Duino in many ways was an ideal stimulus for Rilke who knew that, according to legend, Dante had stayed there. To Rilke it was like living in the ancient hills of human existence. In the setting of the immensely walled castle of Duino "that holds one a little like a prisoner," Rilke experienced somewhat the same emotions that swamped him when he wrote *Malte*, "not so much as a going under but a singularly dark ascension into a remote neglected part of heaven." There, it seems, the first of the famous *Duino Elegies* was born. In the elegy, the hybrid Biblical and mythological angel of the Mary cycle gave way to a sharply different Rilkean concept and vision. Rilke's enormous breakthrough from the minor poetry of the Mary cycle to the marble splendor of the elegies within congruent days of composition is one of the inexplicable acts of creativity. Not even Rilke seemed to be fully aware of the threshold he had passed.

Princess Marie writes in her *Reminiscences*:

On the 23rd January [1912] I received a small parcel, and before me lay the turquoise-blue volume we had bought together in Weimar. . . . A short letter accompanied the First Elegy. . . . Later Rilke told me how the Elegy came to be written. He had made an allusion in one letter to the nightingale which was coming nearer. . . . Perhaps he had felt what was coming. But then it seemed to fall silent again. A deep sadness came over him, he feared that this winter would pass without results.

One morning he received an annoying business letter. He wanted to deal with it as quickly as possible and found himself forced to concentrate on figures and other prosaic matters.

Outside a strong *Bora* was blowing, but the sun shone and the sea was radiantly blue, crested with silver. Rilke climbed down to the narrow path which connects the bastions jutting out to the east and west at the foot of the castle, from where the rocks fall down to the sea in a sheer drop of 200 feet. The poet walked up and down this path, entirely absorbed in thought and wondering how to answer the letter. Then suddenly, as he was pondering, he stopped dead: it seemed to him that he heard a voice call through the roaring of the wind: *Who, if I cried, would hear me from the ranks of the angels?* . . . Taking out the note-book he always carried, he wrote down these words and several more verses that formed themselves without any conscious effort on his part. . . . Then he went up to his room quite calmly, laid his note-book away and dealt with the business letter. Yet by the same evening the entire First Elegy had been written down. Very soon afterwards the Second, the "Angel" Elegy, was to follow.

Just as "the tempest's fury" initiated *The Book of Pilgrimage*, the raging and tumultuous sea of Viareggio accompanied the writing of the *Book of Poverty and Death*, and a stormy night gave birth to the *Cornet*, the elements set in motion the rhythm of Rilke's "First Elegy." It is also likely that Rilke's inner commotions had as much to do with the elegies as the elements, despite the story Rilke had romantically embellished for Princess Marie. From the letters of that period of flareup, we can see that Rilke had been prodding his emotions: the longing to feel "magnificently endangered inwardly," the urge of plunging down "the funnel of solitude." It was to a great extent a self-induced state of calm terror and visionary sublimity. Mario Malvolto in Heinrich Mann's novelette *Pippo Spano Dances* says: "It is essential to me to cheat myself into states of feeling so that I may be able to represent them." Rilke admired this work possibly because it stated his search for inspiration more candidly than he dared.

In the "First Elegy" we see the thoughts that occupied him and the questions that plagued him. Just shortly before, he had translated Giacomo Leopardi's poem "L'Infinito" in which the poet finds solitude and human silence a prelude to experiencing the sounds of nature that are synonymous with endless and ultimate silence; all tenses of time swim together, and the poet fears and simultaneously welcomes inner "shipwreck" in this sea of thought. To save himself from this fate, Rilke needs human companionship but it is this need which perversely drives him into paroxysms of despair: "Dear Lou, I am in a bad way when I wait for people, need people, look around for people: that only drives me still further into the more turbid and puts me into the wrong; they cannot know how little trouble, really, I take with them, and of what ruthlessness I am capable." The angel of the elegies is to be this kind of ruthless and disdaining creature.

God needs man for *his* existence, cried Rilke's monk years earlier; in the elegies the poet turns from the assertion to the questions, whom or what do *we* need to fully exist and what degree of intimacy should enter relationships? The "First Elegy" then begins the search for answers. Were the angel to take one to his heart, one would be extinguished by his stronger being. Yet the experience is still bearable as a form of terror or beauty which we admire because it disdains to destroy us. Instead of being shattered by the haughty and humbling condescension of the angel, Rilke feels an abject pleasure in the imaginary relationship. If we cannot use the angel, the young departed, human beings—and even the knowing animals who sense that we are not at home in our interpreted world—what is left? Perhaps a tree, a slope that we see daily, the street of yesterday, habit, the night wind that contains cosmic space, the Spring seasons. Is the task of establishing identity easier for lovers? Rilke's answer is negative: "Alas, with each other they only conceal their lot." But these are common lovers:

*Sehnt es dich aber, so singe die Liebenden; lange*
*noch nicht unsterblich genug ist ihr berühmtes Gefühl.*
*Jene, du neidest sie fast, Verlassenen, die du*
*so viel lieber fandst als die Gestillten. . . .*        (sw 1,686)

*No, when longing comes over you, sing the great lovers; the*
*    fame*
*of all they can feel is far from immortal enough.*
*Those whom you almost envied, those forsaken, you found*
*so far beyond the requited in loving. . . .*

Unrequited love is greater than requited love, as similarly poetized in Keats' Ode in which the frozen moment, *stasis,* is to be preferred to the moment of fulfillment, *ecstasis.* The act of longing and the moments of anticipation overshadow any possible consummation. The plaint is an echo of Rilke's disappointments in relationships that did not measure up to the emotions engendered by the cumulative excitement of anticipation, rather than a common-stock romantic sentiment.

Characteristic of the elegies are long lines of blank verse whose syntax is prosy and often ambiguous, filled with declamations and injunctions, elegiac sighs, abrupt broaching of ideas, essayistic capsules, rhetorical questions that harbor a foregone answer, didactic monologues, and imagistic metaphors. Rilke freely and consciously employs exaggeration and accentuation in the elegies. So strong is Rilke's fictive-emotional strength [6] that he often persuades the reader of the living reality of the creatures that populate his fantasies. Certainly at the moment of poetizing, Rilke persuaded himself of their reality; the invented became the substance of his experience. The angel is a creature willed into existence by Rilke.

The elegies are a recapitulation of all the ideas he had

ever harbored. What the poetry does, however, is to give them pictorial concreteness and compressed verbal expressiveness. What he wrote in one letter within a few days of the composition of the "First Elegy" is a commentary on the elegy:

> People yield themselves to me only in so far as they themselves find words within me, and then in these recent years they have been communicating themselves to me almost solely through two figures upon which in general I base my inferences on mankind. What speaks to me of things human, immensely, with a calm of authority that makes my hearing spacious, is the phenomenon of those who have died young, and more absolutely still, more purely, more inexhaustibly: *the woman who loves.* (Letter to Annette Kolb, Jan. 23, 1912)

Throughout the elegies eulogistic stanzas are devoted to woman's self-contained love, love that exists independent of reciprocity and needs no requital, as illustrated by Gaspara Stampa, the Lyonnaise Labé, or the Portuguese nun Marianna Alcoforado who wrote to her beloved, "My love is no longer dependent on the way you treat me." Contrasted to the women canonized by Rilke is man's absolute inadequacy in love. In the "First Elegy," Rilke somewhat plaintively shows the way to love's transcendence:

. . . *Hast du der Gaspara Stampa*
*denn genügend gedacht, dass irgend ein Mädchen,*
*dem der Geliebte entging, am gesteigerten Beispiel*
*dieser Liebenden fühlt: dass ich würde wie sie?*
*Sollen nicht endlich uns diese ältesten Schmerzen*
*fruchtbarer werden? Ist es nicht Zeit, dass wir liebend*
*uns vom Geliebten befrein und es bebend bestehn:*
*wie der Pfeil die Sehne besteht, um gesammelt im Absprung*
*mehr zu sein als er selbst. Denn Bleiben ist nirgends.*

(sw 1,686–87)

. . . *Have you so fully remembranced*
*Gaspara Stamp, that any girl, whose beloved's*
*eluded her, may feel, from that far intenser*
*example of loving: "if I could become like her!"?*

*Ought not these oldest sufferings of ours to be yielding*
*more fruit by now? Is it not time that, in loving,*
*we freed ourselves from the loved one, and, quivering,*
     *endured:*
*as the arrow endures the string, to become, in the gathering*
     *out-leap,*
*something more than itself? For staying is nowhere.*

Rilke's constant moving about was hardly conducive to
stability in relationships, yet non-rootedness is a causative
factor in Rilke's creativity. He needed new sights and
sounds and people as stimuli that would inevitably provide
unexpected, epiphanous insights. Relevant to the elegies
he wrote:

> I believe in Naples once, before some ancient tombstone,
> it flashed through me that I should never touch people with
> gestures stronger than those there portrayed. And I really
> believe that I am sometimes far enough along to express all
> the insistence of my heart without loss and fatality when I
> lay my hand lightly on a shoulder. (Letter to Lou, Janu-
> ary 10, 1912)

In the "First Elegy" this theme is struck, and is repeated
with variations in the later ones:

*Es rauscht jetzt von jenen jungen Toten zu dir.*
*Wo immer du eintratst, redete nicht in Kirchen*
*zu Rom und Neapel ruhig ihr Schicksal dich an?*
*Oder es trug eine Inschrift sich erhaben dir auf,*
*wie neulich die Tafel in Santa Maria Formosa.*     (sw 1,687)

*Rustling toward you now from those youthfully-dead.*
*Whenever you entered a church in Rome or in Naples*
*were you not always being quietly addressed by their fate?*
*Or else an inscription sublimely imposed itself on you,*
*as, lately, the tablet in Santa Maria Formosa.*

What happens after parting? Rilke answers his own
questions: "Truly it is strange not to inhabit the earth any
longer, / not to practice scarcely-acquired habits / . . . to
leave behind one's name like a broken toy. / Strange not to
continue wishing one's wishes. Strange / to see everything,

that once held together, flutter / so loosely in space. And being dead is tiring / . . . until one slowly feels / a bit of eternity. But the living / all make the mistake of differentiating too sharply. / Angels (it is said) often do not know if they move among the living or the dead. The eternal / stream tears through both realms / of all ages and outsounds them in both." In language close to prose, the poem with its cumulative tautology (*nicht mehr, seltsam, und*) and violent enjambments shows its rhetorical character, while the ideas posed sum up Rilke's speculation about the afterlife. In the closing lines of the "First Elegy," Rilke repeats the annotation to his translation of de Guérin's *Le Centaure*. He is fascinated by the legendary musicians Linos and Orpheus who, like poets, stand outside of human fate but whose song is the mystic power that enables the dead to sense each other's existence in space without physical contact but in silent movement through all dimensions.

After writing the "First Elegy" Rilke regained his self-confidence, rejecting psychoanalysis whose excavation techniques he thought would result in a noncreative life. He told Baron Emil von Gebsattel, a friend and analyst, that his earlier plans to submit to analysis had been merely pretexts, that the misery and joy of creation was his lot, and that relief would come through enduring and in final achievement: "Let no one tell me I do not care for the present, vibrating as I do within it; it bears me, gives me all this spacious . . . immemorial workday." And in a week the "Second Elegy" followed. Again, the angels and the lovers dominate.

As if dissatisfied with his incomplete pictorialization in the "First Elegy," Rilke tries again in the "Second." He broaches imponderable questions and works himself into an impasse of contradictions, especially in his relations to the angels. In *Malte*, Rilke had viewed the angels as being at home in all realms, but he gave little intimation that they were anything but the angels of his childhood, the holy creatures of Judeo-Christian tradition, as he knew them through St. Augustine's writings. In the elegies he raises them to such monumental figures as those that appear in Milton's and Klopstock's poetry, yet he slowly veers toward a mystical interpretation which Hölderlin had revived. Rilke's angels—male figures—now are embodiments of beauty and terror, "almost deadly birds of the soul," darlings of creation, suprahumans, mirrors which draw their outstreaming images back into their own faces. Man, by contrast, experiences an earthly passing, a literal evaporation and dissolution like fading embers, streaming into the *Weltraum*, the world-all. If this is so, continued Rilke's metaphysical logic, then it may be possible that our essence subtly mingles with that of the perilous angels who step downward from behind stars through vast space while human hearts soar upward into the mythological and neutral territory symbolized by stars. Our essence then remains somewhere, immortal.

Like air we pass over anchored, real objects, and all things in nature conspire to silence, possibly because they are ashamed of man, or partly because they hope for him. At the point where one may feel that Rilke becomes hopelessly lost in transcendental reverie and poetic exaggeration, he brilliantly succeeds in externalizing concretely the intuition and vague feelings that seethe in his heart.

Addressing lovers, Rilke asks, "Does your satisfaction and sufficiency with one another give you proof of your existence?" To show lovers their naïveté, Rilke suggests this analogy: "Look, it happens to me that my hands become / as one or else that my worn / face spares itself in them. That gives me some / sensation. But who dares to presume existence because of it?" The fleeting sensation creates an illusion without offering proof of existence. Love, through physical contact, is for Rilke one of man's most poignant experiences, intensified and made sad by human transience and eventual and inevitable parting.

> . . . *Ich weiss,*
> *ihr berührt euch so selig, weil die Liebkosung verhält,*
> *weil die Stelle nicht schwindet, die ihr, Zärtliche,*
> *zudeckt; weil ihr darunter das reine*
> *Dauern verspürt. . . .*                    (sw 1,691)

> . . . *I know*
> *why you so blissfully touch: because the caress persists,*
> *because it does not vanish, the place that you*
> *so tenderly cover; because you perceive thereunder*
> *pure duration. . . .*

"This," notes Rilke, "means quite literally that the spot on which the lover lays his hand is thereby completely withdrawn from the passing away, the ageing, the continual process of decay that is always at work in our essential selves—it simply *endures, exists* under his hand." [7] Much in Rilke's poetry, that to the reader seems to be poetic conceit or hyperbole, was intended by Rilke to be a matter of literal logic. His interpretation of the elegy passage describing the lover's touch is one of the few Rilke exegeses extant although he had planned to annotate the elegies much as Eliot footnoted *The Waste Land*.

In Rilke's view, human contact and gesture must be light.

> *Erstaunte euch nicht auf attischen Stelen die Vorsicht*
> *menschlicher Geste? war nicht Liebe und Abschied*
> *so leicht auf die Schultern gelegt, als wär es aus anderm*
> *Stoffe gemacht als bei uns? . . .*  (sw 1,691–92)

> *On Attic steles, did not the circumspection*
> *of human gesture amaze you? Were not love and farewell*
> *so lightly laid upon shoulders, they seemed to be made*
> *of other stuff than with us? . . .*

The "Second Elegy" ends on a note of yearning and hope (with which he had teased Clara) to find "some pure, contained, narrow, human, own little strip of orchard."

Although much has been made of the declarative prose style of the elegies, the listener hears the cunning internal rhymes, assonance, and alliteration attuned to rhythm, sensuous sound and changing vowel pairs. Where the necessity of endline rhyme schemes in previous poetizing often led Rilke to say things he may not have meant and allowed sound to dominate sense, the blank verse of the elegies permits him greater flexibility in shaping his meanings and still demonstrate mastery of devices like internal assonances as in the last two excerpts: berührt-verspürt; nicht-attischen-Vorsicht-menschlicher, Liebe-Abschied.

The "Third Elegy" also had its beginning early in 1912 at Duino and was completed about a year and a half later in Paris. As an elegy it stands like an enclave among the rest, a self-contained prose-poem, in which Rilke's habitual etherealization of love, for maidens and mother, yields to terrified admiration of the primordial surge of sex and anticipation-fears, as male passions are unleashed by "the guilty river-god of the blood," that "Lord of Pleasure"— who rouses the night to infinite uproar with the "gloomy blast from his breast, a twisted sea-shell." Psychoanalysis might easily have robbed Rilke of a mystique that permits him the most fearsome embellishments and imagery this side of Puritanism. Here also is one of the rare instances in which the idea of guilt is given direct expression, but only in passing. It is not the maiden, who wanders like morning breezes, but "ancient forces" that shatter him. It is not the loved one who incites the lover's delight but the stars. Rilke implies that love or passion exists independent of a love-object and merely fastens on it to give the illusion of reality. It is the classic Narcissus pose.

The loved one, however, can soothe deep-welling feelings, and a mother can displace the fears that lurk in the night and that surround the child in his chamber. The tempest which raged in the first part of the elegy subsides when remembrance plaintively evokes the slender figure of Rilke's mother who nightly during childhood allayed his anxieties. Yet, in watching over him she also obstructed the way to the strange, the "surging abyss." Gratitude mingles uncomfortably with impatient accusations: "Mother, *you* made him small."

*Und er selbst, wie er lag, der Erleichterte, unter*
*schläfernden Lidern deiner leichten Gestaltung*
*Süsse lösend in den gekosteten Vorschlaf—:*
schien *ein Gehüteter . . . Aber* innen: *wer wehrte,*
*hinderte innen in ihm die Fluten der Herkunft?*    (sw 1,695)

*And he himself as he lay there in such relief,*
*mingling, under his drowsy eyelids, the sweetness*
*of your light shaping with foretaste of coming sleep,*
*seemed to be under protection . . . Within, though: who*
  *could avert*
*divert, the floods of origin flowing within him?*

The pleasure of melting away under eyelids as a foretaste
of the "long sleep" becomes a cherished sensation.[8] In the
elegy, thoughts twist and turn: the love object is needed,
yet it is incidental to the sensation of loving; Rilke is
grateful for the mother's protection, yet regards her as an
intruder who bars the way to the great emotion: he fears
the interior experience, yet invites and even loves it,
immersing himself in feverish dream—the meadow of the
inner world.

*Er, der Neue, Scheuende, wie er verstrickt war,*
*mit des innern Geschehns weiterschlagenden Ranken*
*schon zu Mustern verschlungen, zu würgendem Wachstum,*
  *zu tierhaft*

*jagenden Formen. Wie er sich hingab—. Liebte.*
*Liebte sein Inneres, seines Inneren Wildnis,*
*diesen Urwald in ihm, auf dessen stummen Gestürztsein*
*lichtgrün sein Herz stand. Liebte. . . .*      (sw 1,695)

*He, so new, so timorous, how he was tangled*
*in ever-encroaching roots of inner event,*
*twisted to primitive patterns, to throttling growths, to bestial*

*preying forms! How he gave himself up to it! Loved.*
*Loved his interior world, his interior jungle,*
*that primal forest within, on whose mute overthrownness,*
*green-lit, his heart stood. Loved. . . .*

In the descent, "Yes, Horror smiled at him . . . Seldom /
did you, Mother, smile so tenderly. How could he help /
loving what smiled at him?" This silent interior landscape
contains the immemorial sap of creation, ancestral fathers
and mothers. All this, Rilke almost exultantly proclaims,
preceded maid and mother, echoing Ewald Tragy's last

words. Ewald's "first love" is dramatically identified in the elegy as Rilke's own interior world.

In the "Third Elegy" Rilke's macabre imagination devotes itself to sexual imagery. As the maid conjures up primordial time in her lover she also rouses sinister men in his vein, incurs the hatred of the interior women, and attracts the dead children. The lust of the fathers and the hatred of the mothers make it consciously difficult to approach a love relationship with a sense of balance. Yet, this is what Rilke sought and gives poignant voice to in the last lines of the "Third Elegy": "Maid, Oh gently, gently show him daily a loving, confident task done, —guide him / close to the garden, give him those counterbalancing nights . . . Withhold him." Yet, which maid, mother, or mistress could "withhold" him?

The rush of creativity continued through March, with fifteen lines which were to form the opening of the "Tenth Elegy," the motif of the "Sixth," and part of the "Ninth Elegy." Then a sudden turnabout took place. From the doldrums of elegiac lament arose a note of hope: "Someday, emerging at last from this terrifying vision, / may I burst into jubilant praise to assenting Angels?" This theme is expanded within a fifteen-line preview of the "Tenth Elegy" to indicate clearly that pain is "our winter foliage" which we must bear as a condition of existence; we must accept life without wasting time on sorrow or yearning for its end.

However, the avalanche of poetry subsided and, instead of the "dictated" flow and compulsive utterance, scraps of material had to be laboriously quarried. He thought that a change of locale might help so that from June to September he stayed in Venice where, "Alas, as we waited for help from mankind, angels stepped soundlessly, in a single stride, over our prostrate heart." Because the wait in Venice continued to prove unproductive, he hearkened to a séance-prophecy and the voice of "the unknown lady" who said that he was destined to experience the stars, sky, and angels in Toledo, Spain. Rilke had been curious anyway about the land painted by El Greco and Ignacio Zuloaga. When he finally viewed the prototype, he was shaken: this "unsubdued, undiminished landscape, the mountain . . . of vision,—monstrous the earth issues from it and directly before its gates becomes world, creation, mountain and ravine, Genesis." It is a perfect setting for the prophet and his vision, a city of heaven and earth which "goes right through all existence . . . for the eyes of the dead, the living, and the angels." The inventive vocabulary of the elegies has now become an integral part of his life, providing shorthand symbols for his subsequent poetry.

Momentarily, in the poem "The Spirit Ariel," composed after reading Shakespeare's *Tempest,* Rilke toys with the idea of "abjuring magic" and "entering into destiny like others," but this frequently expressed idea of giving up poetry—which for him is reality created through the magic of words—is quickly abandoned with the next spontaneous verses. One of the superlative poems shaped during those days is an untitled one that exploits the image of rolling pearls and shows considerable allegorical ingenuity.

*Perlen entrollen. Weh, riss eine der Schnüre?*
*Aber was hülf es, reih ich sie wieder: du fehlst mir,*
*starke Schliesse, die sie verhielte, Geliebte.* (sw ii,42)

["Pearls roll away. Woe, did one of the strings tear? / But what is the use, if I string them again: you would be missing, / you, the strong clasp which holds them together, you beloved."] The future beloved of the "Third Elegy" is the missing pearl on a "string of lament," each note like a pearl awaiting its companion in a melody that rises to jubilation. In the second stanza of the poem, Rilke strings simile after simile to illustrate personal incompleteness and desperate need: I am like the gigantic face of an expectant theater audience, like a desert river bed, like a prisoner awaiting the answer of the stars through his innocent window, like a cripple who hangs his crutches over the altar waiting for a miracle. In the third stanza, the similes give way to declarations: Only you do I desire; must not the wretched crack in the pavement sense the urge of the driving grass and want to experience the fullness of Spring . . . the fullness of the future which moves toward us? The poem, like the unstrung string of pearls trails off . . . into three dots.

The poem is full of such violent motion as would cause the severing of a string, and almost every reference to the coming beloved is prefaced by a verb, noun, or preposition implying motion: *Aufgang, Auftritt, aufrecht, entgegenbewegt, bestehen.* At the same time, these words were quite specifically becoming the officially sanctioned expressions in Rilkean scripture to signify ascension, transcendence, sexual excitement, ceremonious motion, endurance, and suffering.

Thirty-two out of the forty-five lines of the "Sixth Elegy," the shortest of the cycle, center around the symbolic significance Rilke ascribes to the fig tree: It almost omits to flower and immediately bears "seasonably-resolute fruit." Man by contrast glories in flowering, in living; in the act of lingering and delaying, the core of man's ultimate fruit is retarded and he is betrayed. Flowering or living is an illusion and the beginning of death is true fruition. In the hero (unconcerned with continuance of life) and in the youthfully dead, the transition from flowering to fruition is brief. The longing for fruition or death is a relative to the Freudian death wish and it is counterbalanced by the desire to exist in the delights of anticipation: "And then how gladly I'd hide from the longing: oh would, would that I were a boy and might come to it yet. . . ."

To Lou, by now only a mother-confessor, Rainer described his physical longing that existed independent of any specific person and that simply waited for someone to walk into its ken; but then always came the letdown. Yeats' phrase, "Desire dies because every touch consumes the myth," applies strikingly to Rilke. Disturbing, however, are his relapses: Mother " . . . keep your cloak open. / I am too big. I will be child again to you. . . . / No beloved could give me refuge. . . ." Neither could the angel. It was Rilke's destiny to be consumed by his own longing.

What Rilke wished for during the drab winter days of 1913/14 in Paris, he wrote to Marie on December 27:

. . . to find a few rooms in the country where I can rave quite in my own way and where the Elegies may howl out of me at the moon . . . also the possibility of taking long solitary walks and exactly the person, the sisterly person!!! (alas, alas!) who would look after the house and would have no love at all or so much that she asks for nothing but to be there functioning and protecting the border of the invisible.

Yet, he craved the kind of experience that would allow the poet to "transfer all affliction and bliss into one's work." The elegies needed life substance for transmutation and Rilke thought that he had found it in his role as protector of the young girl Marthe he had befriended two years earlier in Paris. But any kind of human love was impossible exertion for Rilke, "only in relation to God have I any ease." Precisely because he had little to offer Marthe, his imagination discharged itself into a seduction fantasy played out in twenty-one lines intended for the elegies; but the lines were justifiably discarded. In the lines he seems to envy "the exultant man" at the frightened maiden's garden gates; as a passing stranger and never the "possessor," all he can do is choke his cry of grief into a poetry of suffering.

Because inspiration no longer came easily, Rilke tried to force the great "dictation" by a mystical transformation of the self into what he called the "inner space of night" (*Nachtinnenraum*) and through infeeling become part of the infinite cosmos: "how my being . . . trusts itself in hurling itself close to you." Such metaphysical hyperboles became the reality of several technically impressive "Night Poems."

Although it had been sufficient for Rilke to share his poetry with only a small inner circle of friends (he begged Marie to keep the elegies sheltered, after she proposed that Hofmannsthal read them publicly, until he overcame the frame of mind which had produced them), he became increasingly restless physically. Marie tells of a fear-tormented and nervous Rainer who talked of divorce from Clara and complained that he had always yielded to the emotions and demands of others; now, thought Marie, "he himself wanted to feel, to desire, and to love." Rilke's complaint was sheer delusion, but the urge for a real love relationship seemed sincere. And a few months later, in January, 1914, he had his wish when one of the "future beloved" materialized in the person of Magda von Hattingberg, a young divorcée and a concert pianist of repute.

Magda had been emotionally overwhelmed by Rilke's cloying *Stories of the dear God*, and precipitated a correspondence which was more ecstatic than their suspensefully delayed meeting and communality. Rilke at first admits to being unmusical, to viewing music as an imprecise art form, and of having waged "a valiant fight against the existence of pianos" in his proximity (they reminded him of piano dusting chores when a child), that he, like Orpheus and his unfathomable lyre, was in a period of gestation and not quite ready for jubilation, but that he yearned for his hands to achieve "their mysterious destiny" in the dear hands of Magda. Both seemed to swoon toward each other. Rainer christened her Benvenuta—welcome arrival, and she was like a pilgrim at a shrine. The break, and it was jagged, came when Rilke proposed marriage and Benvenuta made it clear that she wished to memorialize him and not to wash his linen. The union, at any rate, would have been disastrous because for Rilke's part, his mother fantasy removed any possibility of a realistic relationship: "Benvenuta, my darling, darling heart, are you not my maidenly mother, my child, my darling, darling girl?"

In the two months of correspondence-courtship, Rilke clearly expressed the ideas that seem obfuscated in the poetry. The *angel* is a creature that could redeem him: surely the intensity of one's wishing to reach the angel's ear can be transformed into "radiations of extreme emergency" which pass through the dense world and into the angel's domain. Angel, beast, child were imagined by Rilke to have a strangely rich life into which he wished to sink himself in order to experience their paradisial existence; yet he was afraid that they would dominate him. To these symbols Rilke added one that formerly had been touched only peripherally, namely dolls. In one of the courtship letters to Benvenuta, he lists some of his personal debits, among them a "monstrous fault" that consists of assuming people's hostility in advance. He asserts accusingly that whatever qualities of "affection and intimacy" he possesses, he has acquired from play with childhood dolls, resulting in his inability to have "valid judgment about inflicting pain or pleasure . . . dolls never talk back." Further, his was the frequent complaint that his mother played with him as with a doll, possibly stifling any genuine response he would have made as a boy. In German, doll or *Puppe* is female, and Rilke notes the wonderful playthings that boys have as against the horrid girlish dolls. All these accumulated resentments virulently stream into an essay called *Einiges über Puppen* [*Some Reflections on Dolls*], generally acknowledged to be his most powerful and strange essay.

Dolls, Rilke writes mordantly, are things that "allow themselves to be dreamed and to be lived" parasitically in the energy of others as horrible foreign bodies "on which we had wasted our purest ardor"; dolls cause a hopeless misplacement of one's earliest affection; they are things whose lifeless acquiescence does not condition one for the simplest human love relationship; dolls provoke assertiveness, inventiveness and fantasy—without which they are nothing; because of the deadly unresponsiveness of dolls, one is made to feel unloved throughout life. Its silence and constant mode of evasion was a disillusioning foretaste of the silence of "destiny" and of God, and by implication the angel:

A tremendous silence (larger than life) which was later to come to us repeatedly out of space whenever we approached the frontier of our existence. . . . That emptiness of feeling that heart-pause, in which we should perish did not the whole, gently persisting Nature then lift us across abysses like some lifeless thing.

Then quite startlingly, Rilke connects the doll, the lifeless thing, to one named Anna, the same name given to a retarded peasant girl in one of his short stories, "Frau

Blaha's Magd" ["Frau Blaha's Maid"], that dated back to 1899. It is a horror story told with extreme simplicity about the child-like Anna who gives birth to a baby, puts it among her collection of dolls, and when neighborhood children take fright at the exhibition of her menage, Anna calmly goes about splitting the heads of her dolls, including the "large, bluish one." The association of doll and child, his complaint that his mother used to play with him as with a doll, the death of a baby sister he had never known, the necrophilic fascination for lifeless maiden bodies (the doll is "unmasked . . . as the externally painted watery corpse which floated and swam on the flood-tides of our affection"), all these merge in the symbol of doll, "ignorant like a peasant Danaë," the toy of man and the gods. Toward the end of the essay, Rilke says: "Sexless as the dolls of childhood were, they can find no decease in their stagnant ecstasy, which has neither inflow nor outflow," unlike humans or angels.

To the dolls he ascribes the desire to be consumed by "a beautiful flame into which they might fling themselves," and in the letters to Benvenuta he attributes a similar desire to himself: "in the end, there may be no need for anyone to lay my funeral pyre, since I myself have touched the torch of ecstasy to my unblemished heart, that it consume itself utterly and flare up in a single flame to God." Whether the doll as a symbol stands for the poet ("I am become worn and broken—just like a toy") or his art, as some have interpreted it, or a morbid portraiture of the female is of less concern than the knowledge that such thoughts informed his poetry. As Oscar Wilde once said, "There is no such thing as changing one's life: one merely walks round and round within the circle of his personality." And, although Benvenuta could not suspect Rilke's life-pattern, he did give her some warning: "In the same breath with which I implore God to let me love you, I beg him, I implore him to strengthen my will for militant solitude, for such is the destiny of every fibre of my being." With the essay on dolls, which Rilke thrust at her, he plunged her into a profound panic; at that point she saw the dark recesses of his personality and the meaning of his self-description: 'Profoundly Slavic man that I somehow am."

Rilke assigned special importance to a poem he called "Wendung" ["Turning"] "because it depicts *the* turning which probably must come if I am to live." Central to the poem composed June 20, 1914, is the injunction, "Work of sight is finished, do now the heart work / on the pictures within you, those captives." In a manuscript note to the poem, Rilke expressed the wish to free himself from an interior-based gazing outward and substituting "a loving preoccupation with inner fullness"; perhaps this would transform him into a being capable of love and a poet capable of deeper perception: "For see, gazing has a limit. / And the much gazed-upon world / wishes to flower in love."

In the act of wishing to break the limitations of observant gazing in order to permit the images caught in his gaze to ripen inwardly, he creates lines that prefigure the power, grace and breathtaking communion of the later *Sonnets to Orpheus*.

> *Tiere traten getrost*
> *in den offenen Blick, weidende,*
> *und die gefangenen Löwen*
> *starrten hinein wie in unbegreifliche Freiheit;*
> *Vögel durchflogen ihn grad,*
> *den gemütigen; Blumen*
> *wiederschauten in ihm*
> *gross wie in Kinder.*                    (sw 11,82)

> *Beasts trustfully stepped*
> *into the open gaze, grazing,*
> *and the captured lions*
> *stared into it as if it were incomprehensible freedom;*
> *birds flew through it straightway,*
> *the consenting; flowers*
> *reflected each other within it,*
> *great as in children.*

With these lines in "Turning" a metamorphosis is set in motion, but the beasts and children and inner maiden must undergo a long gestation before being born.

THE GLITTER of the war machine and the ringing sounds of patriotic songs at the outbreak of World War I caused Rilke to write Marie, "It is absolutely wrong to lead a life of one's own in these times. . . . my place must naturally be in Austria." Hungry for sensation that would excite every fiber of his being, Rilke submerged himself in the communal hysteria. Perhaps this was the bond that would give him a longed-for contact with humanity. When Rilke inscribed his "Fünf Gesänge" ["*Five Songs*"] in a copy of Hölderlin's mystic hymns and elegies, it was as if the dead poet's memorable fervor to recall the mighty gods of Greece into human life and to quicken it also pulsed through Rilke. And certainly Rilke did not disappoint the shade of Hölderlin. With a mighty roar, the perennially reticent Rilke welcomed the god of battle who "hurls the firebrand: and above his heart, filled with home, / screams his blood-red heaven, which he thunderingly occupies." In Rilke's songs, the scythe of war cuts down the crop, taller than man, and the harvest begins. A nation comes to life, parting becomes the most meaningful of experiences to the bride, the wife, the young, the elderly, the would-be warrior—anything except this call to war seems insignificant.

For mothers, Rilke has this consolation: "Once before, as you gave birth, you experienced parting, mothers,— / now find renewed joy that you are givers." To maidens who relinquish their lovers, Rilke gives the unique assurance that in their parting they will truly be impressed upon the hearts of the beloved and in their *absence* be able to love them eternally. Rilke naively thought that the painful pleasure-experience of parting and joy through suffering, which he periodically cultivated in life and celebrated in poetry, would be equally appreciated by others. "We glow into One, / into a new creature which he [the war god] deadly animates. . . ." "I exist no longer; with communal hearts mine beats in unison, and the communal mouth / forces mine open." But after three days of such poet-izing, he finds it difficult to reconcile himself to the god of destruction, a cynical god: "And yet at night there howls within me like the ships' sirens / the questioning element, howls for the way, the way." The best one can do is to find jubilation in pain, to live more intensely, and to follow the bridal flag, as once did the *Cornet*. To follow the progress of the five poems is to watch a compelling and unparalleled hymn to war falter and fade into an elegiac whimper: "Things are mysterious. See, our heart too / is a mysterious thing." He was embarrassed to be standing idly by while Marie's sons reported for military service and the young generation of poets was drafted into the army. Rilke became disillusioned when, instead of producing civilian idealism, the war encouraged claptrap sentiment, dissipation, hypocrisy, and opportunism. When the war took the lives of several persons he held in affection, when Duino was shelled, when most of his possessions were lost in Paris, and when the arm of the draft began reaching closer to him, Rilke began to distinguish between senti-ment and external reality. Within a year, Rilke's hymnic enthusiasm had changed to appeals for someone to cry out for a stop to the war slaughter, appeals which he confined to those receptive among his most intimate circle of correspondents. Across the seas, in England, poets like Rupert Brooke and Siegfried Sassoon went though a similar cycle from enthusiasm to disillusionment.

With astonishing rapidity, Rilke isolated himself from the contemporary turmoil right after the outburst of the "Five Songs" in August, 1914, and, until his induction into the army at the end of 1915, led a fairly idyllic existence. This came to light emphatically in 1952 with the publication of Lou Albert-Lasard's unambiguous memoirs, *Wege mit Rilke* [*Paths with Rilke*], also releasing sixteen poems unavailable up to then.

In the stillness of a mountain village resort, Rilke besieged Mrs. Loulou Lasard, whom he had followed in previous years through the streets in Paris, Perugia, and Assisi, without daring to strike up a conversation or to give her flowers. She was a painter who traveled with an easel on her back while her husband immolated himself in his science laboratory. Adding to the coincidence of their meeting was the fact that she was also deep in the task of translating Rilke into French. After three days of silent companionship, the dam broke and Rilke presented her with the first of a series of translucent, lyrical, amorous poems. Just as he had renamed Magda "Benvenuta" so he called Loulou his "Armide." In the legend of Armida and Rinaldo (charmingly close to Rainer), Armida rivalled Venus and used her wiles to seduce the crusaders from their vows and duties, luring them into her luxurious palace and gardens, but Rinaldo vanquished Armida in her Bower of Bliss. Some such similar fantasy Rilke had in mind for his relationship with Loulou. Her subsequent insights into Rainer's personality and his compulsion to name changing are worth noting:

> He suffered a curse, tribute to his particular genius, which forced him to penetrate into people and things unto identification in order to draw "the name" out of them, in a magical sense. Through this "name" everything is raised to the absolute and loses its all too human aspect. But his curiosity and unstilled thirst for life forced him to play the game of the Danaïds, which brought him and others so much pain. For him the attraction of life was so mighty that he continually felt himself drawn to the life of others only to remain for the most part on the threshold.[1]

Loulou was more receptive to a symbiotic "ineinander" life than Lou Andreas-Salomé had been. Although they took up a common abode, Loulou assures posterity that they respected the boundaries of their individual quarters, but her husband thought it best under the circumstances to seek divorce. Whether modesty or fact prompts Loulou to give a Platonic aura to their life, aside from some nocturnal bedside dialogue, her memoirs are the least evasive of all in describing Rilke's personality. From depression to impish humor, from mannered gallantry to sincerity, and from childish tantrums to manly tenderness were emotive distances Rilke could traverse quickly. Contrast and paradoxical moods were also mirrored in Rilke's features when he sat for a portrait by Loulou:

> A world of dreams and thoughts lay like an illumination on Rilke's clear forehead. His depthless eyes—intense, penetrating and at the same time receptive—formed a surprising contrast to the lower part of his face which expressed a life thirst through a fullsome mouth with dazzling teeth, framed by a greenish-blond Chinese moustache and a certain weakness in the soft-fleeting chin.[2]

Rilke vacillated between life and work, the need for people and isolation, subjection and negation, jubilation and dejection, inspiration and forced work, human love and immortal love, horror and joy. He showed Loulou a passage in his diary in which he analyzed his unstable position: "He was in the position of a god who had no way out of the world he had overfilled; for whom remained only the vertical—either descent into hell or ascent into heaven." To counter his gyrations and irresolutions, Rilke tried to locate himself somewhere in space and time so that almost all the poetry to Loulou concerns itself with a search for a fixed point in existence. Poetically he tells her,

> *Sieh, ich bin nicht, aber wenn ich wäre,*
> *wäre ich die Mitte im Gedicht;*
> *das Genaue, dem das ungefähre,*
> *ungefühlte Leben widerspricht.*
>
> *Sieh, ich bin nicht. Denn die Andern sind;*
> *während sie sich zu einander kehren*
> *blind und im vergesslichsten Begehren—,*

*tret ich leise in den leeren*
*Hund und in das volle Kind.*          (sw II,224–25)

*See, I do not exist, but if I did,*
*I would be the center of the poem,*
*the precise to whom the imprecise*
*and the unfelt life is contrary.*

*See, I do not exist. The others are, because*
*while they turn to one another*
*blindly and with forgetfulness-inspiring desire,*
*I step softly into the empty*
*dog and into the full child.*

Loulou explains that the dog refers to a creature which is emptied because it lives looking up to man, whereas a child moves in its self-contained world.

Despite inner confusion, his external life seemed rather orderly and even stimulating. We see him in the company of Loulou and Heinrich Mann at a fiery patriotic lecture given by Thomas Mann, and overhear the whisper of Heinrich to Rilke, "My brother has more printable thoughts than I." There are days with Hofmannsthal, Richard Beer-Hofmann (the Jewish patriarch whose Old Testament poetry lay close to Rilke's heart), the stately Karl Wolfskehl (a poet who towered next to George), the brilliant politician Walter Rathenau, the expressionist painter Kokoschka, the notable artist Paul Klee, the trenchant political satirist Karl Kraus, and the writer Stefan Zweig.

Among the stream of visitors were Lou Andreas-Salomé, Clara and Ruth, and Rilke's mother Phia. Loulou pictures Lou in a gray sackdress, accompanied by her howling dog Drujock and an entourage of passionate admirers. She regarded Lou as a human dynamo possessing an almost exclusive intellectuality, a strong sensuality, and a mighty temperament. One can sense her resentment at Lou's bossiness and her treatment of Rilke as a transparent Freudian subject. Particularly, she took exception to Lou's interpretation of Rilke's angels as the projections of a sick person who dreams of a disembodied existence. Lou took Rilke and Loulou in tow, setting up for them "a mad potpourri" of spiritualistic sittings, sessions with astrologists, and conversational evenings with people in the medical profession and in the arts.

With Clara, Loulou struck up a lasting friendship. In her eyes, Clara was a tall, austere, strong, simple, sensible person. Apparently she took all of her errant husband's self-indulgences in stride, but we have little means of knowing her side of the story because her letters have not come to light. As for the chubby and radiant little child Ruth, her father seemed to regard her abstractedly and with the awe he felt for all children. Most upsetting of the visitors was mother Phia, the small, slight figure whose long face was draped by a black veil and who lived under the joyous illusion that both Jesus and Mary came to visit her at the hotel where she was staying. While the projection of angels and beasts was poetic-psychic with Rainer, with Phia it was a literal worship of "the poor wooden saints." It is quite possible that Rainer panicked at the thought of a similar psychotic fate. On October 14, 1915, he gave Loulou a poem that began, "Oh, woe, my mother destroys me." The refrain is accompanied by the assertion that though strangers know him as a real being, his mother alone does not know him as a mature and grown human. "From me to her never was a warm wind / . . . she lies in a high alcove of the heart / and Christ comes and bathes her every day." Rilke rejects even the good moments that were theirs in his childhood and chooses to be plaintive and cutting in his attitude. Lou Andreas-Salomé tried to moderate his exaggerations, but to no avail.

If there is any doubt about Rilke's strong interest in the occult and in its fringes, graphology and astrology, Loulou's account of their itinerary should dispel it. What he had sensed intuitively—the overpresence of the dead, the merging of all tenses into a bottomless present, a belief in the rightness of fate backgrounded by "the all-surviving stars," the reality of the "unknown"—was verifiable through spiritualism, although he could be sarcastic about planchettes and other contact paraphernalia; Rilke's imagination was powerful enough to induce contacts, without resorting to mediating artifice. Aside from occupying himself with the works of the dead poet Hölderlin, he was attentive to a living visionary formerly with the George circle, Alfred Schuler who made a lasting impression; some of Schuler's thoughts bob to the surface seven years later in the *Sonnets to Orpheus* and in the completed *Duino Elegies*. Schuler believed himself to be a reincarnation of an old Roman, and in three lectures that Rilke and Loulou attended he spoke with uncanny convincingness of the dead as those who really exist (as having "a unique, fabulous existence") and of our life as but a temporary anomaly. A motif running through his talks was the contrast between the "open life," open to the side of death, and the "closed life." Here, Rilke found support for his own views. Rilke was also very much taken with the "mystery of concentric circles," the idea that fate was bound up with certain locales (in his case with Paris, Duino, Muzot) and the thought that these circles determine our fate. Loulou suggests a tie between these ideas and Rilke's angel, the eternal coming-one who circles. (In the *Stunden-Buch* Rilke had pictured himself as continually circling God.) Indigenous in the poet's mind was one of the most recurrent primitive myths — the uroboric circle, a symbol of all-containment and origin, a world-womb idea which Rilke uses both in the abstract and the literal sense.

Strindberg's theater was for Rilke a significant experience if for no other reason than that Rilke saw a dramatization of *verzweifelte Liebe,* hopeless or despairing love. These were the emotions that tugged at Rilke as he was trying to grasp a measure of happiness and fulfillment in his relationship with Loulou. The sixteen autobiographical poems written for her are intense conversion of experience into poetry, rising from calm to passion and then subsiding into dejection. In the group of the earliest poems to Loulou we find stanzas like:

> *Einzeln sind wir Engel nicht; zusammen*
> *bilden wir den Engel unsrer Liebe:*
> *ich den Gang, du seines Mundes Jugend.*    (sw II,222)

*Alone, we are not angels; together*
*we form the angel of our love:*
*I, the motion, you, his mouth's youth.*

Here the angel is metaphoric and the love urge euphemistic. A few poems later Rilke's angel asks, "Do you see Eden? Have you divined life?" And Rilke answers, "Eden burns. . . . Life consumes." Again, existence doubts assail him: "Are we, Lulu, are we? Or do within us / deceased figures greet each other." Then there are lines that capture afternoons together in the meadows: "Being distant is only a listening: hear. / And now you are this total silence. / Yet my uplooking will always again / gather you in the object—your body." That Rilke was capable of "almost intoxicated joy," according to Loulou, may be seen in such lines as, "These kisses once were words; / strongly spoken at the door to freedom, / they forced open the portals. / Or, were these kisses cries . . . / Cries above such lovely hillocks / as are your breasts. Heaven cried them / in the storms of his youth-years." Hunger for affection tinged with eroticism is to become even more marked in the subsequent poetry.

One morning Loulou received a splendid bouquet of roses and knew that they were a symbol of "pure parting," and she was determined not to stand in his way. A little earlier Rilke had written to Marie: ". . . incorrigible as I am, I again attempted not to be alone . . . and it is always the same, cruel fate: to be burdened with another life, which eventually proves to be that of a stranger . . . with its complications and bewilderments. . . . I would like to help, and expect to be helped; that is the fundamental error: people always believe that I can help them, while I am actually inveigling them into the trap of my illusory helpfulness in order to get help for myself." Marie remonstrated with him: "But, Dottor Serafico: *Every* human being is lonely, and *must* remain lonely and *must* endure it and *may not* give way and must not seek help in other people but in the mysterious power that we feel within us. . . . And why must you always be saving silly geese, who should save themselves—let the devil take the

geese. . . . And you must always choose those weeping
willows, who are not so sad in reality believe me—it is you,
you yourself, who is reflected in all those eyes. . . ." But
Rilke's letters to Loulou, when he was away for short
times, and his personal entreaties continued to be seductive in their warmth until his gyrations between giving
himself and withholding created an impossible situation.
Loulou surprised him in the midst of writing,

> *Lass mich nicht an deinen Lippen trinken,*
> *denn an Munden trank ich mir Verzicht.*
> *Lass mich nicht in deine Arme sinken,*
> *denn mich fassen Arme nicht. (Lasard, 140; sw 11,219)* [8]

> *Let me not drink at your lips,*
> *for on lips I drank renunciation.*
> *Let me not sink into your arms,*
> *for arms cannot hold me.*

Rilke tore up the verse, threw himself at Loulou's feet and
begged forgiveness. By this time Loulou realized "his need
to deceive and to be deceived" and that she could do nothing to change Rilke's pattern of compulsive flight, the tension between life and work, the identification with the
prodigal son who did not want to be loved, and Rilke's
fantasy of the hero who in the elegies storms through the
delays or brief sojourns afforded by love. Rudolf Kassner,
Rilke's only close male friend, had a simpler explanation
for Rilke's instability: "What do you expect? All these
women are finally beginning to bore him." Perhaps so, but
Kassner also knew Rilke to be a strong sensualist and a
"Platonist of the flesh." The same judgment we have from
other sources as well. Although Friedrich Gundolf belonged to the Stefan George circle, his views of Rilke are
not completely prejudiced. He pointed to Rilke's Pan-like
eroticism which quivered with tireless turmoil wantonly
nibbling, temporizing, and consuming. Even Marie became impatient with Rilke's thinly veiled exercises in seduction and gently told him, "It seems to me that the late
Don Juan was a babe in arms compared to you." [4] These
observations go part of the way to clarify Rilke's prompt-

ings to write a cycle of "fertility" poems during the climax of his involvement with Loulou.

*Sieben Gedichte* [5] [*Seven Poems*] were composed during October–November, 1915, and were first permitted to appear in print exactly thirty years after Rilke's death. A year before his affair with Loulou Albert-Lasard, he broached the idea to Lou Andreas-Salomé of writing a cycle of phallic hymns. Lou was not overly enthusiastic about the project and told him that she regarded the phallus as a ridiculous appendage, compared with the other complicated and more meaningful parts of the human anatomy. Moreover, she felt that sex in the modern world was unduly emphasized and was approached with a mixture of priggishness and dismay, becoming a material rather than a spiritual experience. She equated Rilke's phallic theme with the doll theme, each object being the cause of a mental awareness of the differentiated "other," the recognition that these—doll and phallus—are counterparts of ourselves, sometimes sluggish, inert, or hostile but always making demands upon one. Like many of Lou's interpretations, this was too textbookish an analysis of Rilke's mind. In parts of the *Visions of Christ* and the *Stunden-Buch*, in the "Third Elegy," in the *New Poems* (particularly "Leda" and the "Archaic Torso of Apollo"), in *Malte*, and in the *Life of Mary*, Rilke had already celebrated the awakening male and female as well as sexuality in the broadest sense. These were poetic instances when Rilke crossed the threshhold and the passive stranger becomes the active intimate. Lou ignored the fact that even in the phallic poems Rilke preserved his pet notions. Already in the letters of 1903 to Kappus, Rilke had explained that artistic experience and sex were rooted in the same source of yearning and delight.

The rose as a perennial symbol of sexuality and the idea of transformation are somewhat playfully and crudely combined in the first of the *Seven Poems:* "Suddenly [she] the picker of roses grasps / the full bud of his organ / and at the fright of the difference, the gentle gardens vanish into her being." It is the same fright which was

shared by Leda and Mary. In the second poem, the narra-
tor feels the treelike surge of the phallus and its summer-
drawn seed: "O plunge him so that turned about / in
your womb, he learns the counter-heaven / in which he
really heaves and really towers. / Bold landscape, as clair-
voyants / see them in crystal balls. That inwardness / is
that outsideness. . . ." Even in the act of love, the poet
seeks the absolute, the prototype, the conjoining of all the
realms of being, the erasure of boundaries.[6] The third
poem speaks of the lovers' excitation stimulated by the
magic and potency of the gods. In the fourth he experiences the marvelous spaciousness within the loved one,
but once the climax has been reached he feels himself too
narrowly constricted, yearning for a suprasensuality that is
beyond his power.

Then, in the fifth poem, there is the awakening: "Now
through the silent sieve of kisses / trickles the bitter taste
of 'alsem' and absynth." And several lines later: "Are you,
am I, the one we so delight?" Perhaps, elsewhere there is
joy that vanishes less rapidly? A speculative tone is struck
in the sixth poem: "What are we near? Death or that /
which as yet does not exist?" Lovers would represent
nothing but clay-to-clay if the god did not feelingly infuse
the figure that grows between them, notes Rilke. Like
Yahweh and Epimetheus who created from earth and clay,
Rilke allows himself the fantasy of raising the body of clay
from the "hot grave"; from the body's metaphorical "deep
ascension" into the heaven of the loved one, Rilke
abruptly turns to a literal rendering—"my stiff corpse again
become tender." Beyond pictorialism, *zart*, or tender,
implies here that in sexuality there can also be a shedding
of the callous and, even if only temporarily, a feeling of
contentment. And finally, in the sixth poem Rilke discards
all inhibitions: "How I did call you. Those are the silent
cries / which ripened sweet inside me. / Now I hammer
into you step upon step / and gaily mounts my seed like a
child. / You primal mount of desire: suddenly he sprints /
breathless to your inner ridge. / Oh, give yourself up to the
feeling of his nearing / for you will fall when from high up
he winks."

Love is an elemental means of self-satisfaction and a physical avenue, apart from mystical immersion, to possible transcendence. That the twin ideas of death and immortality beset the poet in the act of love is a principle not unfamiliar to psychoanalysts, but these ideas Rilke had no need to borrow from Lou Andreas-Salomé's dissertations because they were deeply imbedded. With Kafka, Rilke shared the eerie way of talking as if no one else were around to listen. Loulou Albert-Lasard gives testimony to this:

> His outcries of astonishment, admiration interrupted his partner's words. At the same time, I could not fend off the impression that basically they resolved themselves into monologues or dialogues with an absent one—was it perhaps the angel? . . . everything he absorbed, he changed into a Rilkean elixir. In truth, he fulfilled himself with his own. Did he ever take pains even in love to see the partner as she was? Did he not usurp both roles? [7]

Although bitterness is absent in Loulou's reproaches, they substantiate Rilke's extreme narcissism that fed on experience in order to translate it into the "reality" of his poems. Rilke seemed to have no qualms about this narcissism, unlike D. H. Lawrence who wrote in his poem "New Heaven and Earth," "I was a lover, I kissed the woman I loved / and God of horror, I was kissing also myself."

As Rilke had hoped, his random poetizing again kindled an elegy, and in November, shortly after the phallic cycle and the *Requiem on the Death of a Boy*, a "Fourth Elegy" emerged. The critic J. B. Leishman has characterized it accurately as "the most bitter and negative of all the *Elegies*," and almost all commentators have ascribed its tone to the depression he felt because of the war and men's mismanagement of life. These interpretations are impossible to sustain, for the poem is a monument to Rilke's self-preoccupation and carries no hint of the European holocaust. Nor is the view, inspired by Marie's reminiscences, tenable that the opening lines of all the elegies were written down at Duino in 1912. Actually, the "Fourth Elegy" is a regurgitation of the indigestible ex-

periences of his childhood and at the same time the
opening lines are inextricably linked to the phallic poems,
the *Requiem on the Death of a Boy*, and thoughts
confided to his diary fifteen years earlier.

> O *Bäume Lebens, o wann winterlich?*
> *Wir sind nicht einig. Sind nicht wie die Zugvögel*
> *verständigt. . . .*                    (sw 1,697)

> O *trees of life, o when winterly?*
> *We are not at one. We are not like the*
> *migratory birds, complete. . . .*

Interpretations of the opening line of the "Fourth Elegy"
have resulted in a critical free-for-all because of the ambiguous declamation, interrogation, and the absence of
predication. Rilke's language is both literal and figurative
when he says *tree of life*; he accents "Baum" (tree), the
most frequent object in the phallic poems and makes it
synonymous with *Lebensglied* (life organ). We see this
in such lines as, "You, summer, you have suddenly
appeared / and have updrawn my seed into the violent
tree." If summer has this turbulent effect, winter in the
"Fourth Elegy" should have an opposite, relatively calm-
ing effect much as in the "Stanzas for Winter" where
winter's "frost and rawness prepare / the tension for future
receptivities." With these Rilkean concepts of summer
and winter in mind, the elegy reference takes on meaning:
We are like trees because during the summer heyday we
yearn for the peace of winter and calm gestation.[8] Elsewhere he speaks enviously of the completeness of the
migratory bird—unlike that of man and tree who cannot
escape the merciless cycle of the seasons. In contrast to the
bird who naturally and effortlessly yields to the winds, we
humans "force [*drängen*] ourselves upon the winds / and
fall into an unresponsive pond" (lines 4–5, "Fourth
Elegy"). Effective symbolic drama ensues when Rilke
interchangeably calls the angel "bird." For Rilke the
chasm is hopelessly wide between the creatures at home in
the "all" and rejected man.

Contrasts and comparisons course through the entire "Fourth Elegy": the beast, unlike man with his awareness, glories in his simple being; we are participants in life and at the same time observers as in a puppet play; we are aware of the world within and restlessly live outside of it; we are painfully aware of simultaneous flowering and fading. The line which most brilliantly sums up Rilke's existential despair is derived from art: "Wir kennen den Kontur / des Fühlens nicht, nur was ihn formt von aussen." [We do not know the contour of feeling, only that which forms it from without.] (In the phallic poem cycle the profane joy of the lover is graphically described; in the canonical elegies, this temporal and temporary joy is rendered in the abstract.)

In a superb analogy Rilke imagines himself sitting before his heart's curtain which draws open and reveals a stage; the thematic setting or mood is "parting." A dancer appears on the swaying garden-set, but he is a sham artist, acting not being, a half-filled mask, a disguised and commonplace bourgeois who is more objectionable than the wire and chaff-stuffed, unthinking and undivided doll. When the lights go out and nothing is left on the stage and when his fellow spectators fade—ancestors, women, the little cross-eyed boy (cousin Egon von Rilke who appeared in *Malte*), even then, "I stay in spite. One can always gaze." The "act of gazing" projects one into the very contour of feeling and the inexpressible. For corroboration, "Am I not right?", Rilke turns to his father, he "who tasted life so bitterly because of me." Disappointed in René's choice of a vocation, he never gave up reminding his son to build an assured future and to wear presentable clothes, touchingly supporting the penurious son even when he took on the hapless burden of marriage. Josef Rilke wrote such well-meaning admonitions to René and Clara as, "Eggs and milk are very wholesome, but no one can do without meat as well." The solid bourgeois virtues of his father were as much an anathema to Rilke as the warped piety of his mother. Rilke's conflicted attitude toward his father is represented in the most difficult and ambiguous lines of the "Fourth Elegy:"

*der du, mein Vater, seit du tot bist, oft*
*in meiner Hoffnung, innen in mir, Angst hast,*
*und Gleichmut, wie ihn Tote haben, Reiche*
*von Gleichmut, aufgiebst für mein bisschen Schicksal.*

The ambivalence of the emotion is not clearly accented in the various translations attempted:

. . . *my father; you whose fear in me*
*I felt in all my hopes since you are dead.* . . .
                                        V. AND E. SACKVILLE-WEST

. . . *you, who so often since you died, my Father,*
*have been afraid within my inmost hope.* . . .
                                        LEISHMAN AND SPENDER

. . . *you who, my father, since you died,*
*are often full of fear within my inward hope.* . . .
                                        RUTH SPEIRS

. . . *you, father, whom I feel, since you have died*
*trembling for me within my hope.* . . .
                                        NORA WYDENBRUCK

*Mon père, toi qui, depuis que tu es mort, souvent,*
*dans l'espoir que je porte en moi, as peur.* . . .
                                        J. F. ANGELLOZ

The father who fears for or worries about his son's "bit of destiny," surrendering even the serenity or indifference (*Gleichmut*) which the dead possess (a theme which is reiterated in the "Tenth Elegy": "the first condition of the young dead is timeless indifference") is the single meaning which comes through in all the translations. The critic Guardini paraphrases what he believes to be Rilke's irritability: "My father has no real confidence in me, otherwise he would not be afraid." Simenauer notes that the phrase "in my hopes" grammatically is an ablative absolute and that accordingly the sense is shifted to a rendering which says that "finally after the death of his father, the son's hopes are fulfilled: the father stands before the son with fear." The tables are reversed in a drama which Kafka calls "the ascendancy of the son." It seems as if one of Rilke's declarations in the *Tuscan Diary* had come home to roost: As long as authority prevails in the form of the god, and presumably the father, we are all unvocal children; only after his death do we achieve our wish *to become fathers*. There is merit in a translation which would read, "since you are dead, my father, often in my inmost hopes *you* are afraid inside of *me*."

Continuing the "Fourth Elegy," Rilke gazes intently upon his heart's stage until he wills into existence a drama between angel and doll: "Engel and Puppe: dann ist endlich Schauspiel." The obstinacy of willing something into existence through the power of imagination was one of Rilke's most pronounced traits, a trait which put fright into the uninitiated and created a distance between poet and people; but it also was the mainspring of his visionary poetry. Rilke's role as spectator in the cosmic drama between the unaware, pure (existence-for-the-sake-of-existence) doll and the imperious angel glorying in the arrogant consciousness of its own existence reminded him of the similarity of man's unacknowledged condition: in life he stands between the realms of toys and ultimate reality. However, " . . . See, the dying, / do they not suspect how much pretense / everything is that we accomplish here." For Rilke, death and life are eternal, coexistent elements; death hovers almost solicitously over man's life center while man's daily experiences quickly become things of the past like burning embers. "Who shows a child, just how it is? Who places / him among the stars and gives the measure of distance / into his hand?" Who, in other words, tells him these truths and encourages an unlimited cosmic-mythological frame. Instead, the gray wind which earlier in the elegy wafted from the great emptiness across the stage, becomes like gray bread that is allowed to harden and which senselessly chokes a child to death. Rilke abhors unfulfillment and he suggests that one's life determines one's particular kind of death.

Ideally one should cultivate an openness and receptivity toward death without regarding it as a hostile element: " . . . death, / the complete death, to hold it so gently / even *above* life and not to be angry, / is indescribable." A few days before writing this elegy, Rilke pictured an "incomplete death" in a poem called "Der Tod": "There stands death, a bluish concoction, / in a cup without a saucer," a bitter undiluted, poisonous draught for those who cannot read the faded inscription, "hope." When life is extracted from their mouths like a dental plate, "Then they babble. Babble . . . babble. . . ." Theirs is a plain, hideous death, a fugue of fears like that which tormented the hero of Tolstoy's *Death of Ivan Ilych*. Throughout the "Fourth Elegy," with its huge analogy of the stage, we can sense the poet's anguish at the realization that it is impossible to be both participant and spectator at one and the same time. Consciousness is necessary if we are to know what we are missing, but as Shakespeare put it, such knowledge also is "Adam's penalty," the cause of our dividedness which Rilke mourns, and in a final sense, the grim or ironic joke creation has played on man.

In the autumn of 1915, Rilke was caught up in a tremendous period of creativity—*Seven Poems, Requiem,* the "Fourth Elegy," and such short masterpieces as "The Death of Moses" which carried with it the inspiration of his Spanish sojourn. All this was aborted when he was called to Vienna for war service on January 4, 1916. Then, said Rilke, "the dense, grey military cloth covered my illuminated face." This work stoppage, not the war at this point, was his worst aggravation. Three weeks of barracks life that he barely endured was relieved by a call to man a desk in the Austrian war archives; there he found little energy to do more than transcribe military work and to rule lines on paper with inimitable neatness. Sheltered from field service, he was plagued by conscience: "somewhere is a residue of old soldier's blood in me because it pains me that I offer so much to-do and that I resist." Austrian officials would very much have liked to put the poet of the *Cornet* into the propaganda harness. In one of their journals, they reprinted his "St. George" poem, with its tinselled knight, but otherwise he was petulantly unresponsive. The photos of Rilke in military dress look Chaplinesque, and he was glad to get back into conservatively elegant civilian clothes in June, after numerous petitions—with signatures that carried weight—succeeded in freeing him from military service, a grotesque episode at best. "The *poor* child, the *poor* child!" wrote Hofmannsthal with a sigh of relief; he had been one of the recipients of letters from the gloomy depths of Rilke's captivity.

Katharina Kippenberg, Rilke's publisher who was instrumental in his release, compared Rilke to Pegasus in bondage, but once the bonds were removed his "inner paralysis" remained. Loulou returned and Rainer sat for an oil portrait; however, the flame had gone out of their relationship. When Benvenuta tried to reach him again, according to her obviously biased account, the sight of an overly-rouged Loulou heavily clinging to Rilke's arm repelled her into hasty retreat. Were it not for the women who sheltered him and ministered his ego during the war years, his existence would have been reduced to a mere shuffle. An acquaintance, Hertha König, made her Munich flat available to him. There, the wall-sized painting "Les Saltimbanques" by Picasso reduced him to awe, and he spoke movingly to visitors of the strange illusory atmosphere in which Picasso had steeped his clowns and how they stood uniformly with their weights, an image that is reincarnated in the "Fifth Elegy."

Meanwhile, Rilke's fame was soaring, primarily in the wake of his *Cornet* which at the end of 1918 had amassed a sale of 180,000 copies. *The Book of Hours* climbed to nine editions, *Stories of God*, the *Rodin* book, *The Life of the Virgin Mary*, *Malte* went into multiple printings. Katharina Kippenberg tells of the popular adulation that surrounded Rilke as women would pretend to know him and impress their friends by imitating Rilke's gestures and voice cadence, how people would offer to move into hotels so that Rilke might occupy their flats, how one admirer appeared at Rilke's door with a burning, meter-long candle, and how he had to resist other eccentric attentions. Ordinarily, he might have responded to acclaim but the war kept robbing him of young friends like Keyserling and

Marwitz. "Coldly, coldly," he made short restless trips, but everywhere he saw malicious confusion; frightened, he wrote in a heartsick tone, "Losses, losses . . . if only each loss were a full pledge and relentless in demanding of us a life more serious, more responsible and more sensitive to mysteries!"

In several letters, Rilke describes the postwar temper of Bavaria, waning and flaring in beer-halls and at public gatherings, the overstrained anarchists, pacifists, internationalists, and the hastily organized soldier-worker-peasant council. Caught between the Bolshevik and anti-Bolshevik Munich riots, Rilke had little peace from invectives and demonstrators who pounded his door at night. Sliding from spectator interest to weary indifference was an almost predictable course for Rilke; social conservatism, if not a reactionary attitude, was to mark Rilke's life from then on. More and more, he was showing signs of returning to the magic circle of poetry and isolation: "My inclination is now more than ever to do what I really *can*, quite against the call of the time which would like to seduce everyone away from his real ability into political dilettantism."

Five years of relative immobility came to an end, although there had been some thirty changes of address during that period, when invitations came to lecture in Switzerland. By accepting them in June, 1919, he permanently left Germany and Austria—as well as Lou Andreas-Salomé, whom he was not to see again—and made a fresh start in a new geographic terrain that was to be his last home during his remaining seven years as well as the setting for his greatest accomplishments.

RILKE'S ANTIPATHY to Austria and Germany did not immediately result in admiration for Switzerland. The scenic cities, mountains, and landscapes seemed to Rilke, at first, too much of a theatrical up and down. Indelible in his mind were the Bohemian forests, the Russian plains and valleys, the flatlands of North Germany, the spacious highlands of Spain, the sand-and-river settings of North Africa, and the pictorial tradition-fused landscape of France which had profoundly influenced the tone of his poetry. No longer did he seem to be able to take in landscapes: "Spain was the last 'impression.' Since then my nature has been worked on from inside (*travail repoussé*), so strongly and steadily that it cannot be 'impressed anymore.'" Perhaps he now needed the tranquillity of a relatively antiseptic and undistracting landscape that would permit complete concentration on finishing the manuscript elegies which he always carried with him.

Were it not for an October–November, 1919, lecture tour, made necessary by the impossibility of transferring funds from Germany to Switzerland, Rilke would have been content to hibernate at Soglio as a guest of the von Salis family. But indirectly the tour was to have a decisive effect on his life. Although his lectures were received enthusiastically by the Swiss, he sought no public career. Hans Trog, editor of the *Neue Zürcher Zeitung*, told of the unique impression made by Rilke's reading of such poems as "The lady before the Mirror" ["Dame vor dem Spiegel"], a figure which through the voice and words of the poet dissolves into the mirror, and the musically effective "Woman in Love" ["Die Liebende"]. Trog perceptively noted that the selections from the *New Poems* "are not so much devoted to an emotion as intended to provoke one." [1]

Rilke's feelings toward Switzerland warmed during the lecture tour when he met a new benefactress and confidante, Frau Nanny Wunderly-Volkart, who admirably filled in for the distant Princess Marie. Also, he was drawn into an all-consuming affair with a woman who according to Rilke possessed a "tempérament volcanique;" promptly she was renamed Merline, the enchantress. Living in Geneva with her two sons Pierre and Baltusz, the painter Dorothée Baladine Klossowska was the most formidable young woman Rilke had yet met. The critic Dieter Basserman has gone so far as to suggest, with considerable support from the correspondence published in 1950 (*Lettres françaises à Merline*, 1919–1922) that their relation accounts for the complete "psychic reconstitution of the poet, so thoroughly and happily" [2] that it made possible the creation of his last monumental works.

In three November days he wrote what was to be the first part of a cycle of poems which he called *Aus dem Nachlass des Grafen C. W.* [*From the Remains of Count C. W.*]. If ever a great poet produced aborted and maudlin poetry, here it was. From ten poems, it is possible to salvage several presentable stanzas and to see what he was attempting subconsciously: "Let me page gently in your diary / great-grandaunt, ancestress, let—. / I know not which sentence I seek. / Unrest, doubt, worry, love, hate— / all this is equivalent no more." But the images that arise from the past are as skimpy as the lines that evoke them, except for a few that recall his travels—the granite Egyptian cats and pylon at Karnak or the lonely, romantic Provençal shepherd. Almost at once, Rilke recognized most of these poems to be travesties, but his immediate disappointment found an outlet in mischievous irony. He blamed the spirit of Count C. W., a former inhabitant of the castle, for having dictated the poems to him; Rilke finally called a halt to the ventriloquism when the count started to recite in Italian. The apparition of the count at the fireplace was Rilke's invention, yet it is not unlikely that Rilke autosuggestively became persuaded of the count's reality.

Childhood, religiosity, and eroticism seemed to play tug-of-war within Rilke. In the letters to Merline, he reverted to signing his name René; in cancelled passages of the Karnak poem in the *Count C. W.* cycle, he invokes the name of Amelie, a childhood sweetheart he had poetized when he was a military school captive; in a Christmas letter to his dear Mama, René consecrates with loving remembrances "Christmas days of longest ago." Intoning the terror and jubilation of childhood, Rilke shortly after the *C. W.* cycle composed an elegy on childhood,[3] "for timelessly does the heart hold it," and plunged into a vortex of prenatal recollection, into the "fore-world" that precedes mother. It seemed that the path to a most terrible regression lay open again—a bleak vista in which the distorted dolls again make an appearance. However, the elegy remained a fragment and his mood was dispelled by the call of life.

Toward the end of 1920, he wrote to Merline, "I kiss your letter, lingeringly, religiously;" "[I] remain at times with my face in my hands, so as to feel nothing but the contents of my heart, increased magnified, multiplied to infinitude." This time he did not seek a mother-mistress as with Lou, but someone who would unreservedly share all his emotions and yet be moldable. To his new priestess-elect, Rilke wrote:

> No, Merline, I am not at all surprised to find you so strong . . . to penetrate into the sanctuary of our love and kneel down there, not merely as adorer, but as a priestess-elect holding up to the god the final sacrifice, with arms straining under the delicious weight. . . . A "Hunter of images," I go up into my mountains, unsociable, taciturn; I loose myself. But you my delicious valley, you flute of my heart, you

vase of clay to which I, a humble artificer of love, have given the inspired curve that marks you for divine uses for ever,—may you have the innate imperturbable patience of the landscape and the flute and the sacred vase! (November 18, 1920)

Intoning this incredible benediction, Rilke is overpowered by a god-fantasy; he is the divine potter of universal folklore and she his sacred vessel, a holy virgin who radiates divine stigmata that Rilke compares with those of Saint Theresa. Romanticized paganism, borrowed Christian theology, and earthy metaphors reflect the René-Merline relationship. Some passages of letters to Merline uncannily preview, image for image, the *Sonnets to Orpheus*, but as yet they are prose-bound and have not soared into poetry:

> . . . where I am going no name can count, no memory dare persist, one must arrive there as one arrives among the dead, surrendering all one's strength into the hands of the Angel that is leading one. I am going away from you Merline, but as I am going all the way round, I shall come nearer again at every step. The bow is bent for shooting the arrow at the celestial bird; but if the arrow drops down again it will have passed through the bird without killing it, and from on high it will fall into your heart. (November 18, 1920)

To help Merline understand his views, Rilke again emphasizes that art is an act contrary to nature, a terribly self-willed act that resembles sacrifice in that it seeks the point of intersection between extreme danger and personal salvation. The religious meaning of salvation is transvalued by Rilke into the secular motive of art. Yet, a slight change in nuance is detectable as Rilke places love on the same plane as art in its power to heroically transcend human conditions. The apostrophe to childhood, the recurrence of the mystical moment of the *Book of Hours* (the *Nu* when eternity is revealed in a split second), the conceit that all women (even the widowed or the married) who came into his ken brought with them their virginity—all these are thoughts which swell with abandon in the letters. The height of his ritualistic love is reached when he combines the Friday commemoration of the Nativity and the death of Merline's father, "the blest patriarch whose force lighted the flame of your ardent life in your mother's womb." Completely overwhelmed by his own sacral tone, Rilke vows, "I shall kneel before him, so that he may give me his blessing too; may my arm around you protect you as well as the two hands of that old man, which, coming from the heights of prayer, laid themselves on his head." Whatever extravagances he permitted himself, the profundity of his experience with Merline is unshakable: "From that moment on . . . I can die." In the second part of the Count C. W. cycle which Rilke finished in February, 1921, he crowns his Merline experiences with astonishment: "To have survived this, also to have survived this happiness / quietly and thoroughly . . ." Still, Rilke feels that he is the subject rather than the master of his emotion and he rationalizes that "because no one masters life, it remains pure."

Rilke's readings, as before, were prolific and his discovery of the magically crystalline poetry of Paul Valéry, especially "Le Cimetière marin," roused him to unrestrained enthusiasm and to the immediate task of translating some of Valéry's poems. Their eventual friendship and Rilke's warm introduction of Valéry to a German-reading public were additional rewards of the encounter. More than that, in the absence of writing his own poetry, but in prepration for it, the translations and letters to Merline, written for the most part in French, show a greater preoccupation with theoretical and technical aspects of poetry than ever before. It was a sound way of filling the vacuum and anticipated the time when he would mellifluously write volumes of poetry in French.

Rilke reported to Marie about having revisited the locale of Sierre and Sion with "a friend" (Merline) and having fallen under the spell of the Château de Muzot: "If you could only see it! When one approaches it from the valley it seems to stay there like magic, rising above the rose arbors (now withered) of the little garden, the color of its age-old stones, which have grey and purple tints but have been roasted and tanned to gold by the sun, again like certain walls in Andalusia." [4] Muzot, renovated at the turn of the century, dated back to the thirteenth century and its fortress-like aspects filled Rilke with anxiety and depression, but his intuition reassured him that this place of terror, like Malte's Paris, among a vast site of mountains was fated to be his isolated abode. A macabre air enveloped the place and Rilke treated the susceptible Marie to the legend of Isabelle de Chevron whose inconsolable spirit roamed Muzot. Isabelle, a 16th century inhabitant of Muzot, after being widowed had the additional misfortune of having two suitors run each other through during a duel. She lost her mind and one morning was found frozen to death in the graveyard at Miège that housed her suitors. (Rilke himself was either so impressed or frightened that in his will he specified that he was not to be interred in Miège in order not to revive the night wanderings of poor Isabelle.) Marie was hoping that Rilke would return to her hospitable wings, but Rilke had already confided somewhat ungratefully to his new benefactress Frau Wunderly that Marie had "neither the understanding, the love, nor the patience" to realize the minimum needs of his existence. Rilke plainly was tired of the rigamaroles and pretensions a pet poet had to follow in order to obtain aristocratic shelter. However, when Frau Wunderly's cousin Werner Reinhart put at his exclusive and unconditional disposal the medieval manor of Muzot, a symbol of austerity and tradition, suitably enshrouded in gothic legend, Rilke eventually accepted. At the end of July, 1921, after Merline had spent weeks helping to make Muzot habitable, Rilke made himself at home. A suite that contained a three-hundred-year-old oaken writing desk and chests, large double windows, a workroom connected by a doorway with his bedchamber, and a small balcony were to give Rilke a secluded setting for work.

All his theorizing failed, however, to remove the block to the great poetry which was penned up until he was able to isolate his difficulties: "As long as you catch the self-cast, everything is / dexterity and indulgent winning—; / only when you suddenly become catcher of the ball," partner of an eternal female player, then "out of your hands steps the meteor and careens wildly in his spaces." [5] An equally superlative analogy of the ideal state of mind for the creation of poetry—simultaneous submission and action—is Rilke's envious description of the perfect balance and exhilaration shown by a flock of birds trajected over the seas by their old, warm instincts and the seasons. This is unmediated experience and spontaneous participation, permitting oneself to be caught up in the natural flow of things. Rilke was still vibrant with the emotions aroused by Merline and surprised by his uninhibited reciprocation.

Together, he and Merline had discovered a postcard reproduction of a pen and ink drawing of *Orpheus* by the 15th century artist Giovanni Battista Cima da Conegliano. It is a disconsolate portrait of Orpheus and his lyre, attended by faintly outlined and reposeful animals. Merline put the card on the wall which faced Rainer's writing desk, and around the figure of Orpheus, sonnets were to gather rapidly.

Early in January, 1922, Rilke received news from Frau Gertrud Ouckama Knoop that her nineteen-year-old daughter Wera had died. Rilke devoured the details of Wera's illness and death and he asked the mother to send him a memento of something the girl had cherished. All he knew of the girl he had briefly met in Munich at the Knoop home was that she caused great excitement among those who had seen her dance; suddenly she declared that she could no longer dance, foreshadowing her illness. Her preoccupation with music, however, remained until the end. His letter to Frau Knoop has touches of delirium, for Wera (whose photo impressively shows large, lustrous eyes in a mature face framed by massive black hair) fitted his obsessive hymnology to the young departed: "Oh how, how she loved, how she reached out with the antennae of her heart beyond all that is graspable and encompassable here—, in those sweet hovering pauses in pain which, full of the dream of recovery, were still vouchsafed her . . ."

He ascribes to Wera a pure intuition of heart, no longer subject to the physical (as manifested by suffering) "that drives its wedge, its stony wedge, into the unity between heaven and the earth," a heart open to "this unity of the existing and enduring world, this assent to life, this—joyous, deeply moved, capable of the ultimate—belonging in the here-and-now—ah, in the here-and-now only?" Another cause for his posthumous concern for Wera was her mother's writing to Rilke that Wera dreamed she saw Rilke at her bedside.

Ideas, phrases, and images were shaping themselves for the Orpheus cycle. Rilke's hand almost automatically sketched a lyre growing out of foliage and he accompanied the visual concept with several short poems. In these preludes, he casts a profound silence over the figure of the self-viewing Narcissus and the forests, creating an 'audible silence' and a perfect telepathic hearing. But the poet is fated to be a mouth that speaks and sings rather than to be an inconspicuous listener, falling into the contradiction of singing about something which escapes him, something that can be only retained in hearing. At best, the reality of a poem captures a fragment of the poet's illusions. Almost in despair because he needed to poetize, Rilke wrote on the evening before the Orpheus sonnets: " . . . When will, when will, when will lamentation and saying / be enough?" Although man has cried louder than storms and seas, there must be an overbalance of silence in the universe with its toneless stars to permit us to hear crickets. When do we become listeners to the most ancestral of sounds, when do we resolve the conflict between the artifice of language and the totality of contact with nature? Rilke is preparing to lead the reader into the realm of the dead and to hear the sound of silence.

From the second to the fifth of February, 1922, all the sonnets—except the 26th, were formed into Part I. The cycle is intoned *to* Orpheus, but unlike the poetry and drama from Vergil to Cocteau, which adhere faithfully to the tragic myth of the poet who almost succeeds in wresting his wife Eurydice from the shade of the dead,

Rilke fashions the 14-line sonnets [6] into lyrical metaphors that express his *own* psychic experiences and resolute convictions. It is not the detailed Orphic myth that concerns him [7] but the concept of metamorphosis as a key to life's meaning. Already in the first stanza we are given notice that the sonnets are not regurgitations of the classical myth, but poetry full of private symbols and emotions. As in all the sonnets, Orpheus is the singer and lyre-player and Rilke the poet-narrator.

> *Da stieg ein Baum. O reine Übersteigung!*
> *O Orpheus singt! O hoher Baum im Ohr!*
> *Und alles schwieg. Doch selbst in der Verschweigung*
> *ging neuer Anfang, Wink und Wandlung vor.*   (sw 1,731)

> *There rose a tree. O pure transcendence!*
> *O Orpheus sings! O tall tree in the ear!*
> *And all was silent. Yet even in silence*
> *appears new beginning; beckoning and change was near.*

At work is the procreative force, "Wink and Wandlung" or the "Wink and Wendung," of the fourth fertility poem of 1915 with its dominant tree symbol. The transformation of Adam's rib into Eve is paralleled by the Orphic, male tree from whose branches springs the feminine lyre that Rilke described in the prelude to the cycle. With Orpheus' appearance, silence ensues among the beasts, and Rilke marvels: Orpheus, "you have built temples for them in their hearing." As they listen, the Rilkean myth develops: From song and lyre a girl emerges and beds herself in the poet's ear, sleeps in him, "and everything became her sleep." (Sonnet 2) "See, she arose and slept. / Where is her death?" The poet pleads with Orpheus to deal with this motif before his song consumes itself, before the maiden glides away. How close all this comes to Rilke's psychic experience is clear from his reflections: "For myself, those things that have died have, in dying, entered my own heart. When I searched for the vanished one, it was so moving for me to feel that his only existence was now within me." [8]

Orpheus' song is not desire, not wooing—"Song is existence," easy for the gods. A youth's love song is not love; it is temporary ecstasy. Learn to forget, repeats Rilke from a notable passage in *Malte*, for real singing is purposeless, a wafting in God, a wind. (Sonnet 3) It recalls Goethe's maxim: "Our whole art consists in this that we must give up our existence in order to exist." In order to exist, says Rilke in the "Fourth Sonnet," "Fear not to endure; give back the heaviness to the weight of the earth." Since Orpheus comes and goes, is metamorphosed in all things, and is recognizable by his song, erect no tombstone for him but let a rose bloom for him yearly: "Is it not sufficient when he outlasts sometimes by a few days the bowl of roses?" Orpheus must vanish so that we grasp his significance; before anxiety takes hold of Orpheus, he already has transcended the being-here. (Sonnet 5) Orpheus is the perfect myth-figure for Rilke because he belongs to both the realm of the living and the dead.

> *Geht ihr zu Bette, so lasst auf dem Tische*
> *Brot nicht und Milch nicht; die Toten ziehts—.*
> *Aber er, der Beschwörende, mische*
> *unter der Milde des Augenlids*
>
> *ihre Erscheinung in alles Geschaute; . . .*    (sw 1,734)

> *Going to bed, leave on the table*
> *no bread and no milk; it attracts the dead—.*
> *But he, the conjuror, mixes*
> *under the mildness of eyelids*
>
> *their appearance in everything that is viewed . . .*

For Orpheus it is possible to work any transformation because he has the magical willow branch, the symbol of sorrow; instead of abracadabra, his magical word is "praise" (*Rühmung, rühmen*). Just as a magician names an object and it comes into being so Orpheus can make visible the dead in all objects that humans view; he can transform image ("be it from graves, be it from apartments") into objects by naming them: "finger-ring, clasp, and jug." These were among the objects that according to ancient tradition were buried with the dead. (Sonnet 6) Through praise, contradictions became complements; Orpheus' "heart, oh ephemeral press / of a wine that for men is eternal"; Orpheus is a staying messenger, again a contradiction in terms but not in meaning. (Sonnet 7) "Only in the realm of praise may lamentation go / . . . Jubilation knows, and longing acquiesces, — / only lamentation still learns . . ." (Sonnet 8) Then follow the memorable, limpid lines:

> *Nur wer die Leier schon hob*
> *auch unter Schatten,*
> *darf das unendliche Lob*
> *ahnend erstatten.*

> *Nur wer mit Toten vom Mohn*
> *ass, von dem ihren,*
> *wird nicht den leisesten Ton*
> *wieder verlieren.*　　　(sw 1,736)

> *Only one who has lifted the lyre,*
> *as well among shades,*
> *may intuitively render*
> *unending praise.*

> *Only who with the dead has*
> *eaten of their poppy*
> *will not lose the quietest tone*
> *ever again.*

"Only in the dual realm / do voices become / eternal and mild." (Sonnet 9) Pictorial ideas — rather than narrative or regularity of metrics — link the sonnets so that the duality of the realms mentioned in the last line of the "Ninth Sonnet" is given capillary extensions in the *"Tenth"*:

> *Euch, die ihr nie mein Gefühl verliesst,*
> *grüss ich, antike Sarkophage,*
> *die das fröhliche Wasser römischer Tage*
> *als ein wandelndes Lied durchfliesst.*　(sw 1,737)

> *You, who have never left my feeling,*
> *I greet, antique sarcophogi,*

> whom the happy waters of Roman days
> flow through as a wandering song.

Memory has no boundaries. As reminders of antiquity and the dead stand the sarcophogi of Rome and those of the cemetery of Aliscamps near Arles. They created impressions which he recorded in *Malte* and poetized in the *Neue Gedichte*. Their evocation in the sonnets reflects the internal continuity of his work and experience. But Rilke's poetry is not an emotion recollected in tranquility; it thrives on cacaphonous contrasts and meaningful disarrangements. "Happy waters . . . as a wandering (or changing) song" flowing through Roman sarcophogi that were also used as troughs, would have had a more conventional meaning as "wandering waters and happy song;" yet, the disarrangement of attributes effectively mirrors metamorphosis. The sarcophogi open like eyes and like mouths and both "build the hesitant hour / in the human face." Man's face symbolically harbors his fate in Rilke's surrealistic fusion of eyes and grave. At first the image is bold and static but then it becomes fluid when the poet analogically relates the eternal waters in sarcophogi to the tears in human eyes. (Sonnet 10)

For the human figure he seeks a celestial counterpart. Rilke asks, "Is there no constellation called 'rider?' " Because the rider and ridden understand each other through simultaneous touch and turning, they are one on a path or in the open spaces. But this contact really is illusion because the human and the animal are separated by "table and pasture." No sooner had Rilke fragmented the celestial conceit through logic than he retrieved some of the fragments by saying that momentary gladness through belief in the "figure" is enough. The logic of reality need not interfere with the pleasure of abstraction. A figure of substance becomes a figure of speech, and reality is turned into a metaphor as the poet seeks an eternal equivalent among the stars for man's fleetingness. (Sonnet 11) "Hail to the spirit who is able to unite us; / for we truly live in figures. / And with short steps, clocks accompany our real day."

Although we do not know where we stand, we act out of relatedness: "The antennae feel antennae." It was to Wera that he had ascribed antennae of the heart that reach beyond the graspable on earth. In the sonnets, relatedness is achieved similarly through intuitive touch. Kaleidoscopically the metaphors and analogies change but the theme of yearning for relatedness despite fated separateness remains constant. Even the farmer who works and worries cannot reach with sight or mind into the place where summer-seed transforms itself. (Sonnet 12) Things that grow—vineleaf, flower, fruit—are bestowed on man by the earth: Is it not the dead though, the masters, who sleep near the roots who grant us these things out of their own overflow? Fruit therefore conveys "life and death into one's mouth." The named fruit—apple, pear, banana, gooseberry—become nameless, become taste in the mouth. Where once words had been, discoveries and intuition released from the fruitflesh take their place. The modality of word-sound is changed into taste-sensing joy: "Read it from the face of a child." (Sonnets 13, 14) Sense and sensuality meet in the actual and symbolic fruit whether it is Eve's apple or King Solomon's pomegranate or Rilke's known gustatory delight in the fleshfruit of apples. It is difficult to say if Rilke's vegetarianism has a physical or philosophical base, but the thoughts in the sonnets have an intuitive affinity with Hindu concepts on transmigration and metempsychosis that link the spirit world with the human.[9] In an essay *Primal Sound* Rilke had toyed with the possibilities of synesthesia that he now puts to practice. Taste is transferred to sound—music—as Rilke enjoins the maidens: "tanzt den Geschmack der erfahrenen Frucht!" ("dance the taste of the fruit experienced! Dance the orange . . . create the relationship / with the pure, resisting rind, / with the juice which fills the happy fruit.") (Sonnet 15)

If Rilke had not explained in a note that Sonnet 16 is addressed to a dog, it would have been difficult to guess. The dog is lonely because it cannot be like humans who make the world their own through words and finger-pointing. Yet humans cannot point to a smell; it is a dog that senses the dead and is terrified by the magic spell. Man and dog must bear things together, but Rilke warns the dog not to plant humans in his heart. Rilke's attitude to dogs was ambiguous. He liked the idea of their companionship but, half-humorously, feared that their dependence and pitious needs would require him to give up his profession and live entirely for their consolation. This attitude is but a paraphrase of his fear of entering human relations that would use him up and dissipate the concentration of his life's work. At the close of Sonnet 16 he seeks his master's hand, referring to Orpheus, and guides it in blessing the dog, a creature disguised in Esau's pelt in order to share vicariously human joy and sorrow.

Rilke's ingenuities in demonstrating metamorphoses are boundless and somewhat tiresome as the song-like language flows hypnotically and unabated through the rest of the cycle. Unlike anything he had done before, the weight of thought is gracefully transformed into the airiest of language; everything seems abstract, but nothing really is. Possibly because the sonnets were completely unplanned and written within the quick sweep of several days, there is more of an intoxicated, associative and uneven quality about them than the studied perfection of the New Poems. Notably, no anguish is spent on the scenes of childhood that had assumed proportions of horror elsewhere. Whatever memory brings, for instance the white horse that hobbled toward Lou and Rainer on a Volga meadow, is commemorated with joyousness and sanctity: "Sein Bild: ich weih's." ["His picture: I consecrate it."] (Sonnet 20)

Almost sarcastically, Rilke tells Orpheus about the harbingers of the "new" who exalt the droning and throbbing machine. It "wreaks revenge, distorts and weakens us," yet wants to be praised despite the fact that through its noise it prevents our "listening" from being whole. (Sonnet 18) Still, Rilke says almost consolingly, "Although the world keeps changing rapidly / like cloudshapes, / everything completed falls / home to the primal." The cycle of seasons in time, and the never-wooing gods, are celebrated in the next sonnets. In Sonnet 25, Rilke returns the focus to "the playmate of the invincible cry," Wera, and echoes her actual death cry, "Now I shall dance," as she enters "the inconsolable and open portal." In the closing sonnet of Part I appears the god with the lyre and the myth of the disdained maenads who dismembered him: "O you lost God! You unending trace! / Only because finally enmity tearingly dispersed you / are we now the listeners and a mouth of nature." The god endures and survives in metamorphosis; the song of Orpheus is in everyone's mouth, and Orpheus' art brings order into chaos and assumes a constructive role.

One would be content to let these sonnets rest as some of the happiest and most spontaneous creations in modern poetry were it not for the impression of artifice Rilke creates by expressing greater concern for the perfection of the poems than for the memory of Wera. On the seventh and ninth of February, Rilke wrote letters to Frau Knoop, with editorial putterings and sounds of urgency:

> It makes me so uncomfortable to think of that XXIst poem, the "empty" one in which the "transmissions" occur ("O das Neue, Freunde, ist nicht dies") . . . , please paste over it at once this *Child's-Spring-Song,* written today, which better enriches the sound of the whole and stands not badly, as a pendant, opposite the offering to the white horse. . . .

Intent and technique blend lyrically in the *Sonnets to Orpheus.* Rilke's intent is to celebrate transformation as a condition of existence. His technique consists of verbalizing and visualizing this continual transformation: a feeling becomes its name, the drinker becomes wine, the dancers of the orange become an orange, a body of substance becomes a disembodied splendor, the material changes into metaphor, verbs change into nouns, nouns into substantives, transience to permanence, time into a literal being.

The days which followed were to Rilke like the first days

of creation. On the seventh of February the "Seventh Elegy" appeared (with final touches on the twenty-sixth); on the seventh and eighth, it was the "Eighth Elegy"; on the ninth, the "Ninth Elegy" was shaped (also a fifth elegy later called "Antistrophes" which was supplanted by the new "Fifth Elegy" on the fourteenth of February); and on "Saturday, the eleventh, at six o'clock in the evening," the "Tenth Elegy" was finished. It was at Muzot, then, that Rilke joined the fragments and entities born in Duino, Paris, and Ronda and gave them an architectural configuration. Throughout these days he telegrammed and wrote his friends, telling them—with unaccustomed immodesty—of the cosmic events taking place at Muzot.

Sweeping hortatory lines characteristic of the elegies open the difficult and exhausting "Seventh": "Werbung nicht mehr, nicht Werbung, entwachsene Stimme, / sei deines Schreies Natur . . ." The parenthetical phrase "outgrown voice" sets up an ambiguity that permits several renderings of the lines: not wooing or wooing no longer be the nature of your cry, *or* not wooing but a voice that has outgrown wooing be the nature of your cry. Some commentators see in the lines a determination to cease wooing, an arrogant tone that comes from *hybris*. But this view ignores the distinctions Rilke develops between voluntary and involuntary wooing. In the "First Elegy" the poet wooed the angel with notes of hopefulness, despair, terror, love, and recognition-seeking, but he had to swallow his birdlike cry. An almost forcible wooing occurs in the "Fourth Elegy" ("an angel must come") and stems from the poet's deep, existential need. The wooing and pleading tone is not confined to the angel; Rilke adopts it whenever he asks anyone, especially lovers, for enlightenment. Wooing seeks an outside response, yet in the elegies Rilke has been responding to his own questions, forming tight little circles of limited satisfaction. With the "Seventh Elegy," he hopefully declares an end to wooing that *seeks a response*, an objective, or a fulfillment: let wooing be a disembodied, objectlessly striving voice, for song is not wooing, it is existence (as he postulated in the *Sonnets to*

*Orpheus*). Humans, like birds with their pure cry, do evoke a response "so that, still invisible, / a companion feels you, the silent mate in whom an answer / slowly awakens and warms itself in hearing . . ." Sound is transformed into visual "call-steps" (*Ruf-Stufen*), the voice-trill into cascading and diminishing fountains—a favorite Rilkean image of visible change; transformation and ascension reign, death and life are affirmatively joined in Rilke's Orphic world. This elegy triumphantly weds feeling to expression.

We can feel, see, and hear all of nature's echoing response to the involuntary and spontaneous wooing of the poet: "First that small / questioning upsounding which with heightened silence a pure assenting day mutely surrounds afar." He celebrates the many unfolding forces in nature, prefacing each with a tautological *nicht nur*: "Not only" the morning of summers that change into days . . . the days wrapped tenderly around flowers . . . the walks . . . the meadows; "not only" the sensed coming of sleep "but also" the nights, the lofty summer nights . . . the stars so close that they become the stars of earth. The pulsing upward beat of cumulative verbs that imitate ascent ends in a crescendo and fusion—"stars of earth." This momentary, unforgettable joy granted one in life is a foretaste of the endlessly intimate contact and sensation that is experienced in death: "O, at last, to be dead and to know them [the stars] unendingly, / all the stars: for how, how, how does one forget them!"

To share these perceptions, the poet calls up a dead loved one; but since his wooing is no longer confinable to any purpose or object, he is not surprised when a host of maidens rise from their graves. Rilke's sermon on the grave contains a series of epiphanal homilies: a single grasped thing here is as good as many; fate is no more than the richness and density of experience in childhood; being here is glorious; existence is an end in itself; the most visible of joys first reveals itself when it is inwardly transformed. The relativity of our being, hardly measurable between two durations, is posed against the durable: "Nowhere, loved one, will there be world as it is inwardly. Our / life passes in transformation. And ever diminishing passes the outer."

Rilke takes the measure of man and holds it up to the angel as not undeserving. Lest he be misunderstood, Rilke adds, "Do not think that I woo. / Angel, and if I did woo you! You would not come." The hopelessness of wooing the angel is clear to Rilke, but he can never reconcile himself to it nor can he cease involuntary wooing. By redefining his wooing-call as *Hinweg*—indirection, indifference, sidestepping, a lightly passing over—does he proclaim an independence that no longer seeks the angel directly. Why does the angel not come? In earlier elegies it is because the angel, a self-contained creature so powerful that we would be destroyed by his embrace, is disdainful and even unaware of our existence. In the "Seventh Elegy," Rilke explains that the angel would not come "aus Rücksicht," out of solicitude for man. But, on second thought, Rilke felt that this compassionate figure of the angel would be too deeply incompatible with all he had said and would probably be misinterpreted as a stereotyped Biblical angel; it would also have contradicted his aim of objectless wooing. After all the elegies had been written, he crossed out *Rücksicht* and instead added several assertive and rationalizing lines in temporary farewell to the angel of the elegies: you do not come "Because my call / is ever full of indirection; against so powerful a / current you cannot advance. Like an outstretched / arm is my call. And its graspable open hand afar remains before you / open, like repulsion and warning / untouchable one, far up." The circuit between the thought of the first and last lines of the elegy seems to be closed with astonishing finality; the contact and contest between Rilke and the angel is over when the limits of sense experience has been reached. Yet the subject is reopened two elegies later.

The "Eighth Elegy" comes like a respite. Its tone and images are uncomplicated; there are no harsh, metallic edges, no sharp turns from hymn to shattering lament, no reproaches, no tension, and no involuted thought. In this elegy Rilke develops his primitive, if not atavistic, mythology of the various realms of being and the relative place of man and beast.

"With all eyes" the animal sees the open. In the elegy Rilke makes a distinction between two kinds of openness: "Offen" as the open vistas of the landscape for instance, and "das Offene" as a mystical concept of pure space (*reiner Raum*) or the inner-world space (*Weltinnenraum*), a silent communal space that courses through all beings. Just as all beings are surrounded by an outer space that gives them a visible contour, so for Rilke there is an inner space continuum, the other side of nature, that forms a realm jointly for all beings. This philosophic speculation, inherited partly from Novalis, makes it readily possible for Rilke to say poetically and graphically, "I look outward and the tree grows within me," "Birds silently fly through us," a maiden "made herself a bed in my ear;" the outer-viewed object (*Ding*) is metamorphosed into an inner image and the inner side of nature becomes the magic mirror into which outer representations swim dimensionless.

Rilke's mystical open space is seen and inhabited directly by the animals while man, living in his circumscribed material world (*Welt*) of illusory reality, can only surmise from the face of the animal what the space-outside-the-world is like. Living unintrospectively and unselfconsciously in the open space, the animal is not aware of death; only man sees death. The animal, free of death because it cannot conceptualize it, "has his decease perpetually behind him / and God in front / and when it moves, it moves / into eternity, like flowing wells." "Das Offene" becomes synonymous with God and eternity. Man has not a single day of pure space, the nowhere-without-nowhere; man is trapped in his real and interpreted world (*gestaltete Welt*) — "Ever is it world" — and he conditions children early to look "backwards," away from the open space. Where man sees a material future tense (*Zukunft*), the animal sees everything (*Alles*).

Man's destiny (*Schicksal*), Rilke laments, is always to be opposite to the inner world and for lovers to block each other's view of it. Memory, however, is an experience common to both man and beast. It clings to the warm, wakeful, unsmiling, and sadness-weighted beast and may be likened to his first home; the second or the present, by comparison, is drafty. Man is often overwhelmed by memory but he cannot live with it. Most to be envied are the simplest of creatures:

> O *Seligkeit der* kleinen *Kreatur*,
> *die immer* bleibt *im Schoosse, der sie austrug;*
> o *Glück der Mücke, die noch* innen *hüpft,*
> *selbst wenn sie Hochzeit hat: denn Schooss ist Alles.*
>
> (SW 1,715–16)

["O bliss of the *small* creature / that always *remains* in the womb which delivered it. / Oh, joy of the gnat that still hops *within,* / even on its wedding day: for womb is all."] Some critics have been tempted to give these lines an exclusively Freudian interpretation, but what Rilke has in mind, in context, is the biological phenomenon of the non-mammalian creatures, hatched from eggs; all of nature automatically is their home and womb, and that is all they know. The romanticists' noble savage is replaced by Rilke's joyous gnat. Four years earlier, he had written to Lou about the multitude of creatures that come from externally exposed seed and have the spacious, open nature for their maternal body; they need never leave the maternal body's security at all. Whether he knew it or not, Rilke's speculations are poetic counterparts of Freud's interpretation of birth as a traumatic experience. He ascribes full security to the simplest creatures, "half-security" (*die halbe Sicherheit*) to creatures like birds whose nest is a kind of nature-womb not wholly exposed to the open, and bemoans the insecurity of womb-born man. The half-security of birds, bats, moths, he imaginatively sees evident in their erratic flight. If man, in his imagination should seek flight, his self-consciousness would unbalance him as it does a bat:

*Und wie bestürzt ist eins, das fliegen muss*
*und stammt aus einem Schooss. Wie vor sich selbst*
*erschreckt, durchzuckts die Luft, wie wenn ein Sprung*
*durch eine Tasse geht. So reisst die Spur*
*der Fledermaus durchs Porzellan des Abends.*   (sw 1,716)

["And how distraught is one that flying must / and originates from a womb. As if frightened by its own self / it rends the air like a crack / through a cup. So tears the track / of a bat through the porcelain of evening."] No amount of philosophic exegesis can equal the impact of such suggestive metaphors. Turning to man, Rilke observes sentimentally, "And we: spectators, ever, everywhere . . . We arrange things. They fall apart. / We shape things anew and decay ourselves." Who has fashioned us so awry that everyone of our attitudes harbors departure? We linger and survey the landscape we have traversed, hold it fast for a moment: "so do we live and ever take our leave." Never are we part of the inner open spaces of ultimate existence, our first home. Rilke's catalogue of the insufficiency and insecurity of man has no other purpose than to voice pure lament, an acceptance of a *de facto* situation. Rilke's envy of the mindless state of the gnat, the admiration for the child in its naiveté, and the romanticizing of the vacuity of animals and their illusory serenity are projections of his own longings for tranquillity. Man's uniqueness and loneliness stem from his awareness and emancipation from nature. Rilke twists these perceptions into a knot of pain, into a cosmic tragedy, and a vision of life as an evanescent and transitory place. He laments the loss of primal memory (*Erinnerung*), a recollection from *within*. In this mood, Rilke commented that the "Eighth" is "my silent elegy."

At Duino in 1912, Rilke had written nine lines of what was to be the "Ninth Elegy" but could not continue beyond the essential question: Why not be content for the short duration of life to be like a laurel (a modest symbol of existence-victory) and submit to dignified plantlike being without destiny? "Oh why the urge to pursue things human and avoiding destiny, / long for destiny? . . ." In various guises the question appears throughout the elegies. After ten years of intense living and then stock-taking at Muzot, Rilke decided in favor of an emphatic and ecstatic answer: "Oh, not because happiness *exists* / . . . Not out of curiosity or to exercise the heart, / . . . But because being here means much and because seemingly / all that is present, this fleetingness, needs us / . . . Us, the most fleeting of all. *Once* / for everything, only *once*. *Once* and no more. And, we too, *once*. Never again. But this, / *once* to have been, if only *once*: to have been *terrestrial* seems not to be revocable."

It was as if he had recaptured the enthusiasm of the days in 1912 at Duino when he also penned the introductory lines of the "Eighth Elegy." At that time, he wrote to Lou: "You came, that can be only once, just as there is only one birth;" and to a friend, the psychiatrist Gebsattel: "I am still struck by nothing so much as by the incomprehensible, incredible wonderfulness of my existence." The "Eighth Elegy," completed at Muzot, revives this rapture in a style whose intensely rhetorical stress falls like blows on certain words. Rilke's habit of using Roman capitals — sometimes even underlining them, and using multiple underlinings for emphasis and meaning is reproduced by levelling italics in the published texts; still, they mark fairly accurately the poet's emotional intensity and declamatory intent.

In the "First Elegy" the poet had asked: Who can use us and who can make use of us in order to give us a true sense of existence? The partial answer he gave was that we could use no one nor could we anchor ourselves to anything but the daily objects against which we move; nothing except the spring seasons needed us. In the "Eighth Elegy," he sweeps aside all reservations and exclaims that all the here-and-now needs us and that glory of a life experience, even if only *once*, is purpose enough. The phrase "Being here is glorious," from the previous elegy, now becomes an elaborate theme. The things we can take with us into the beyond are the weightiness and sufferings of life, love's long experience, and others unnamable (*unsäglich*). The things of the world that we should hold up to the angel in a hymn of praise are the art of seeing, the art of naming—house, bridge, fountain, gate, jug, olive tree, window (among Rilke's favorite significations).

"Is it not the uncanny slyness of this secretive earth" which urges lovers on and insures posterity? "*Here* is the time of the namable, *here* its home," "Praise the world to the angel," show him the simple things transmitted from generation to generation, tell him about the ropemaker in Rome and the potter in Egypt (artisans whose tradition goes back to most ancient times and who remained in Rilke's mind after seeing them during his travels), show the angel how happy and innocent can be a thing that belongs to us, how a sorrowing lament becomes a form and serves as a "thing." Whoever we may be, all these fleeting things are transformed in our invisible heart. Tell these things to the angel and he will be astonished. Again, Rilke has discarded his intention of not wooing the angel or of wooing without purpose; he seeks the astonished response of the angel. Despite fervent avowals and pretended indifference, Rilke cannot let go of the angel.

The naming, forming, and interpreting things of the world are the tasks of the poet and by distilling them into abstractions he makes possible their transfer into the inner space.[10] The creative act of the poet, Rilke implies ingeniously, enriches the life beyond and the inner space. This is an inversion of the Platonic idea that all things here are but reflections of absolute prototypes. Why does Rilke go to such metaphysical extremes? It is not likely that these ideas spring solely from momentary impulse or that their illogical shifts imply careless contradictions that can only be resolved by quibbles. Rilke is trying by various means to impress the angel and to establish a firm relationship. All his impetuous lament and praise has not helped, and many of his poetic attempts and differing approaches have not bridged the distance. What has been lacking is patience and total submission to the process he called transformation (*Verwandlung*).

Although Rilke does not always clearly distinguish between the types of transformations that he poetizes, separable outlines are discernible. The first type of transformation is purely biological, a natural process of decay and change, a dissipation and disappearance of things. The other is a type of controlled transformation, a creative act that changes experience into poetry and the material into eternal elements transferable to the space beyond. The parallelism of the two kinds of transformation is an immeasurable consolation for Rilke. The knowledge that there is an open space where some form of identity and intelligence is retained and where one is a timeless co-habitant with all, including the angel, makes it possible for Rilke to accept life. One transformation, moreover, is a step to the next. And so he closes the "Ninth Elegy" with a songlike coda to the earth: "Earth, is it not this that you want: invisibly / to rearise in us?—Is it not your dream / someday to be invisible?—Earth! Invisible; / What if not transformation is your urgent mandate? / Earth, you dearest, I will." I will submit without reserve and be part of your transformation; it will not be necessary to win me over with your spring seasons. "Nameless" am I, as opposed to the ephemeral and therefore namable things, determined and destined to belong to you. "Ever were you right, and your holy inspiration / is that friendly death." More than a note of acceptance is struck here: Rilke has come to a peaceable resolution with a personal mythological framework. Life is natural metamorphosis; death (without recriminations) is the portal—and not a terminal point—into the open space that surrounds us. The concepts are no longer forced; it is as if Rilke had worked out a simple and reassuring formula, a happy capitulation.

The elegiac invocation of the opening stanza of the "Tenth Elegy" ("Someday, emerging at last from the grim insight, / may I sing-out jubilation and praise to assenting angels . . .") had been written in Duino. Subsequent continuations too intimately reflected his relationship with Marthe Hennebert and were discarded, so that according to Rilke "the rest of the elegy all new and, yes, very very very beautiful" originated at Muzot. Rilke's self-praise should have been heaped on almost any other but the "Tenth Elegy" which, far from being beautiful in any lyrical or thought sense, is a virtuoso wedding of elegiac allegory and crude expressionistic caricature; intended ascent to the visionary declines too rapidly into broad farce.

The invocation's main theme that we are "wasters of sorrows (*Schmerzen*) . . . our winter foliage, our somber evergreen," is pervasively illustrated in the body of the elegy. Rilke leads us over an eerie topography: the City of Pain, the Annual Fair, and the spacious landscape of the Land of Pain. The City of Pain (*Leid-Stadt*) is a deathlike city "cast from the mould of vacuity," a reconstruction of the Spanish towns that he had described ten years earlier. Sound and vision clash in such imagery as "gilded noise" and "bursting gravestone," the antiseptic and disappointed church stands shut like a post office on Sunday, and if an angel wished, he could tracelessly wipe out the city's marketplace where illusory consolation (*Trost*) reigns. In contrast to the city where life is neglected or abdicated, sounds of life come from the Annual Fair adjoining the city. It is the fair he had playfully satirized in the *Visions of Christ* twenty-two years earlier, but this time an unsparing mockery infects his view. Aside from the horrendous bawling of hawkers, the tinny noise from the shooting galleries, and other surface vulgarities, Rilke sees those who are in pursuit of "happiness" on the mechanical Swings of Freedom or the luck-seeking target shooters as senselessly reeling figures of misguided zeal and self-deluding humanity. Most graphic is his scorn when he points to booths that advertise their wares for adults only: on view are the anatomical procreation of money and the sex organ of money, "the whole works which instructs and makes fertile." The poet's eye then moves to placards that say "Deathless," encouraging the drinking of bitter beer that seems sweet when accompanied by the chewing of Distractions. Behind the placard, children play, lovers hold each other "serious in pathetic grass, and dogs do what they must."

Quite abruptly turning from mordant social criticism,

Rilke introduces the figure of a youth who probably has seen the City of Pain and the Fair and is drawn beyond all these scenes into the realm of "reality." The youth is compelled by something: "perhaps he loves a young Lament?" Quite possibly the youth is an incarnation of the Orphic figure, the "almost godly youth" who at the end of the "First Elegy" enters forever into the "frightened space," the emptiness that is beset by "vibrations that pull us in and console and help." Whatever the force that has attracted the youth and urged his lone separation from the mass of humanity at the fair, it takes the shape of a female; her poise, shoulders, and neck indicate the offspring of a superb stock. But the uncomprehending youth merely shrugs, "She is a Lament." Of what use is she to him? There is to be no direct answer to the question.

At first, like Orpheus, the youth is only a visitor to the land beyond, in contrast to the early departed (already canonized in the "Fourth Elegy") who in their first condition of being weaned from the earth have attained timeless serenity or indifference (*Gleichmut*). The youth lovingly follows the figure of Lament attired in "pearls of pain" and "delicate veils of patience." The visions that unfold during his journey are sketchy, and Rilke avoids the categoric fictions and cosmological details lavished by Homer, Vergil, or Dante. Rilke's vista of the beyond is similar to the topography of our earth, but through Rilke's strength of imagery we slowly begin to feel and see things uncannily from the inside out. The youth has questions that the "young Lament" does not answer, but in the Valley one of the older Laments takes an interest in him and explains that they were once a great generation whose fathers were miners in the great mountains so that humans occasionally find a polished stone of "primal pain" or ossified "stone-formed rage." (Rilke's lament for the uninhibited passions of the ancients and their primal directness in life is reflected here.) The older Lament escorts him through the immense "landscape of pain" and shows him the ruins of temples and towers, the tall "tear trees" and meadows of flowering sadness which "the living

know only as tender foliage," the grazing animals of
sorrow, the graves of the sibyls and prophets; everything
seems to be preserved here, and there is even a hint that
the deceased may suffer further decease. Sometimes a bird,
startled perhaps by an awareness of being in the land of
lament, moves flat-flying—like the flickering picture of a
soundwave, through the youth's upward vision. Night
approaches as they wander silently, and soon "it moons"
upward so that in the light they can admire the regal head
of the Sphinx that, eternally mute, "has placed the human
face on the scale of the stars."

It was Rilke's intention to render whatever the youth
saw in terms of the desert clarity of a dead person's
consciousness. The descriptions here are remnants of
memory drawn from his Egyptian journeys.[11] And imper-
ceptibly the youth joins the early departed as a new
sensation and a strange life experience takes shape; it takes
time, said Rilke in the "First Elegy," before the dead
perceive a bit of eternity. That point is reached when
visions become audible and sound becomes visible, a form
of synesthesia that Rilke had put to poetic practice in the
*Sonnets to Orpheus.* The youth's glance is still dizzy, but
that of Lament is so strong that it shoos an owl from
behind the double crown atop the Sphinx's head. If the
double crown is symbolic of the two realms, life and death,
then the owl becomes a token messenger. The owl,
"brushing the cheek with the ripest curve, / with slow
strokes, softly etches into the hearing of the dead / . . . an
indescribable outline." In these dazzling lines that attempt, nevertheless, to describe the indescribable, the
youth is initiated into the land of ultimate being. Now, as
he looks up at the stars of the Land of Lament he is told
that the figures in the constellations are the abstractions of
the essences that concern us, the polarities around which
life moves: rider, staff, fruit-garland, cradle, way, the
burning book, doll, window, mothers. Each has a particular significance for Rilke—human relationships, pilgrimage, achievement, birth, childhood, longing, revelations—
but he singles out as especially resplendent the symbol of

the mothers, imbedded in one's palm. (Through palmistry Rilke learned that an "M" appears if one upstrokes the second onto the third line of the left palm.)

Finally the older Lament brings the dead youth to a gorge that gleams in the moonlight and indicates that this is the source or spring (*Quelle*) of joy which humans call "the carrying stream." Alone he descends into the mountains of Primal Pain, "and not once does his tread resound from the soundless fate." It is the last we see of the youth; yet there are intimations that the dead engage in ceaseless activity, retaining their individuality. If the dead were to awake in us metaphoric insights, they would point to the rain that *falls* and enrichingly vanishes and to the *fall* of the catkins from the hazel husk, typifying *in*florescence.[12] The brief life-duration of rain and catkins in nature and their fertile fall into the realm of death are analogies of our condition. Rilke, in the gentlest manner, reminds the reader who is accustomed to think of happiness as an ascending feeling that there is happiness too in descent or falling; the realm of the dead is that into which everything falls and converges to have its ultimate existence.

Rilke's mythology of the death realm — an occult-tinged inner open-space of consciousness — is unique precisely because it is so similar to the features of our world, except that the vantage points are opposite and terminologies of the dead and the living differ. An object may be a "tear" tree to the dead but a "willow" to the living. The same holds true for every object of the world that is transformed into an abstraction in the realm of the dead, as if the dead looked at things from the inner rind-side of existence. Rilke's personal vision is sharply different from the ancient mythmakers, from that of the Judeo-Christian view in the center of which lies atonement and resurrection, and from modern scientific or existential-philosophic thought that holds death to be no more than a necessary terminal point of life.

After having written the final lines of the "Tenth Elegy," Rilke described his heady experiences to Lou on February 11th: "Think! I have been allowed to survive up to this. Through everything. Miracle. Grace. —All in a few days. It was a hurricane, as at Duino that time: all that was fiber, fabric in me, framework, cracked and bent. Eating was not to be thought of." Then he plunged into the sun of the Sunday air; upon returning to his study he was ready to labor again.

During the next two days, Rilke wrote a prose piece *In Memoriam* to the Belgian poet Émile Verhaeren, who ever since the Paris days remained his "great friend." In a section called "The Young Workman's Letter," he restates his credoes, possibly as an antidote to any notion that the elegies are no more than mystical effusions. The letter, which was published posthumously in 1930, underlines some key points in the elegies and is a huge polemic directed against those who, in Rilke's view, misunderstand the meaning of God, Christ, life, death. God is a conviction within Rilke and not something learned. Using the language of the *Sonnets to Orpheus*, Rilke sees Christ as a tree in God on which we could ripen like fruit. The teaching of the Old Testament, the Koran, Christ are all *pointers* to God; Christ is a pointer, a gesture, and not a dwelling place.

On February 9, 1922, at Muzot, Rilke completed the "Fifth Elegy" begun in Venice during the summer of 1912. With unambiguous admiration, he characterized the essence of women: "Flowers of the deepest earth-realm, / loved by all the roots, / you, Eurydice's sisters, / ever filled with holy return / behind the ascending man." Because in style and tone these lines have an independence apart from the elegies and the sonnets—although the spiritual bridge between the two cycles is visible, Rilke decided to title them "Gegen-Strophen" ["Antistrophes"] and to replace them on February 14th with the new "Fifth Elegy." As a result, the new elegy is a pictorial continuation of certain scenes in the "Tenth" and has subtle links to the "Fourth" as well as to the "Antistrophes."

Rilke composed the "Fifth Elegy" under extreme emotional compulsion. The verses were so rapidly pencilled onto fourteen pages of note paper that they often resemble shorthand; in the draft there was no coherent sequence. Rilke contended that he was at the mercy of a dictating force. The elegy can easily stand the strain of diverse interpretations, but all major signs point to it as being a highly autobiographical resumé. Lou responded almost immediately to the autobiographical significance of the elegy:

> I would not let the "Fifth" talk to me as anything but that which stems from your most distant experience in regard to will to victory and apprehension, extreme withdrawal and almost steerlike and compressed inner strength ("of neck and nun") . . . and ripening *in the Nu* . . . How could it be other than that the "Saltimbanques" trailed you from far afar . . . (Letter, March 6, 1922)

We know of some notes that Rilke made when viewing a performance of Père Rollin and his troupe on July 4, 1907, in front of the Luxembourg in the direction of the Pantheon. Later this scene merged with Picasso's painting "Les Saltimbanques" on view in the König apartment which Rilke inhabited in Munich during the war years. In the elegy, the personages of the Paris scene and of the painting spring alive with special meaning.

Rilke puts himself amid the spectators of the acrobatic troupe, but, as in the "Fourth Elegy," once the "heart's curtain" is drawn open his identification becomes close to what takes place on stage. Who are these travelers, asks Rilke, and for whose sake are they driven by a never-contented will? It is this vague will or the iron grip of playful fate, as well as power, which wrings, bends, slings, swings, tosses and catches the acrobats. As if through oiled and smooth air, they glide down on their carpet worn threadbare by their "eternal upspringing." And suddenly Rilke has glided into the abstract: the carpet becomes a cosmic carpet which like a strip of adhesive is laid on the place where the outer-city sky has abrasively injured the earth; the figures on the carpet and, by a stretch of the imagination, the figures in Picasso's painting, form the letter D for *Dastehn* (Being There), existence.[13]

Shedding its leaves, the rose of onlooking (*die Rose des Zuschauns*) blossoms, and in its center is the carpet where the acrobats play out their existence. It is a contradictory center where nothing takes place (the acrobats are driven by a seemingly purposeless will) and yet symbolically everything significant takes place. Rilke compares the troupe to a rose and its pestle, pistil, and pollen. The self-fertilizing action of the troupe bears sham fruit whose glowing, thin, and superficial surface is like their audience-directed smiles that hide boredom. The German words for the rose components admit to more than botanical meanings: *Stampfer* (pestle, stamper, stomper), *Stempel* (pistil, stamp), *Staub* (pollen, dust). Rilke plays with multiple *entendres* as he begins to focus on every member of the troupe.

First comes the father or grandfather: "Da, der welke faltige Stemmer . . ." *Da*, the prefix of *Dastehn* (rooted in existence, Being There), introduces him as the flowerwilted, faded *Stemmer* (symbol of authority, strong man, weightlifter, one who stems, stops, or possibly prohibits). He is the old man, now drumming or marking time for the troupe, who has entered his tremendous skin, distended as if it had previously housed two men, one of whom was already in the graveyard and the surviving other remaining deaf and sometimes a bit dizzy in the widowed skin. This deaf drummer cuts a clownish, pathetic figure, hanging on to life.

In contrast to the caricature of the father, the young man is introduced "as if he were the son of a back-of-the-neck / and a nun: tautly and robustly filled / with muscles and naiveté," making the young man an heir of the profane and the sacred.

Rilke turns from this modern-day minotaur and becomes intrigued by the grandson in the troupe. Rilke compares the child acrobat to an unripe fruit which falls from a tree and bounces up and away from the grave. The draft version of the poem shows that Rilke put the word grave (*Grab*) in double-sized capitals to emphasize the child-acrobat's physical hazards and his spiritual closeness

to the grave by reason of his unripeness. The poet projects
his own boyhood feelings into the child-acrobat: "Sometimes, in a half-pause, a loving expression / will shape your
face as it turns to your seldomly tender mother." Unrecip-
rocated, the instantaneous expression vanishes, there is
hardly time for pain to set in "near the heart" as the father
claps his hand and the child-performer's soles begin to
burn. A few lively tears have formed in the boy's eyes and
yet there blindly appears a smile. From the insensitive
mother and the stern duty-demanding father who has
come between them, the poet turns urgently to the angel
and asks him to pluck the small-blossoming smile—a
self-healing herb that tastes bitter on the tongue of the
boy—to place it among the joys not yet revealed, and to
preserve it in an apothecary-like urn that is praisingly
inscribed "Subrisio Saltat," the Acrobat's Smile.[14] Aside
from the autobiographical childhood drama of mother,
father, and angel, Rilke successfully puts into images his
veneration of the emotion engendered by sorrow and pain,
though in the boy's case it was but a "small" pain.

The family portrait would hardly be complete without
the maiden, costumed and mute, like one whom the most
exquisite joys have passed over. (For the maiden, Rilke
used the word *Übersprungne*, literally one who is jumped
over, in perfect consonance with the acrobatic troupe
pictorialization.) She is the incarnation of the deceased
sister he never knew and all the other maidens he
idealized:

> *Du dann, Liebliche,*
> *du, von den reizendsten Freuden*
> *stumm Übersprungne. Vielleicht sind*
> *deine Fransen glücklich für dich—,*
> *oder über den jungen*
> *prallen Brüsten die grüne metallene Seide*
> *fühlt sich unendlich verwöhnt and entbehrt nichts.*
> *Du,*
> *immerfort anders auf alle des Gleichgewichts schwankende*
> *Waagen*
> *hingelegte Marktfrucht des Gleichmuts,*
> *öffentlich unter den Schultern.*          (sw 1,703–4)

["You then, lovely one, you / mute one whom the exqui-site joys have passed over. Perhaps / your tassels are happy for you—, / or over the young / taut breasts the green me-tallic silk / feels itself endlessly spoilt and relinquishes nothing. / You / evermore different on all of the balance's scales, / proffered market fruit of indifference, / exposed under the shoulders."] The infinitely tender tone toward the maiden, modulated by the soft vowelling *ü* and *ö*, is in contrast to the agitation of the poet, exhibited by his highly erratic line lengths. Indignation and sensuality heighten the poet's fantasy which lingers on the public dis-play of the maiden, a violation of privacy. For publication, Rilke deliberately blurs the final version of this passage somewhat, permitting the interpretive but inexact transla-tion of the last lines as the maiden "publicly shown among shoulders" [15] of the spectators. Rilke's first draft was much more explicit: "the silk / the black one in swoon / on your / warm . . . breasts / under the shoulder / not secretly, / open to public view / under the shoulder." This to Rilke was tantamount to sacrilege. Ironically, everything and everyone who comes in contact with her gains a pleasure that is denied her.

The remaining stanzas of the elegy are quite disarranged and somewhat difficult because the poet is conscious that he is putting his most inward emotions on exhibition. He must do it, but he attempts it with a minimum of clarity. What holds the discordant stanzas together is the poet's search for locales—designated by the shifting synonyms *Ort, Stelle, Platz*—where love might seek fulfillment: in some area of the heart, in the tumult of life, in the space-realm of the dead. At first, he cursorily looks into his own heart and observes the play of his emotions and finds an inability to devote himself to the kind of love that, like art, requires work. Rilke uses the gross image of mounting animals who fall away from the act, "not properly paired," like humans, acrobats who in their apprenticeship clumsily handle weights, hoops, and stick-twirled dishes. The insufficiency of lovers, pathetic in their transitory intoxica-tion and incapable—in this life—of matching Rilke's idea of true love relations, is legion in Rilke's writings. Here, through the analogy of the acrobats, temporal love, though capable of sudden transformation from a wearisome learning (the stage of the pure too-little) to a routine perfection (the empty too-much), is likened to an equation that balances and cancels out into meaninglessness. Rilke has turned from poetic to didactic and punsterish prose. Yet we expect surprises from Rilke, and in the next stanza we find a great, expressionistic thought-portrait:

*Plätze, o Platz in Paris, unendlicher Schauplatz,*
*wo die Modistin, Madame Lamort,*
*die ruhlosen Wege der Erde, endlose Bänder,*
*schlingt und windet und neue aus ihnen*
*Schleifen erfindet, Rüschen, Blumen, Kokarden, künstliche*
*   Früchte—, alle*
*unwahr gefärbt,—für die billigen*
*Winterhüte des Schicksals.*                    (sw 1,704–5)

["Place, oh places in Paris, unending showplace / where the modiste *Madame Lamort* slings and winds the restless ways of the world, endless ribbons, / and from them devising new / bows, frills, flowers, cockades, artificial fruits—, all / falsely colored, for the cheap / winter hats of fate."]

A more spectacular place than that within the heart is the life in Paris, which alternately repelled and attracted Rilke in his *Malte* days; it is also the market fair of the *Visions of Christ* and the "Tenth Elegy" as well as a general view of the here-and-now. Madame Death, a flamboyant sister of the Greek fate-spinners, doles out superficialities and illusions and, by implication, the "small" or mass death which Rilke abhorred in *Malte* and in *The Book of Hours*. Catering to tasteless fashions of the days she gleefully creates "cheap winter hats of fate," including the clownish caps of the acrobats. With a shock we realize that her garish cockades and frills are also those that ornament the costume of the girl acrobat and that Madame Death is the willful creature for whose sake the acrobats are driven by a "never-contented will." *She* is the force that wrings, "slings and winds" humans as if they were ribbons. Rilke has answered the question which introduces the elegy.

The final stanza belongs to the angel of the elegies. Almost humbly, Rilke tests a hypothesis that could be verified by the angel, a lofty inhabitant of the inner space realm. Rilke assumes that somewhere is a place where on an "indescribable carpet, lovers show / what they are unable to accomplish here: their hold, / high figures of heart-flight, / their towers of pleasure . . ." In Rilke's fantasy, the human spectators are replaced by countless and "toneless" dead who ring the lovers; there the lovers are *able* to perform, encouraged by the "eternally valid coins of happiness" thrown by the dead; then, finally, will there be a truthful "smiling pair on the stilled / carpet?" The elegy, the last to be written at Muzot, ends with a question mark and the last word "carpet" is a synonym for existence. At the beginning of the elegy, the carpet on earth was threadbare and the "smile" was fleeting; at the end, the carpet is "indescribable" and a place of fulfillment in the realm of the dead, while the smile becomes truthfully lasting. The elegy's final question may be read as a desire for assurance, "Isn't it so that in the realm beyond, all our expectations for absolute happiness will be realized?" The routine perfections and all the preparatory aspects of earthly life will become intuitive, "true relatedness," as he said in the sonnets, in the realm where "antennae feel antennae." If anything extends through all realms, it must be the relatedness we call love. Since death is deeply imbedded in love and contradicts it at no point in Rilke's thinking, the drama of lovers calmly confronting the dead becomes a pictorial rendering of the poet's wishful thought. On this muted note, Rilke closes the entire elegy cycle.

Because they were written under diverse tensions and during different periods of his life, the elegies do not possess a complete unity of thought or emotion. Whatever the extremes—elations and depressions, excessive hymnology to life or death, they exhibit Rilke's efforts to say the unsayable, to stray into regions that defy our knowledge. To call the elegies thought-lyricism (*Gedankenlyrik*), as some commentators have done, would imply an attempt at pure and polished philosophical reflection that just is not there; in the sonnets and the elegies the poetry *is* the thought of the moment in all its fine-veined convolutions and associations. Rilke made intuition an extension of reason and what he called mysterious "dictation" was a euphemism for narcissistic compulsion.

Rilke was elated because the elegies undeniably were stunning artistic and personal triumphs. On February 15 he sent a communiqué to Frau Wunderly, describing his "divine tempest" and telling how from the top of Muzot he trumpeted tremendous command calls and received signals from the cosmos, answering them with immense cannonades of salute. We have here a spectacle that is both heroic and quixotic: despite the demonic activity, his mind survived the self-imposed task and at the same time the artist-warrior was the victim of his own fantasy—what he heard were not signals from the cosmos but the echo of his own voice. Caught in the net of human limitations, he had done as much as few creative geniuses had ever been able to do.

With sustained excitement, Rilke spent the next eight days writing twenty-nine poems that were to form Part II of the *Sonnets to Orpheus:* "It was very strange how my pen was literally guided." Orpheus, mentioned only twice more, has almost disappeared, rent and scattered but alive in the rhythmic being of all animate and inanimate things. By virtue of this legacy—the Orphic god within all men, Rilke is able to see himself in close identity with everything in the cosmos "in which I rhythmically occur" as a silken thread woven into the eternal tapestry (Sonnets II, 21). This orientation clarifies what would otherwise be the strangest of associations when he calls himself "the gradual sea of a solitary wave," when he reflects that "many a wind is like a son to me," or that "the once-smooth rind of air is the perfection and page [*Blatt* also means a leaf of nature] of my words." Mystically he is the cosmos and at

the same time he is only an elemental part of it, as in the
*Book of Hours*. In the sonnets the reader must be prepared
to read Rilke's "open universal map" which charts a
boundaryless multi-dimensional sense field and to see
associative themes at play rather than to search for a
non-existent narrative continuity.

Symbols and ideas recur in the sonnets, with an un-
matched translucence. The mirror of Narcissus and the
companionate virgin and unicorn appear in Sonnets three
and four (Part II). Through concentrated willing the
unicorn came to *be* and to "a virgin it became hither white
— / and was in the silver mirror and in her." The mirror
temporally captures fleeting intuitions, the impalpable, the
unproven, and turns figments of imagination into realities.
Only to the profane and unbeliever is the unicorn non-
existent. The purity of the virgin permits the unicorn
image to live both in the mirror and in herself. Rilke
emphatically rules out any hint of a Christ parallel in the
symbol of the unicorn.[16] In all these visions are mirrored
the poet's preoccupation with himself, the isolated and
undistracted interior-listening, the relieved and pleasurable
return to himself after demanding exterior relations.

Wonder, admiration, and praise of life within nature
course softly through the sonnets, not in a romantically
descriptive sense but always as wistful analogies to the
human condition:

> *Blumenmuskel, der der Anemone*
> *Wiesenmorgen nach und nach erschliesst,*
> *bis in ihren Schooss das polyphone*
> *Licht der lauten Himmel sich ergiesst . . .*
>
> *Wir Gewaltsamen, wir währen länger.*
> *Aber wann, in welchem aller Leben,*
> *sind wir endlich offen und Empfänger?*    (sw 1,753–4)

> *Flower muscle that opens for the anemone*
> *a meadow-morning bit by bit,*
> *until into her womb the polyphonic*
> *light of pure skies pours itself out . . .*

> *We, violent ones, we last longer.*
> *But when, in which of all lives,*
> *do we at last open and become receivers?*

Rilke had intended to use the dark violet-furred species of
*Pulsatilla* as symbol of something rare, being under the
impression that it only grew in the Valais region, but he
yielded with typically gracious humor when he learned
differently:

> Someone passed through who with disgraceful familiarity
> called the little flower "cow-" or even "kitchen bell" and
> assured me *que c'etait tout ce qu'il a de plus commun* . . .
> Well, that would not, after all, detract from its beauty, but
> it surprised me, because as it first comes up here among the
> rocks, in the protection of its silver fur equipped for all
> disaster, it looks really rare and noble.[17]

Rilke's botanical knowledge (he had read much but hastily
in the natural sciences) here and elsewhere falls far short
of the poetical reality he created. Although the rose in the
next sonnet has many conventional and traditional signifi-
cances, Rilke shuns them all by uniquely describing the
"throning" rose in an Orphic context: "In your richness
you seem like garment upon garment / about a body of
nothing but light. / . . . For centuries your fragrance calls
across to us / its sweetest names / . . ." Cut flowers, in
Sonnet 7 (Part II), are likened to tired maiden-hands,
having started to die and then being revived by water and
the "streaming poles of feeling fingers." Implied is the
alliance of flowers and maiden, a brilliant flowering death,
and then revival. What started as a simple analogy has
become a bold interplay of images, personifications, and
animization through Rilke's uniquely transforming touch.

Childhood devoid of terror but full of irreality, except
for a few recapturable moments as the picture of his
young-deceased cousin Egon at play, marks a new and
significant change of tone in the eighth sonnet (Part II).
Life is magical *despite* all the problematic elements
symbolized, for example, by the arrogant machine: "in
hundreds of / places there is still primal origin. A playing

of pure / forces, touched by no one who does not kneel and admire." (The "mystic kneelers of El Greco" were for Rilke the visible personifications of reverent feelings.)

Just as rhetorical anguish and the outcries of lament weight the elegies, praise and acceptance buoy the sonnets—yet it is an acceptance of life without forgetting its "scaffold" and grim aspects. The calmly established rules of death that men mete out as hunters are meted out to man in return. The eleventh sonnet (Part II) contains a sharp analogy-vignette remembered from a scene he witnessed in 1912 in the hinterlands of Trieste: ". . . Strips of sail / which one used to dangle into the cavernous Karst. / Quietly one lowered you [sails] as if you were a sign / to celebrate peace. Yet then: at the edge, the helper gave you a twist, / —and out of the caverns the night threw a handful of pale, / staggering pigeons into the light . . ." to be killed by the hunters during the terrified escape. Rilke quickly adds: "But even *this* is right / . . . *Killing is a figuration of our wandering sorrow* . . ." To the ideas of the great and the small death, the death in the bluish cup, the infinitely tender death, *Madame Lamorte* and her frivolity, now is added the capricious and treacherous death. The inevitability of death in its various guises haunted Rilke as did the question of which death would strike him. But whatever life would dole out, he conditioned himself stoically to accept as an inner, inexorable logic of existence.

Of Sonnet 12 (Part II) he told Frau Knoop that it was the closest to him and the most valid. In it he states categorically: "Whatever shuts itself up into remaining already *is* petrifaction / . . . Whoever pours himself out as a spring, he is accepted by Awareness; / and she leads him entranced through serene creation / that often ends with beginning and begins with ending." By means of key terminology ingeniously dispersed throughout the sonnet, Rilke charts his own philosophic enlightenment and human progression. First one must *will* a change (*Wandlung*), pursue changeful transformings (*Verwandlungen*), love the turning point (*wendenden*

*Punkt*), accept the happy space of parting (*Trennung*) and be able to ethereally wander through it (*durchgehn*), then the creatures already transformed into the elements of nature will beckon and wish that you too change or wander (*wandelst*) and experience a relationship like wind to a laurel.

Rilke's consummate illustrations of the will to transcendental relationships are carried on a wave of sentiment, hymnic and sacral. Rilke's praise and blessing culminates in "Be ever dead in Eurydice," ["Sei immer tot in Eurydike"], a paganistic substitute for the common orthodox phrase, "Rest in God." From this focal phrase, lines radiate throughout the remaining sonnets and form hymns to the immortal gods who speak through nature's creations—if man would only learn to listen and understand his affinities. Rilke admires the capacity of the ancient Greeks to "listen" and devotes a lovely lyrical sonnet (Part II, 28) to the essence of Greek vase pictorializations.

The sermons Rilke issued from Castle Muzot have two recurring aspects in the second part of the sonnet cycle: first, anticipatory mitigation of human pain through acceptance of fate and, second, the continuity of life through transformation. "Be prepared far ahead for all parting, as if it already were / behind you, like the winter which just now has passed," is typical in its anticipatory protectiveness. In various ways Rilke tried to visualize the nature of "transformation" through injunction like, "Be a ringing glass which shatters itself in sounding," "Be and know, at the same time, the condition of not being, / the infinite depth of your inner vibrations," count yourself jubilantly onto the infinite sums of things in nature and cancel the count by integration. No longer does the cancelling result in zero or meaninglessness as in the "Fifth Elegy;" here it means the totality of transcendental communion with "all those quiet sisters in the wind of the meadows," manifestations of the gods. Orpheus resurrected at the close of the sonnets becomes the "singing God."

In the C. W. cycle Rilke had said, "Then, who is not fearful: where is a staying, / where a final *being* in all this? / Staying is nowhere." In the sonnets, he has come to the jubilant conclusion that staying is *everywhere*: "And when the earthly has forgotten you, say to the still earth: I flow. / To the rapid water say: I am." This ringing self-affirmation closes the sonnet cycles and the relation between the poet and Orpheus becomes clear. The poet's function in the sonnets is to fashion a hymn of adoration to the creative elements in nature, while Orpheus is to personify the surging vitality, reconciliations, and relatedness among all the elements in all realms of being.

Like Odysseus, Rilke has tasted the full power of the fictive emotion by making death a life experience; he made a descent into the other realm and accomplished the ascent (as well as assent) to life. He made Orpheus' fate his own through an emphatic recapitulation of a mythic vision: each man lives and dies for himself and not as a sacrificial atonement or as a redemptive act or figure for mankind. In the *Duino Elegies,* the poet is downcast by the unattainable, amid mainly hostile forces, and is in need of consolation. In the *Sonnets to Orpheus,* he is uplifted by his pure relatedness to receptively friendly elements and he rejoices; his emphatic awareness of the isolating spaces that surround man, angel, and the dead in the elegies yields to a vision of the spontaneous transformations that ignores boundaries. An immense melancholic loneliness, however, streams through both elegy and sonnet cycles: "Between the stars, how distant; and yet, how much greater the distance / one learns in the here-and-now . . ." between all humans.

THE MANY superlative poems—still undiscovered by the
general reader—which followed the *Sonnets to Orpheus* in
February, 1922, are distillations of thankfulness; the poet
has made his peace with the past, as far as possible. Rilke
celebrates his new "inclination" (*Neigung*), a gracious
acceptance of relatedness which he compares almost
literally to the inclination of hill to meadow. He reversed
an earlier position and almost grandiosely saw the Valais
landscape as "offering manifold equivalents and corre-
spondences to the expression of our inner world." Rarely
do nature analogies leave his poetry from that time on; it
was as if he had made an Orphic pact. Even toward
childhood, his tone mostly is conciliatory, attributing his
adult bewilderment not to barrenness but to an over-
abundance of experience: "Everything is overflow . . .
how can we ever feel cheated, knowing that we have been
overrewarded by life?"

This new tone is emphasized in several lyrical poems,
previewing the last four years of sheer exuberant creation
and indicating a state of mind he characterized as *si
incomparable bonheur*. The accents are shifted from the
elegiac to the festive and from dark to light symbols:

> *Wann war ein Mensch je so wach*
> *wie der Morgen von heut?*
> *Nicht nur Blume und Bach,*
> *auch das Dach ist erfreut.*

*Selbst sein alternder Rand,*
*von den Himmeln erhellt,—*
*wird fühlend: ist Land,*
*ist Antwort, ist Welt.*

*Alles atmet und dankt.*
*O ihr Nöte der Nacht,*
*wie ihr spurlos versankt.*
*Aus Scharen von Licht*
*war ihr Dunkel gemacht,*
*das sich rein widerspricht.*          (sw II,470)

*When was man ever so awake*
*as today's morning?*
*Not only flower and brook*
*but the roof, too, is overjoyed.*

*Even its aging edge,*
*lit up by the heavens,—*
*becomes feeling: is land,*
*is reply, is world.*

*All breathes and thanks.*
*O you afflictions of night,*
*how tracelessly you faded.*

*From legions of light*
*was their darkness made—*
*a pure contradiction.*

The afflictions of night give way to the delight of morning
(like an echo of the Psalm-line, "Sorrow tarries at night
but joy comes in the morning") and lament gives way to
praise. With equal fervor, Rilke pursues the idea that in
the realm of "pure contradiction" there is not only a
reconciliation of opposites but an organic relationship and
the motive power for transformations, an idea that was to
receive final, canonical significance in his epitaph. Reconciliation, propitiation, and consolation became his poetic
keynotes.

Weigh things "with the carat of the heart," enjoins
Rilke, let art be an exemplary for humans through reason
of art's "innate disinterestedness, freedom and inten-

sity"—a poem means least of all to arouse in the reader the potential poet; poetry is a discipline "not concerned at all with any effect." Unfortunately, said Rilke, the arts have attracted the wayward and the fugitives from life. Rilke began to dispense stern warnings against pursuit of art unless one were to accept it as an all-consuming way of life in which the artist creates for himself and, if need be, interposes long silences as shown by Valéry's twenty-five-year-long refusal to publish and his own long gestatory pauses.

Visitors, who came to Muzot to pay homage to the poet of the elegies and the sonnets, encouraged a feeling of veneration that made Rilke stand in awe of himself, investing his pronouncements on politics, art, and psychoanalysis with an *ex cathedra* sanctity. His publisher's wife, Katharina Kippenberg, describes the poet at his pulpit, reading from the elegies with strong emphasis, pauses, and modulations: Rilke "looked as if he had descended from Mount Sinai, his forehead flowed with holy emanations, a godly breath enveloped it . . ." [1] No less was Princess Marie moved; choking with tears, she kissed the forehead of her "wonderful son" who was kneeling to kiss her hands. To her, he was the incarnation of "the singing god." Such were the modest beginnings of a biographical and critical literature that reached hagiographical proportions.

Rilke, not yet fifty, was looking forward to enjoying life to the fullest. Ironically two things stood in the way, namely money and health. He was hoping that the Nobel Prize would be bestowed on the poet of the *Duino Elegies*, but it was William Butler Yeats who was to receive it instead. As for his health, every excitement, he complained, made his solar plexus "annihilable" and subject to week-long upheavals. Though "a prisoner in the old walls of my Muzot," Rilke rationalized that being sheltered from the distresses besetting postwar Europe had its advantages. The great years of wandering were almost over and except for an eight-month stay in Paris in 1925 and several visits to the races at Thun and the bathing resort of Ragaz, most trips involved sanataria, clinics, and health cure centers.

Long letters were dispatched from Muzot in response to questionnaires about his life and works in an attempt to guide editors, scholars, and an assortment of laymen in creating a Rilke biography and a body of interpretations that would meet Rilke's approval. In some cases it meant a subjective rewriting of old experiences and interpretations; in others, a completely candid statement of his position on specific issues. To Professor Hermann Pongs,[2] Rilke made it clear that he wished none of his work to come under the rubric of "social," that he did not espouse the cause of either the poor or the rich, that when he talked of the dwarf and the beggar in his poems he wanted to extol their "incomparable destiny" and not to wish for an alleviation of their miseries: "I unquestioningly claim for my poem the justified impartiality of artistic expression." He thought that to take up a cudgel for human betterment would be a presumption based on the uncertainty of whether or not change would indeed bring about improvement; one's soul is not affected by the conditions of the world. Not wishing to appear callous, Rilke added, "Something of a human likemindedness, something brotherly is indeed spontaneous in me." In Rilke's mind brotherliness was not incompatible with an aversion and disinclination for advocating social reform. Stability seemed to be Rilke's overriding criterion and he even subscribed to the necessity for capital punishment, probably on this premise. His impartiality, at times synonymous with naïveté, was so broad politically that he—still a Czech citizen—could offer his respects to Czechoslovakia's first president, Tomáš Masaryk, "A man of universal intellectual significance who assumed the topmost place in my native country," and could intone admiration for the beautiful speeches of dictator Mussolini, "cet architecte de la volonté italienne," [3] seeing him also as the forger of a new conscience.

Eager to set the right tone for the interpretations of the elegies and the sonnets, Rilke laid down his creed in a letter to his Polish translator Witold Hulewicz. (Rilke addressed him as "von" Hulewicz, an improvised honorific.) The letter of November 13, 1925, is a mélange of splendidly stated insights but at times poses clear contradictions to the poetic texts. Unfortunately, this famous epistle to future disciples has been accepted uncritically by many Rilke commentators. Neither the letter nor the poetic text should be read without remembering that Rilke's instinctive creation did not always correspond with his deliberate thinking. In the Book of Hours and in a poem about Da Vinci's "Mona Lisa," the artist defied transience by immortalizing his subjects; yet in the last elegies, it became the earth's and artist's urgent mission to transform the visible transient into the invisible. We read in the Hulewicz letter, "Transience itself everywhere plunges into a deep being." To compound the difficulty of finding a firm meaning, Rilke also notes in the letter that what is intransiently visible to us already is transiently invisible in the angel, a proof of the existence of a higher order of reality. The angel is "terrible" because "we still cling to the visible," but hypothetically the elegies, among other things, suggest the *undesirability* of a contact through which man would perish.

In the elegies, the angel was a transcendental figure and in the sonnets Orpheus was an immanent one against a pantheistic backdrop. These differing concepts Rilke tries to unite in one grand scheme of life and death as unbounded realms, both of which nourish our existence. Rilke is eager for the reader to agree that "*Affirmation of life-AND-death appears as one in the 'Elegies'* "; but this retrospective synthesis of divergent moods expressed in the elegies—some are ten years apart in composition—severely forces the issue.[4] Rather than adopt new metaphors and terminologies, Rilke broadens his old ones so that over the years they themselves are transformed by new contexts. In a letter of 1903 (to Kappus, December 23) during his most intense period of religiosity, Rilke had this to say: "As the bees collect honey, so do we fetch the sweetest out of everything in order to build him," the god still being created. The same metaphor appears in the Hulewicz letter twenty years later, yet the context has drastically shifted: "We are the bees of the invisible. We pilfer distractedly the honey of the visible to collect it in the big golden hive of the invisible." Further:

The *Elegies* show us at this work, at the work of these continual conversions of the beloved visible and tangible into the invisible vibrations and excitation of our own nature, which introduces new vibration-frequencies into the vibration-spheres of the universe. (Since different elements in the cosmos are only different vibration exponents, we prepare for ourselves in this way not only intensities of a spiritual nature but also, who knows, new bodies, metals, nebulae and constellations.)

Rilke's notion about the fading of human essence into what seem to be atomic particles that through vibrations are reconstituted into different and new elements is at variance with his own acceptance of identity transposition from life into death and his Orphic myth.

It is difficult to see Rilke's method as other than an act of intellectual desperation in attempting to piece together an original vision of the condition and fate of man. He nibbled at all ideas, gathered congenial kernels from fields as far apart as science and occultism, and in final alarm at the heterogeneity of the idea-stockpile, he attempted a fusion. To the reader who saw in the sonnets evidence of belief in soul-migration, noting the Etruscan bird that transported the human soul, Rilke said "no"; though his letters consistently carry the religious dateline of the Catholic calendar, it was a fetish that seemed not inconsistent with his anti-religious views; when the angels of the elegies were viewed as Christian, he objected by saying that they were Islamic instead, although Mohammed's hieratical angelic hosts are completely un-Rilkean. Rilke's strength lies in his persuasive and subtle poetic expression of hypotheses and intuition, and not in the formulation of an integrated, doctrinaire system.

Relieved of the immense strain of the elegies, Rilke for two years contented himself with prolific correspondence and a devoted translation of the bulk of Valéry's volume of poetry *Charmes* before continuing with his own. It was an ascetic pause that Rilke thought necessary before searching for other "inner resources" as means for a new personal transformation. From then on flowed poetry of every description from the impressionistic to the metaphysical, a profusion of styles that reminds one of the *New Poems* period. Two main strains alternate: a lyrical one that finds most of its expression in the songlike poems written in French and abstract poetry composed in German. Marga Wertheimer, his secretary, in describing Rilke's work habits at the time, tells us that he felt it necessary to live in a language other than that in which he wrote, so that when writing in German he would speak French and vice versa; he wanted to shut out any conflicting sound while listening with his inner ear and writing with pure concentration.[5] Rilke was testing the absolute limit of language and at best he achieved a purity that surpassed some poetry that had gone before.

Just as Liliencron, Jacobsen, Baudelaire, Kierkegaard and Hölderlin had been midwives to his poetry in previous days, Valéry — the magician who wove spells (*charmes*) — served the same function in Rilke's last years.[6] Whenever Rilke made what he felt to be a significant consolidation in his poetry, he regarded it as a base for self-transcendence. Periodically certain key poems would injunctively point to new conquests to be made.

> *Oh, ich weiss, ich begreife*
> *Wesen und Wandel der Namen;*
> *in dem Innern der Reife*
> *ruht der ursprüngliche Samen,*
>
> *nur unendlich vermehrt.*
>
> *Dass es ein Göttliches binde,*
> *hebt sich das Wort zur Beschwörung,*
> *aber, statt dass es schwinde,*
> *steht es im Glühn der Erhörung.*
>
> *singend und unversehrt.*    (sw ii,256)

> *Oh, I know, I understand*
> *the essence and change of names;*
> *in the inmost of ripeness*
> *rests the primordial seed,*
>
> *only endlessly multiplied.*

*Because bound by something godly,*
*the word rises in conjuration,*
*but, instead of fading, it*
*stands in the glow of favorable hearing,*

*singing and unconsumed.*

The Rilkean act of naming, a magical incantation, aimed to reveal the essence and root meaning of words and their relatedness to phenomena. In fragments and a completed poem called "Der Magier," the poet is equated with the magician who penetrates into the powerful circle of language, binds words to his will, and creates an equipoise between himself and everything he is not: the conjuring word shrinks the world into a confronting essence.

Several programmatic poems reveal Rilke's intention:

> *Da dich das geflügelte Entzücken*
> *über manchen frühen Abgrund trug,*
> *baue jetzt der unerhörten Brücken*
> *kühn berechenbaren Bug.*        (sw ıı,157)

> *Just as winged rapture carried you*
> *over many an earlier [7] abyss,*
> *now build for the incredible bridges*
> *a boldly calculable arch.*

With calculated daring he intends a new and "clear, purified achievement," an intimately inwoven language. To make the transition from the poetry of intuition and dictation to the calculated, magical naming-language, he must transcend the idea of *Mitwirken*, the spontaneous participation in the flow of things extolled in the poem "As long as you catch the self-cast . . ." that had programmatically set the stage in January, 1922, for the elegies and sonnets.

Another programmatic poem, dedicated to Merline, celebrates the beginning of work during the fall of 1923 at Muzot. In it he compares his heart to a swing: "not to stay is the essence of swinging / . . . and now, the commanded return (*Umkehr*)." Not only does a swing return to the position it has left (for Rilke this meant the time of the deliberately constructed "object" poems contained in the *Neue Gedichte*), but when it receives the proper push (*Stoss*) the swing overshoots or transcends the original position. This intention Rilke brilliantly metaphorized in the heart-swing poem.

From theory to practice was one short step that resulted in the magical enunciation of a keyword analogically defined and then elaborated. The action of naming, defining, and transforming may readily be seen by sampling the line openings of some typical poems:

*Lächeln . . . , beinah Gesicht*
*dieser gelockten Gelände.*                    (sw II,147)

*Smile . . . almost face*
*of this curly-haired landscape.*

*Dies ist Besitz: dass uns vorüberflog*
*die Möglichkeit des Glücks.*                    (sw II,152)

*This is possession: that which flew past us,*
*the possibility of happiness.*

*Flugsand der Stunden. Leise fortwährende Schwindung . . .*
                                      (sw II,159)

*Wind-sand of hours quiet, continuous fading . . .*

*Innres der Hand. Sohle, die nicht mehr geht*
*als auf Gefühl.*                    (sw II,178)

*Innerside of the hand.*[8] *Sole that no longer walks*
*except on feeling.*

*Nacht. Oh du in Tiefe gelöstes*
*Gesicht an meinem Gesicht.*                    (sw II,178)

*Night. Oh, you in depth dissolved*
*face, close to my face.*

*Wege des Lebens. Plötzlich sind es die Flüge,*
*die uns erheben über das mühsame Land; . . .*
                                      (sw II,475)

*Ways of Life. Suddenly it is flights*
*that lift us over that wearisome land; . . .*

*Spiegel, du Doppelgänger des Raums! . . .*    (sw 11,471)

*Mirror, you double of the space! . . .*

*Schaukel des Herzens. O sichere, an welchem unsichtbaren*
*Aste befestight? . . .*                     (sw 11,478)

*Swing of the heart. O secure one, on which invisible*
*branch are you fastened? . . .*

*Königsherz. Kern eines hohen*
*Herrscherbaums. Balsamfrucht.*              (sw 11,500)

*King's Heart. Kernel of a tall*
*ruler's tree. Balsam fruit.*

*Urne, Fruchtknoten des Mohns—*             (sw 11,502)

*Urn, fruitknot of poppy—*

*Die Puppe. Versuchung!*
*Die geladene Puppe die in den Abgrund fällt*    (sw 11,460)

*The doll. Temptation!*
*The stuffed doll which falls into the abyss*

*Schweigen. Wer inniger schwieg,*
*rührt an die Wurzeln der Rede.*             (sw 11,258)

*Silence. Who fervently remains silent*
*touches the roots of speech.*

*. . . Klage? Wäre sie nicht: jüngerer Jubel nach unten.*
                                            (sw 11,272)

*. . . Lament? Was she not: younger jubilation, downward.*

*Dumpfe Erde: wie hiess es, ihr jeden*
*Stein entringen als wie aus Fäusten; . . .*    (sw 11,145)

*Torpid earth: how was it to wrest*
*every stone from it as out of fists; . . .*

*Weinbergterrassen, wie Manuale:*
*Sonnenanschlag den ganzen Tag.*           (SW II,147)

*Vineyard Terraces, like keyboards:*
*Sunbeat the entire day.*

*. . . . Wandlung*
*Hymnen im Innern, Tanz vor der Arche,*
*Aufruhr und Aufzug im reifenden Wein.*   (SW II,480)

*. . . . Transformation*
*Hymns of the inner, dance before the ark,*
*commotion and rise in ripening wine.*

Tough, aphoristic thought-kernels—around which images accrete—mark these new poems and fragments. The abstract is concretized and the concrete is conjuringly transformed into the abstract so that nothing is what it seems but yet possesses a relativistic meaning. Rilke imperatively says: "From indescribable transformations stem such structures—: Feel and believe!" A disciplined intuitive logic, a description of phenomena by viewing things in action, all these create a third dimension of experience in poetry. In this pure field of experiential consciousness, the poet seeks the essence or *eidos* of occurrences by momentarily isolating an object from its environment. Contemporary philosophers who, like Husserl, espouse phenomenology have found a mine of illustrations in the poetry of Rilke's last years.

By giving unusual and antithetical attributes to objects, by intellectualizing figures of speech, intensely personalizing abstractions, and depersonalizing specific objects Rilke achieves some peculiar surrealistic effects: Weight falls from a sleeper like rain that falls from a reclining cloud, gravitation hurls through a standing person as does a drink through thirst, odors stand in alleys, a center withdraws itself from everything, noise attends the breaking of silence from a mountain of silence, birds dive

upward, hands walk on waters, streets wander, our possession is loss, loss is our possession. Many of the lines have an
experimental roughness, but others attain a stunningly
polished permanence. What gives these lines and poems
their Rilkean stamp is the aching transience and mo-
mentariness of all experience viewed; little solidifies into
framed and graspable moments of time, "nowhere does the
circle close."

A brilliant compactness of lines that enclose difficult
ideas and concretize the metaphysical is evident in almost
all of the new "magical and naming" poems:

> *Durch den sich Vögel werfen, ist nicht der*
> *vertraute Raum, der die Gestalt dir steigert.*
> *(Im Freien, dorten, bist du dir verweigert*
> *und schwindest weiter ohne Wiederkehr.)*
>
> *Raum greift aus uns und übersetzt die Dinge;*
> *dass dir das Dasein eines Baums gelinge,*
> *wirf Innenraum um ihn, aus jenem Raum,*
> *der in dir west. Umgieb ihn mit Verhaltung.*
> *Er grenzt sich nicht. Erst in der Eingestaltung*
> *in dein Verzichten wird er wirklich Baum.*

(sw ɪɪ,167–68)

["Through that which birds hurl themselves is not the /
intimate room that intensifies your form. / (In the free
space, there, you are self-denied / and fade further without
return.) // Space reaches out of us and translates the
things; so that you / achieve the reality of a tree / throw
inner space around it out of that space / that resides in
you. Surround it with mastery. / It does not bound itself.
Only when it takes its place / in your renunciation does it
truly become a tree."] By renunciation Rilke implies a
giving up of the ordinary life-reality concepts and turning
one's self inside-out so that the all-containing inner space
(as distinct from the viewable space of birds) absorbs
external objects into the inner realities.

Of the many poems that aim at magical naming and
capturing the essence of the object or concept in its
metamorphosis, two particularly illustrate Rilke's compres-

sion of language and its immense suggestibility. Plausibility is gained by the pictorial and realistic treatment of the abstract as well as through a dynamic syntax.

### HANDINNERES

*Innres der Hand. Sohle, die nicht mehr geht*
*als auf Gefühl. Die sich nach oben hält*
*und im Spiegel*
*himmlische Strassen empfängt, die selber*
*wandelnden.*
*Die gelernt hat, auf Wasser zu gehn,*
*wenn sie schöpft,*
*die auf den Brunnen geht,*
*aller Wege Verwandlerin.*
*Die auftritt in anderen Händen.*
*die ihresgleichen*
*zur Landschaft macht:*
*wandert und ankommt in ihnen,*
*sie anfüllt mit Ankunft.*          (sw 11,178)

### INNERSIDE OF THE HAND

*Innerside of the hand. Sole that no longer walks*
*except on feeling. That holds itself upward*
*and in the mirror*
*receives celestial streets, that themselves*
*change.*
*That has learnt to walk on the waters,*
*as she ladles,*
*she who walks on the wells,*
*transformer of all ways.*
*That reappears in other hands,*
*transforming its like*
*into a landscape:*
*wanders and arrives in them,*
*fills them with annunciation.*

The infinite tenderness of the hand and its power to transmit through gesture and contact the inmost feeling was a thought that Rilke had often wished to capture. Here he has done it magnificently with puns on wandering and change, through shifting motions (walking, going, appearing, wandering, transforming), and allusions Bibli-

cal and mundane. It is the magician's conjuring hands—
showing his open palms to the audience and then working
a transformation. Through illusion, essence is caught, but
in the gesture of allusion it fluidly points to the future.

### VERGÄNGLICHKEIT

*Flugsand der Stunden. Leise fortwährende Schwindung*
*auch noch des glücklich gesegneten Baus.*
*Leben weht immer. Schon ragen ohne Verbindung*
*die nicht mehr tragenden Säulen heraus.*

*Aber Verfall: ist er trauriger, als der Fontäne*
*Rückkehr zum Spiegel, den sie mit Schimmer bestaubt?*
*Halten wir uns dem Wandel zwischen die Zähne,*
*dass er uns völlig begreift in sein schauendes Haupt.*

(sw II,159)

### TRANSITORINESS

*Wind-sand of hours. Quiet, continuous fading*
*even of happily blessed building structures.*
*Life ever flutters. Already without joining,*
*the unsupporting columns range up.*

*But decline: is it more sad than the fountain's*
*return to the mirror, pollinating it with shimmer?*
*Let us stay between the teeth of Change*
*so that he fully understands us in his contemplative head.*

Rilke attains tension through conflict between structure
and content as well as through the clash of contrasts. In
the poem "Handinneres," the lines are irregular and rhyme
schemes are absent; yet links of metaphors are so strong
that we are confronted by a single dramatic allegory. In
"Vergänglichkeit," Rilke's cross-rhymes tightly lock ideas
and lines; yet, paradoxically, within the body of the poem
there is a complete dissolution of reality. Life, the poet
implies, is as transitory as the gusts of wind which through
attrition make a desert of man's creations; the only con-
stancy is transitoriness. Provocative effects are obtained
by juxtapositions like *wind-sand* hours, *blessed* building,
*unsupporting* columns, *stay* between teeth of Change; yet

the proliferation of unorthodox attributes becomes a technique so glaringly artificial that at times no amount of poetic ingenuity can hide it. Rilke's poetic ingenuity abounds in devices like hovering accents and vocalizations that imitate the sense of the words, devices that barely prevent these poems from becoming cadenced prose. But more rewarding is Rilke's sensitivity for nuances that branch out of the basic image. The wind-sand in "transitoriness" that has such a devasting effect in the first stanza happily turns into pollen dust in the second. No sooner does this happen than Rilke deliberately questions the difference in value between either event; by indirection, one is as melancholic as the other.

The cryptic nature of many of the lines in the poems of this period require acquaintance with Rilkean terminology and metaphoric play. Here we again meet the symbols of fountain, turn, change, and others that belong to Rilke's special vocabulary. For instance the fountain visually symbolizes the unity of the recurrent ascent into life and the descent into death and becomes an idea synonymous with transitoriness. The last two lines of "Transitoriness" yield their meaning if we recall Rilke's strenuous questions as to what awareness the angel and other creatures have of man. Here the concept "change" is itself personified as a creature which eventually will grind us to dust or pollen (does it matter?), but if we are able to assert ourselves and momentarily stay (*bleiben* or *halten*, Rilkean keywords), perhaps "change" will become aware of us. Later Rilke was to give this idea another turn by saying, "you are nowhere more secure  as in danger" (SW II,291). Rilke's frequent personification of concepts and placing it in a realistic context constitute pure intellectual and experimental play.

Among other distinct types of poetry Rilke wrote during the last years are what we might call, with qualification, praise and nature poems.

> *Aber die Winter! Oh diese heimliche*
> *Einkehr der Erde. Da um die Toten*
> *in dem reinen Rückfall der Säfte*

*Kühnheit sich sammelt,*
*künftiger Frühlinge Kühnheit.*
*Wo das Erdenken geschieht*
*unter der Starre; wo das von den grossen*
*Sommern abgetragene Grün*
*wieder zum neuen*
*Einfall wird und zum Spiegel des Vorgefühls;*
*wo die Farbe der Blumen*
*jenes Verweilen unserer Augen vergisst.*

(sw 11,183–84)

But the winters! That mysterious
inward turn of the earth. Where around the dead,
in the pure recession of sap,
boldness gathers itself,
boldness of future Springs.
Where contemplation occurs
under the frozen; where the worn-out green
of the great summers
again becomes a new
invention and a mirror of premonition;
where the color of flowers
forgets the lingering of our eyes.

Here, Rilke pulls together the various strands of thought in praise of winter that fragmentedly appeared in early diary entries, in the bitter "Fourth Elegy," and in the *Sonnets to Orpheus*. For the first time his thoughts on the hibernating strength of winter are given a unity, without personal intrusion or strained analogy. It represents a picture of serene withdrawal into a Rilkean realm where the dead nourish the roots of the future.

VORFRÜHLING

*Härte schwand. Auf einmal legt sich Schonung*
*an der Wiesen aufgedecktes Grau.*
*Kleine Wasser ändern die Betonung.*
*Zärtlichkeiten, ungenau,*

*greifen nach der Erde aus dem Raum.*
*Wege gehen weit ins Land und zeigens.*

*Unvermutet siehst du seines Steigens*
*Ausdruck in dem leeren Baum.* (sw II,158)

EARLY SPRING

*Hardness faded. Concern suddenly lay*
*upon the meadow's uncovered gray.*
*Small brooks change the emphasis.*
*Tendernesses, vague,*

*reach for the earth, out of space.*
*Paths go far into the land and point.*
*Unexpectedly you see its rise*
*express itself in the empty tree.*

At times the songlike nature poems receive a startling
impetus from the "conjuration" technique as waters
intoxicate the land and the breathlessly drinking Spring
staggers blinded into the green, springs "mouth" upward
almost too rapidly, or maidens arrange the grape-locks of
the curly-haired god. But the nature poems could also take
a seriously subjective turn:

*An der sonngewohnten Strasse, in dem*
*hohlen halben Baumstamm, der seit lange*
*Trog ward, eine Oberfläche Wasser*
*in sich leis erneuernd, still' ich meinen*
*Durst: des Wassers Heiterkeit und Herkunft*
*in mich nehmend durch die Handgelenke.*
*Trinken schiene mir zu viel, zu deutlich;*
*aber diese wartende Gebärde*
*holt mir helles Wasser ins Bewusstsein.*

*Also, kämst du, brauch ich, mich zu stillen,*
*nur ein leichtes Anruhn meiner Hände,*
*sei's an deiner Schulter junge Rundung,*
*sei es an den Andrang deiner Brüste.* (sw II,166)

*On the sun-accustomed street, in the*
*hollow half-tree-trunk that long*
*has become trough, surface water*
*quietly replenishes itself; should I still my*
*thirst: the water's gayness and origin*
*I could absorb through the wrists.*

*Drinking seems to me too much, too obvious;*
*but this patient gesture*
*brings clear water into my consciousness.*

*Then, if you came, I would need, to quiet myself,*
*only a light resting of my hands,*
*be it on your shoulder's young rounding,*
*be it on the urging of your breasts.*

In many of the poems after the elegies, Rilke seems to have found tranquillity: no longer is there a lament about the impossibility of love or the lost future-beloved; the tender contact of water on the wrist or the resting of hands on the loved one are sufficient. But the vast and tranquil landscape of Rilke's poetry is at times disturbed by lightning outbursts, erotic storms. Without going into the question of sexuality and artistic productivity in late age, we know that the septuagenarians Goethe, Gide, and Yeats exhibited emotional proclivities that would have done justice to younger men. Though Rilke was close to fifty, his failing health added years to his age but not to his capacity to respond to the stimulus of the eighteen-year-old Viennese Erika Mitterer. A two-year exchange of correspondence in verse ensued after she sent him a poem in May, 1924. In turn of phrase and terminology, hers was a Rilkean poem: "You were within me . . . / And much that I built in silent hours was no longer dreamable." Rilke could not resist Erika's plea and veneration: "grant me one smile, a small one / . . . as you rest in the autumn shade of your grove"; "let me be incense in your dome." Up until then, Rilke had been responding to his own questions and emotions in his essentially monologuistic poetry, so that the new dialogue in verse has the fascination of a relation in which the partners spur each other on. From his Orphic grove, Rilke answered in the unmistakable voice of the sonnets: "And were I the dance-exhausted dead, / since you recognized me, I exist; / obeying your inner promptings, / I silently partake of your bread; / you nourished me, and I came into being. . . ." Few of the love duets that follow are distinguished poetically; still, the various Rilke poems that touch on childhood and his progressing illness are relentlessly honest and self-revealing.

Erika had become for Rilke a confidante who responded in tune with his fantasies and intimate thoughts. By confessing his occasional nightmares to Erika, he seemed sure of her indulgent approval and understanding. Of all the poems on childhood, perhaps the following permits the closest view of Rilke's memory-limbo:

> Warst Du's die ich im starken Traum umfing
> und an mich hielt—und der ich mit dem Munde
> ablöste von der linken Brust ein Ding,
> ein braunes Glasaug wie von einem Hunde,
> womit die Kinder spielen . . . , oder Reh,
> wie es als Spielzeug dient?—Ich nahm es mir
> erschrocken von den Lippen. Und ich seh,
> wie ich Dir's zeige und es dann verlier.
> Du aber, die das alles nicht erschreckte,
> hobst Dein Gesicht, als sagte das genug.
> Und es schien schauender, seit die entdeckte
> geküsste Brust das Auge nicht mehr trug.    (sw ii,305)

> Were you the one whom I embraced, held close,
> in a strong dream—pulling a thing away with
> my mouth from your left breast, like one of those
> brown glassy eyes of creatures children play with:
> eye of a dog perhaps . . . , or else a roe,
> as this serves for a toy. In sudden fright
> I snatched it from my lips. I see myself show
> the thing to you, then how it rolls from sight.
> But you, whom fear meanwhile had not affected,
> lifted your face, as [if] that said all you'd say:
> which more beholding seemed, since the detected
> kissed breast had had the eye taken away.

Resenting the illness that was alienating him from his "brother body," Rilke more and more frequently raises cries of pathetic protest: "I who went out in assent to both life and death now recoil from the battle called sickness." He speaks of an open wound into which he feels himself slipping, "I stand in my own blood, / in the torture-bath of my own blood. . . ." Erika wished to see him but he fended her off: "Partly do I call you, partly do I keep you from me / so that I do not destroy the beautiful magic. / I say to myself as I hear your pulse: are you not here?" Her insistence won out and Erika visited with him for two days in November of 1925. Several poems followed the encounter and the last of these is as unusual for Rilke in structure as is the poignancy and harmony in his relationship with Erika.

*Taube, die draussen blieb,    ausser dem Taubenschlag,*
*wieder in Kreis und Haus,    einig der Nacht, dem Tag,*
*weiss sie die Heimlichkeit,    wenn sich der Einbezug*
*fremdester Schrecken schmiegt    in den gefühlten Flug.*

*Unter den Tauben, die    allergeschonteste,*
*niemals gefährdetste,    kennt nicht die Zärtlichkeit;*
*wiedererholtes Herz    ist das bewohnteste:*
*freier durch Widerruf    freut sich die Fähigkeit.*

*Über dem Nirgendssein    spannt sich das Überall!*
*Ach der geworfene,    ach der gewagte Ball,*
*füllt er die Hände nicht    anders mit Wiederkehr:*
*rein um sein Heimgewicht    ist er mehr.* (sw ii,318–19)

*Dove, that remained outside,    outside the dove-cot,*
*again in orbit and home,    one with the night, the day,*
*she knows mysteriousness    when the insinuation*
*of strangest fright clings    in the felt flight.*

*Amid the doves, the    most sheltered one,*
*never endangered one,    does not know tenderness;*
*recuperated heart    is most inhabited:*
*freer through disavowal    jubilates capableness.*

*Above the nowhere-being    vaults the everywhere!*
*Alas the thrown,    alas the hazarded ball,*
*fills it not the hands    other than with return:*
*pure with its native weight    it is more.*

The poem was his "thirteenth answer" to Erika—a display of virtuosity and restrained sentiment. In structure it is one of its kind in Rilke's repertoire. It can be read straight through line for line, read in either column or chiastically from one line in the first column to the next in the second. Elements of contrast and appositeness are tightly laced into the lines. The boldness of structure defies the metrical confinements of the poem and exquisitely is one with Rilke's existential thought: Dare to transcend the limitations of life which will be all the more meaningful for the experience; the dove, the ball that have been outside their sphere have felt terror and strangeness—the sheltered have not.

Rilke's most effective weapon in his battle with illness was the translation into poetry of the joy he found in the natural surroundings of Muzot and especially in the massive rose garden on the estate. Although he had delighted in walking about barefoot to feel himself close to the earth, more often than not he could be seen about the Sierre locale wearing spats and a monocle, affecting the airs of a Parisian boulevardier consonant with the floodtide of poetry that came to him in French. During his preschool days in Prague, his mother snobbishly had made French his first language and in his youth, like Stefan George, he had to make a choice between French and German as a language for poetic expression. Up until 1922 a negligible number of French poems, some 28, were composed, but from then until the end of 1926 he wrote about four hundred. In his lifetime he saw to the publication of the volume called *Vergers* [*Orchards*] and edited *Les Roses,* and *Les Fenêtres* [*The Windows*].

Hardly could Rilke have foreseen the storm that would be caused in petty and unenlightened German circles by Valéry's publication of some of Rilke's French poems in the publication *Commerce* and other poems in Gide's *Nouvelle Revue Française.* The disdain shown by the George group's unwillingness to publish Rilke in its noted *Blätter für die Kunst* was the reason a number of paltry writers gave for Rilke's turning to French; they felt it to be an act of revenge and treachery, a deserting of the mother-tongue, and a slur on patriotism. Rilke, who claimed that he never read criticism, was aghast. What may have shaken him even more was Lou Andreas-

Salomé's accusation that many of his French poems were "the rapture of a blasphemous masochism." Weakly he defended himself against something that should only have merited his contempt, mumbling phrases like "happy inspiration" and "irrefutable dictation" as the cause of the French poems "which for me signifies the happiest having-been-given." [9]

Rilke's French poems do not measure up to those of his admired figures—Baudelaire, Mallarmé, and Valéry—but they have a graciousness of tone and a shadowy delicacy unlike anything he ever wrote in German. He needed to write these poems—exercises for the left hand, or cooking, as he described their creation. For one thing, Rilke was fascinated by the transformation that ideas and images undergo when rendered in two different languages; language, he felt, has a life of its own, which he wished to experience and to dominate. The ease, mastery, and creative abundance of these poems made Rilke feel young again and sure of his instincts. Alternating between the writing of French and German poems, the contrasts he achieved between subtlety and boldness illuminate their differing potentials. The "untamable god," Eros, seems formidable in the German poem of that name, but his "indomptable feu" and "mouvement hagard et hasardeux" in the French poem ("O faisons tout pour cacher son visage") are lean and weak. On his favorite theme of farewell, his French lines have a nostalgic distillation that would be hard to duplicate in German:

> *Tous mes adieux sont faits. Tant de départs*
> *m'ont lentement formé dès mon enfance.*
> *Mais je reviens encor, je recommence*
> *ce franc retour libère mon regard.*
>
> *Ce qui me reste, c'est de le remplir,*
> *et ma joie toujours impénitente*
> *d'avoir aimé des choses ressemblantes*
> *à ces absences qui nous font agir.*  (sw II,553)

["All my farewells are made. So many leave takings / have slowly formed me since my childhood. / Yet I again return. I begin anew; / this frank return shall liberate my gaze. // It remains for me to fill it, / and my joy always will be impenitent / in having loved the things resembling those absences which set us to act."]

> On arrange et on compose
> les mots de tant de façons,
> mais comment arriverait-on
> à égaler une rose?   (*From* Vergers, sw II,551)

["One arranges and composes / words in all ways, / but how shall one be able to match a rose?"]

Rilke composed twenty-four rose poems in French, so that slowly the rose joins Rilke's other transvalued symbols of orthodoxy—fish, wine, bread. The petals of the rose, each like a shroud, repose one against the other in the heart of sleep and silence; they are like leaves in a half-open book. A thing *par excellence*, the rose embodies the supreme essence of our fleeting sojourn; it is forlorn and surrounded by loneliness; it is the tender interlude in our continual parting, the expression of love and pain. The rose is a contradiction: ardent and at the same time cool. When the poet places it against his closed eyes, it is as if a thousand eyelids have been superimposed, "O musique des yeux" [O music of the eyes]. It—or "she"—is the consoler during hours of despair and life-rejection, a single identity-conscious rose amid roses, a flower shrine to "Saint Rose," it is the perfect friend, and its uniqueness among flowers which merely decorate consists in transfiguration. It shares our existence; its relation to other flowers, however, is as ineffable as the relation of the angel's song to the words of man. More than being rooted in existence and in the death realm of "the mothers," the rose experiences the simultaneity of birth and death.

Instead of having answered his original question, "How shall one match a rose?", Rilke asks "Does she wish to be a solitary rose, nothing-but-rose? / Her own sleep under all the eyelids?" With slight modification this became his choice for his tombstone inscription. Although the question mark is omitted, we hear the echo.

*Rose, oh reiner Widerspruch, Lust,*
*Niemandes Schlaf zu sein unter soviel*
*Lidern.*

*Rose, oh pure contradiction, desire,*
*to be no one's sleep under so many*
*lids.*

Rilke's rose has been a constant companion symbol throughout his works, gathering so many associative meanings that any one meaning could easily be contradicted by another. In the earliest poems, including the *Cornet,* the rose connoted festive and sentimental love, and it was essentially the esthetic rose of longing, death, and a graveyard flower. In the period of the *New Poems,* the rose became a work of art and a transcendental, impressionistic flower whose open, inner sea mirrored the heavens. Only in the French poems does it flower into an existence symbol, joining life and death, with cultic significance that links antiquity and modern times. Never is Rilke's rose a realistic botanic specimen.

At Worpswede he had found a new, self-engendered therapeutic tenderness by placing a rose on his closed eyes. Both the petal and the lid of the eye could be restfully protective against the intensity of gazing that would often weary Rilke. But he could turn this feeling into the most tender expression in poetic lines that describe a quiet submerging into the sleep of a loved one and kissing her eyelids from within. Such pretty conceits could, without warning, change into the most macabre associations of the rose with the dead and the opening of the lids to find thousands of eyes, eyes that could be broken like stems of flowers or eyes that could kill. In contrast to the life and agitation within the rose, he could also see the untouched *center* of the rose, "an angelic space where one remains quite still." In a relevant connection Rilke wrote, "See, I do not exist, but if I did, / I would be the center of the poem, / the precise to whom the imprecise and the unfelt is contrary." The poem is like the rose, the poet at its center whose open but fulfilled space is a contradiction to the world of man. Rilke was to make this space-center a rendezvous for lovers, in one of his last poems.

The words "pure contradiction" in the epitaph poem are perfectly descriptive of Rilke's life which was rooted in "contradiction" (*Widerspruch*). It harbored the conflict between life and art, narcissism and relatedness, staying and parting, anticipation and rejection, saintliness and sensuality, to existing in isolation for one's self or sharing with others, metaphorizing and concretizing, submission and assertion, lyricism and didacticism, neo-romanticism and mysticism, inspiration and dictation or programmatic work. The rose is the memorial flower of Orpheus and a thematic representation of Narcissus' prayer answered, but also it is the pure space in which the lovers meet. Although the out-going Orpheus and the self-centered Narcissus are spiritual antagonists, each is related to the rose and each is a pseudonym for the artist. The eternal aroma (*Duft*) of the rose is an inspirational and narcissistic source for the artist, but so is the music of the rose ("rose . . . o musique des yeux") the song of Orpheus. In short, the rose is the embodiment not only of contradiction but *pure* contradiction because it reconciles all opposites and it resolves all tensions. In the rose, the very ancient and universal object of the *unio mystica*, Rilke had found a symbol for the great unity he attempted to impose upon such diversities as life and death, especially in the elegies.

No definitive interpretation of the rose-epitaph is possible because each word collides and merges and pulls away from the meaning and parenthetical thought of every other word. Lurking in the epitaph are elements of the playful, the dark, the apodictic, and exclamatory astonishment. A huge pun sweeps through the lines that suggest the poet at the pure (*reiner*, Rainer) center with his songs (*Lider, Lieder, musique des yeux*, eyelids of man and petal-lids of the rose). "Lust" in German has the multiple meanings of carnal lust, desire, caprice, pleasure, passion, inclination, longing; each could appropriately carry different nuances for the entire thought of the lines. "Lust" applies equally well in grammar and thought to the pleasure of "contradiction" and the desire of the prodigal son to belong to no one, to be no one's sleep, not even God's. It also applies to the dead, "du leidenschaftlich Toter" (you passionate dead); the dead live and the self-contained rose extends into their realm—contradiction upon contradiction.

Dark undertones rage in the lines which suggest that sleep is not sleep. At the same time, the interjection "oh," expressing critical surprise at the audacity of the symbolic rose to yearn for the impossible. Ultimately, then, the rose is a surrogate for Rilke; both have an exterior tenderness but a thorny, stubborn, assertive inner will to independence. With the epitaph, Rilke achieved what for Kafka had almost always been elusive, namely the equilibrium point of a perfect paradox.

Rilke could not tear himself away from the unlimited possibilities of the rose symbol so that amid the superb cluster of his very last poems is "Ankunft" ["Arrival"]: "In a rose stands your bed, loved one / . . . . suddenly: facing you, I will be born in the eye." The *standing* bed, the *future* birth, the *deathless* sleep, birth in the eye of the rose and the beloved, these are Rilke's fond paradoxes and juxtapositions. That "arrival" and the symbolic birthbed should appear when Rilke felt his strength slipping away fast was not intended to be ironic but a willful attempt to replenish the resources that had created the constellation of French poems. Even then Rilke was ready for another turning, another transcendence:

> *Jetzt wär es Zeit, dass Götter träten aus*
> *bewohnten Dingen . . .*
> *Und dass sie jede Wand in meinem Haus*
> *umschlügen. Neue Seite. Nur der Wind,*
> *den solches Blatt im Wenden würfe, reichte hin,*
> *die Luft, wie eine Scholle umzuschaufeln:*
> *ein neues Atemfeld. O Götter, Götter!*
> *Ihr Oftgekommnen, Schläfer in den Dingen,*
> *die heiter aufstehn, die sich an den Brunnen,*
> *die wir vermuten, Hals und Antlitz waschen*
> *und die ihr Ausgeruhtsein leicht hinzutun*

*zu dem, was voll scheint, unserm vollen Leben.*
*Noch einmal sei es euer Morgen, Götter.*
*Wir wiederholen. Ihr allein seid Ursprung.*
*Die Welt steht auf mit euch, und Anfang glänzt*
*an allen Bruchstelln unseres Misslingens . . .*

(SW II,185)

Now it were time that gods step out of
housed things . . .
And that they overturn every wall in my house.
A new page. Only the wind, which such a
page would throw in turning, sufficed
to upturn the air like sod:
a new breathing space. O gods, gods!
You oft-comers, sleepers in things,
who gaily rise, who wash neck and face
at the wells we surmise
and who lightly add their rested state
to that which seems full, our full life.
Once more let it be your morning, gods.
We repeat: You alone are origin.
The world arises with you, and beginning
shines through all the gaps of our failing . . .

The rose of antiquity and the gods of antiquity resurrected
were for Rilke a wish for the return of greatness—epochal
and personal—and a rebellion against the incurable leukemia that was upsetting the delicate balance between his
mind and body.

Pathetic and human are his cries for a new breathing
space and a new beginning, even an enigmatic new birth
that notably has no tense:

*Unaufhaltsam, ich will die Bahn vollenden,*
*mich schreckt es, wenn mich ein Sterbliches hält.*
*Einmal hielt mich ein Schooss.*
*Ihm sich entringen, war tödlich:*
*ich rang mich ins Leben. Aber sind Arme so tief,*
*sind sie so fruchtbar, um ihnen*
*durch die beginnliche Not*
*neuer Geburt zu entgehn?*    (SW II,184)

["Relentlessly, I want to complete the path; / it frightens me when a mortal thing holds me. / Once a womb held me. / Outstruggling it was deadly: / I struggled into life. But are arms so deep / are they so fruitful that through them one can / escape the beginning travail / of a new birth?"] To see life through despite the inevitable pains and terrors it holds is Rilke's clear wish in these knotted lines. If the lines hint at the need for renewal of life and poetry, little time was left for either. Amid the trickle of poems late in 1925 and the intermittent ones of 1926, several show the last flash of Rilke's genius—"A Sequel to 'The Bowl of Roses,' " a poem for Count Karl Lanckoroński, "Ankunft" ["Arrival"], "Vollmacht" ["Full Power"] (or "Power of Attorney"), and an "Elegie" to Marina Zwetajewa-Efron.

How conflicting moods could invade Rilke's poetry is rarely seen more clearly than in the two poems he composed on the same day (June 9, 1926): "Vollmacht" and "Elegie." "Vollmacht" revives the tone and thought of one of the *Sonnets to Orpheus* (II, 2) as Rilke "in hot youthfulness" joins the hunters in their destined activity, "eternally in the right . . . urgently close to life." Awkward as it may seem to visualize Rilke as a hunter of anything but images, the sudden urge for a robustness of experience at this point of his life has a powerful rationale. Just as quickly, however, he struck a long and deep note in what might be called the "Eleventh Elegy," with lines that rival those written earlier. He felt the descent into the "all" near: "whoever falls, diminishes not the sacred number. / Every renouncing fall plunges into primal origin and heals," a Rilkean wish phrased aphoristically. And again, on the purpose of being and the relation of life to death: "Would it then be all a game, an equation, a transportation / . . . ." "Not-being. Do you know how often / a blind command carried us through the icy anteroom / of new birth . . . Carried: *us?* A body composed of eyes / refusing under countless lids." This is as close to the notion of reincarnation as Rilke cared to come in his poetry. Praise and lament, memory and future-intimations, rhapsodic and melancholy strains inform this extraordinary composition. With utter finality, Rilke says, "no one helps us ever again to fulfillment as does / our lonely, solitary walk over the sleepless landscape."

Romantically, the Circassian beauty Nimet Eloui Bey, "a woman in love with dreams and tortured by destiny," is associated with his last friendship and his death, although the very last friendship distinction seems to belong to a Beppy Veder. At Muzot while gathering a bouquet of roses for Madame Bey, Rilke stung himself on some thorns and incurred blood poisoning; as we know, however, leukemia already was well on its destructive course.

If we need any evidence that Rilke's thoughts in poetry are organic convictions rather than literary flourishes, we might briefly look at the provisions he made in his last will and testament, written on the evening of October 27, 1925. He implored his friends that in the event his mind should be destroyed by illness, priestly assistance was to be rejected: "Bad enough that in the physical afflictions of my nature I have had to accede to the mediator and negotiator in the doctor; to the movement of my soul, toward the open, any spiritual intermediary would be offensive and repugnant." Again, Rilke's private religiosity brooked no institutional mediation. To avoid arousing the restless spirit of Isabelle de Chevron, he ruled out burial at Sierre and Miège but chose the graveyard situated high up beside the old church at Rarogne: "Its enclosure is one of the first places [in Switzerland] from which I received the wind and light of this countryside" as well as the promises that were later realized at Muzot. Rilke requested an old stone "of the Empire . . . as in the case of my father's grave in Vienna," with the coat of arms used by his geat-grandfather and the "rose" epitaph inscription. He stressed that he regarded *nothing* as his actual personal possession; family pictures were to go to his daughter while other objects were to be at the disposal of Frau Wunderly and her cousin, the owner of Muzot. Since "I was accustomed occasionally to direct a part of the creativity of my nature into letters, nothing stands in the way of the publication of my correspondence"; he also gave his publisher a loyal nod. Letters addressed to him, Rilke bound in tight bundles with notations for each and placed them alphabetically in a heavy oak chest. None of his pictures did he regard as essentially valid, except "those evanescent ones still surviving, in feeling and memory, with a few friends."

In December of 1926, the deathly ill Rilke laboriously penciled a note to Frau Wunderly from the sanatorium at Val-Mont, the "annex" to Muzot, "Day and night, day and night . . . hell! one will have known it." In the same vein, he told his friend Rudolf Kassner about the gruesome cell explosions in his body which he had been ignoring but now had to learn, despite a hundred resistances and sad astonishment, to accommodate with their incommensurable pain.

Under these painful physical and mental conditions, he made his final poem entry in his notebook, accepting death: "Komm du, du letzter, den ich anerkenne," wrote Rilke, "Come you last harbinger whom I acknowledge, / incurable pain in fleshly web." He compares himself to wood that has long resisted fire as well as to the flame which death fans and to which he consents by burning within it. Free, pure, planless as to the future he *ascends* pain's funeral pyre: "Is it still I who burn unrecognizably? / I do not force memories to come to me. / O life, life: to be outside. / And not in flame. No one who knows me." But Rilke, like Wordsworth, was a poet of memory. He could not resist writing four lines in which he reflects that childhood illness was not like the one he presently suffered; then it was "pretense for growing," when everything whispered intimations. The last, unfinished line reads: "Do not mix into the present that which astonished you at the earliest." Rilke was unable to banish memory in his last breath of poetry, and in the act of denial that which was denied emerges with irresistible force. The image of childhood seen by the mind's eye stood so stark and symbolic in his last four lines that he crossed them out immediately; they contradicted his conscious intent.

The devoted concern of his friends reached him in many ways. Princess Marie had timidly suggested that he consult a certain Höller-Hansl, a peasant healer who lived deep in the hills of Styria; all he needed was a person's age and male or female identification in order to send hand-picked curative herbs. Or, she would try to rally his spirits, "You, Serafico, are essentially a magician, and it is from magic that you must take the occult power." Marie's Höller-Hansl and her plea fell on indifferent ears; he was much more attentive to the letters of Lou, which were more abstruse than even his own, on the relationship of the physical to the psychic or spiritual; never did he wish to discuss the medical terminology or meaning of the illness that erupted in black pustules and virulently painful internal aggravations, nor did he accept any ameliorative drugs except those that would permit him to retain clear consciousness at all times. He did not want the "death of the doctors," but, as he said to the trusted Frau Wunderly, "Help me to *my own* death . . . I want my freedom!" Even when talking about the hell he was experiencing, he could in the next breath affirm to his friends that life is infinitely glorious and express his satisfaction at having stood on all the peaks of it.

Dr. Theodor Hämmerli, who attended Rilke in the last critical days put down his impressions [10] with a preciseness which disallows any imaginative tales that might have converted Rilke's human demise into a canonical ascension. "Death," Dr. Hämmerli wrote, "was among the problems of his *oeuvre*, and yet the idea of having to pass away so young was unacceptable to him; he did not believe it possible, perhaps up to the last day of his illness." Rilke "accepted his illness more or less as though it were an inevitable mystery which should not be analyzed too deeply." Quite soon Dr. Hämmerli saw through the Rilkean method of rationalizing and was not offended by "our poor friend" who enjoyed explaining his negative views on medicine and who at the same time implied "that one should insist on curing him, under the condition that he was never to be made aware that what one was going to do was contrary to his view." On the morning of December 29, 1926, Rilke had lost consciousness. "At 3:30 A.M.," Dr. Hämmerli records, "he raised his head slightly, his eyes wide open, and sank back dead into my arms. Mme. Wunderly and the nurse were there."

A few days later, January 2, Rilke was interred in the Swiss graveyard at Rarogne, as he had wished. Of all the accounts of the scene, it is Rilke's friend J. R. von Salis' dramatically simple rendering that has a dignity which Rilke would have appreciated: "A small entourage, consisting of friends who had hurriedly come from all distances and the villagers, after the celebration of the mass for the dead, stood around the open grave on that bitterly cold winter day. The *Gemeindeammann* [the community magistrate] carried the cross and school-children held wreaths in their freezing hands. Eduard Korrodi closed his tribute with verses from the 'First Elegy':

> *They have finally no more need of us, the early-departed,*
> *one is gently weaned from terrestrial things as one mildly*
> *outgrows the breasts of a mother. But we, that have need*
> *of such mighty secrets, we, for whom sorrow is so often a*
> *source of blessed progress, could we exist without them?*

In three words René Morax expressed the feelings of French Switzerland: 'Adieu, grand poète!' "

Even here fortuity and paradox intervened. It was a *René* who spoke the last words as clods of earth poured on Rilke's casket, and standing by in affectionate tribute were the peasants whose religion he scorned but to whom he had endeared himself with donations to restore the nearby Chapel of St. Anne; solitary amid Rilke's friends was Rilke's seventy-six-year-old mother. Of everyone in the locale about Muzot, she was to ask for memorabilia of the son she had brought into the world and now had seen buried. If she, as many others, had never really understood him during his lifetime, it was because his pilgrimage took him audaciously through many dark and lonely landscapes. These have been made visible to us through the visions, anguish, and delights evoked in Rilke's poetry.

# NOTES

[References contained in the bibliography are abbreviated in the notes. SW in the book and in the notes refers to *Rainer Maria Rilke: Sämtliche Werke*, published by the Insel-Verlag and edited by Ernst Zinn.]

## 1—*Between Day and Dream*

1. Rilke's concept of time past and tradition are uniquely personal: ". . . every genuine person must feel himself to be the first, for in the world, which begins with him, there is no history; his fathers and ancestors—from whom he receives culture, strength, manner, and disposition—are contemporaries of his soul and exist within him. . . ." This idea, expressed in the Worpswede diary of 1900, is pervasively real in his life and writings.

2. Information about Rilke's ancestry is a tangle of fact and fiction. Through his Swedish admirer and correspondent Ellen Key, Rilke gave vogue to the notion that he belonged to the ancient Kärnthner nobility. A few of Rilke's contemporaries balked, however, at implications that his lineage went back to heathen kings and regarded it as an affectation similar to Nietzsche's claim to Polish nobility (von Oppeln-Bronikowski, p. 194). Toward the end of his life when status seeking was not a serious criterion, Rilke occasionally was able to admit the legendary aspects of his ancestry (*Letters*, Nölke, p. 55); Simenauer, pp. 105, 399, and Mason, *Rilke*, pp. 204–5, concisely summarize the situation.

3. Vally's tune changed when René broke their engagement. If the more than one hundred unpublished letters

by René to Vally are as idolatrous as the several poems that have survived, she has cause for grievance. With her permission, C. Hirschfeld published Vally's recollections in "Die Rilke-Erinnerungen Valéry von David-Rhonfeld," *Die Horne* (Berlin, 1928–29), VIII. The scorned Vally claims that her pity overcame the physically repulsive features of the young René.

4. A picture of René's "castle" days may be found in a firsthand account by Siegfried Trebitsch, *Chronicle of a Life* (London, 1953). Trebitsch writes of René, "Here was a fellow sufferer . . . who summoned up the courage to declare his unconditional faith in himself" (p. 60). René told Trebitsch that it is one's sacred duty to fulfill God's eleventh commandment: Become what you are.

5. SW IV: "Das Christkind," pp. 63–72 (1894); "Pierre Dumont," pp. 407–14 (1894, published 1932); "Die Näherin," pp. 414–62 (1894, published 1961); "Die Goldene Kiste," pp. 426–32 (1895).

6. Butler, p. 29 f.

7. SW IV, 512–67. Rilke's untitled and undated novella was written sometime between the end of 1898 and the beginning of 1899; first published 1927–28.

8. Ruth Mövius, RMR, p. 152, obtained this statement in conversation with Lou Andreas-Salomé. From the Rilke and Lou correspondence, it is clear that Rilke regarded the *Visions of Christ* as great poems.

9. Parallels between the thinking of Nietzsche and Rilke are provocatively discussed by Fritz Dehn, "Rilke und Nietzsche: Ein Versuch," *Euphorion*, 37 (1936), pp. 1–22; Erich Heller, *The Disinherited Mind*, pp. 123–96; and Walter Kaufmann, *From Shakespeare to Existentialism*, pp. 219–41. Heller's generalization about an early short story, novella, and poem cycle respectively is accurate: "In *Der Apostel* (1896), *Ewald Tragy*, and *Christus-Visions* (1896–97), the effects of Nietzsche's hammering and dynamiting are unmistakable; yet there is not the slightest trace of the depth and complexity of Nietzsche's thought and feeling" (p. 127). Attempts by Heller and Kaufmann to intimately relate Rilke's later poetry to Nietzsche's thoughts steer a hazardous course between discovery and invention. Rejection of traditions in order to start anew, openness to experience, admiration for antiquity, homelessness, ecstatic visions, and

much else Nietzsche and Rilke have in common, but they part ways in attitudes toward the otherworldly, women, childhood, among others. If Nietzsche errs in outer-directed callousness, Rilke errs in favor of self-directed sentimentality. See also, Guardini, *Deutung*, p. 59; Mason, *Lebenshaltung*, p. 65.

10. SW III, 827 (note).

11. Heerikhuizen, p. 271 (facsimile of a letter by Phia Rilke).

12. *Tagebücher aus der Frühzeit*, p. 36.


## 2 – My God is Dark


1. Butler, p. 52.

2. Typical among Rilke's discussions of what prayer meant to him is the following: "Pray: to whom? I cannot tell you. Prayer is a radiation of our being suddenly set afire; it is an infinite and purposeless direction, a brutal accompaniment of our hopes, which travel the universe without reaching any destination. Oh, but I knew this morning how far I am from those greedy ones who, before praying, ask whether God exists. If He no longer or does not yet exist, what difference does it make? My prayer will bring Him into being, for it is entirely a creative thing as it lifts toward the heavens. And if the God that it projects out of itself does not persist at all, so much the better: we will do it over, and it will be less shabby in eternity." (Letter to Mimi Romanelli, January 5, 1910, translated from the French by Moore, p. 108.) Prayer, religion, and love slowly acquire a consonant meaning for Rilke.

3. The various parts of *Das Stunden-Buch* [*The Book of Hours*] originated in 1899, 1901, and 1903; they were edited and revised during April and May of 1905 and published at the end of that year. Revisions were made until 1909. (SW I, pp. 253–366 contains the final version; SW III, pp. 307–73, contains the original first part, "Die Gebete"–"Das Buch vom mönchischen Leben," of *The Book of Hours*.) I have used text illustrations from both the final and the original version which has appeared since 1937. The most complete discussion of origins and text variants is found in

the Mövius study. Rilke's title was inspired by the memory of the *Livres d'heures*, miniature-decorated 15th and 16th century French imitations of Latin breviaries. Rilke transposed these formal liturgical books into personal hours of communing with God.

4. R. Blakeney, *Meister Eckhart* (New York, 1957), p. 206; Mövius, p. 143 f., and others point to differences between the concepts of the mystics and Rilke in regard to God and death. Rilke implies that only after editing *Das Stunden-Buch* for publication was he introduced to the writings of Meister Eckhart: "Without knowing about him, I have for years been his pupil and proclaimer . . . I have grown out beyond him" (Letter to Countess Schwerin, June 5, 1905). As yet we do not know enough about Rilke's early readings, but some contact with the writings of the mystics probably did exist in view of the tone and terminology in *The Book of Hours*.

5. SW III, 291–304.

6. *Tagebücher*, p. 252. Rilke's Worpswede diary shows his swift oscillation in moods from unburdened happiness to necrophilic thoughts and reflections on death. He was fascinated by talk of bodies and remains found in the moorlands, dating back to Roman times.

7. *Ibid.*, p. 388 f.; SW I, 469–74. The text of the poem in the diary and that in *Das Buch der Bilder* differ mainly in matters of punctuation and typography.

8. *Ibid.*, p. 238.

9. *Ibid.*, p. 396 (Nov. 22, 1900).

10. In her memoirs, *Lebensrückblick*, p. 183, Lou wanted to retain the following memory of their essential relationship: "Was I your wife for years, it was because you were the first reality to me, the body and the human indistinguishable one, the undoubtable fact of life itself. Literally I could have confessed to you what you had stated as your confession of love: 'You alone are real.' In this sense we became mates even before we became friends, and were befriended hardly through choice but through similarly complete espousings. Not two halves sought each other in us: it was a surprised entity which recognized itself awesomely in ungraspable unity. In this fahion then, we were brother and sister—although as in ancient times before brother and sister marriage had become a sacrilege."

### 3—*To Survive is All*

1. The original lines of those translated here are found in the poems to Clara, SW III, within pp. 711–55, published in 1959.
2. Exemplary translations of these works were made by C. Craig Houston, *RMR: Selected Works*, I.
3. Holthusen, *RMR in Selbstzeugnissen*, p. 86.
4. *Rilke's Craftsmanship*, p. 193.
5. Letter to Clara, Dec. 17, 1906.
6. Translated from the French text of the letter to Mimi Romanelli, May 11, 1910. Rilke's initial letters to Mimi contained such extravagences as "Mon coeur continue de vous contempler tout à genoux."
7. Gottfried Benn (1866–1956), a figure as controversial in German literature as Pound is in American letters, attests to the fame of Rilke's line by saying that it was one "that my generation will never forget"; *Primal Vision: Selected Writings* (New York, 1960), p. 113. When Benn equated Rilke's thought with his own pessimism that followed his espousal of Nazi ambitions up to 1934, he was guilty of taking the line out of context. Benn's acidic and grudging view of Rilke as a "meager person and font of great poetry," seems to be motivated primarily by Rilke's cosmopolitanism.
8. The extracts for the most part are from the *Letters to a Young Poet*, translated by M. D. Herter Norton.

### 4—*Love is Fear*

1. The *Malte* quotes in this chapter are from the fine translation by John Linton, *The Journal of My Other Self*.
2. Marie, p. 19. Rilke ends his letter of July 21, 1911 to Marie with the following: ". . . and so I close and leave everything for the good time soon to come, in which you must really turn me into a *Dottor Serafico*. . . . In the meanwhile still—*il Dottor Provvisorio*." Marie's *Reminiscences* then state: "*Serafico*, as I now always called Rilke . . ."
3. SW III, 699–700.

4. Other representative examples may be found in such books as *Dürers Marienleben nebst einer Auswahl der schönsten Marienlegenden und alten deutschen Marienlieder*, Deutsche Buch-Gemeinschaft, Berlin, undated.

5. The composer Paul Hindemith ingeniously has caught the shifts in Rilke's poetry and has fashioned the various sections of the Mary cycle into passacaglia, 14th century motet, and Gregorian passages.

6. *Fiktiv-emotionale Phantasiekraft* is an apt phrase used by Fülleborn to characterize Rilke's extraordinary capacity to make the products of his inventions synonymous with life experience. In that sense, poetry is life to Rilke. One may also call this phenomenon *controlled* hallucination, dream, or vision because although Rilke succumbs to it, he always manages to return from the borderland he mentions in the diaries and essays.

7. Letter to Marie, December 16, 1913.

8. Monique Saint-Hélier in describing the difference in personality between the two friends André Gide and Rilke comments that Rilke saw things by closing his eyes. "Deux Visages d'André Walter," *Nouvelle Revue Française* (Nov., 1951).

## 5—Arms Cannot Hold Me

1. Lasard, p. 17.

2. *Ibid.*, p. 133.

3. "Lippen," lips, in the second line is replaced by "Munden," mouths, in SW II,219. Mrs. Lasard's version probably is the more correct for reasons of parallelism; similarly, in the third and fourth lines, Rilke repeats "Arme."

4. Rilke's proclivity for short, fiery attachments is illustrated in the report given by Maurice Betz, Rilke's French translator and biographer, about offers from many women to sell "rendezvous" cards and letters written in the poet's hand. Don Juanism in the life and work of Rilke has not escaped biographers and critics (an aspect concisely reviewed by Graff, p. 173 ff.). The ideas of desireless bliss, self-sufficiency in love, narcissism, and the ability to excite love were his own attributes which he projects into the figures of Christ and angel.

5. SW II, 435–38.

6. Rilke's prose version of the thought in poetry reads: "Lovers do not live out of the detached here-and-now; as no division had ever been undertaken, they enter into the enormous possession of their heart, of them one may say that God becomes real to them and that death does not harm them:*for being full of life, they are full of death*." (Letter, Nov. 8, 1915.)

7. Lasard, p. 146.

8. As early as September, 1900, an entry in Rilke's diary reads: "I will submit to snow for the sake of a coming spring, so that what germinates in me will not rise prematurely out of the furrows." Winter for Rilke is a season where a mysterious inward turning of the earth takes place, "an inward swing," a biological withdrawal and gathering of sap infused with the strength of the dead to give courage to the spring ahead. In the *Sonnets to Orpheus* (I, 4; I, 6), all this is restated emphatically. Other notable instances occur in the "Tenth Elegy" ("Sorrow is our winter foliage") and in the beautiful poem "Ô Lacrimosa" which was put to music by Ernst Křenck.

## 6—Being Here Means Much

1. *Letters to Frau Gudi Nölke*, p. 99 f.

2. Bassermann, *Der Andere Rilke*, p. 100.

3. SW II, 130–32 and 457–60.

4. To Marie, July 25, 1921.

5. Translated from "Solang du Selbstgeworfenes fängst," SW II, 132.

6. Technically, the Rilkean Orpheus sonnet has 14 lines: 2 quatrains and 2 triplets. The metrical scheme consists of abab or abba endline rhymes in the quatrains while in the triplets there is a dazzling variation that most often links the triplets to each other. Frequently the rhyme words are trisyllabic. In these respects Rilke breaks with the classical sonnet and achieves a natural rhyme and sound cadence whose graceful expression have no peer in modern poetry.

7. In the poem cycle there is the barest Rilkean suggestion that because Orpheus doubted the reality of the other world and turned back to life did he lose Eurydice. For the most part, however, Rilke insists that Orpheus belongs to both worlds.

8. Letter to Countess Margot Sizzo-Noris Crouy, dated "Epiphany [January 6], 1923." Since the countess was a new acquaintance, Rilke regaled her with his noble genealogy, "I am the last male member of my clan;" but more important in the letter is his clear and detailed exposition of his thoughts on immanence (the dead live within us), the affinity of man and nature in this life and the absorption of man into nature as part of nature after life, and the idea that death is the averted and complementary side of life.

9. Rilke strenuously asserted that his thoughts are rooted in European cultural traditions. Some of his ideas, however, do bear a resemblance to Eastern thought, especially in regard to the equivalence of immanence and transcendence and the perfect reconciliation of contradictions, but Rilke departs in at least one major respect by not accepting the possibility of identity loss.

10. An earlier version of these ideas are contained in Rilke's *Stories of the Dear God*, written more than a decade earlier: "A fence, a house, a well—all these things are indeed of human making. But when they stand in the landscape for some time and have taken on characteristics of the trees and shrubs and other environment, they come into the possession of God and by the same token into the possession of the artist. For God and the artist have the same inheritance and the same poverty." (SW IV, 372)

11. Rilke, who was quite knowledgeable about the Egyptian death cults, may have known the myths in which the dead wander as stars across the heavens. Star images abound in the elegies.

12. Rilke discusses "catkinology" with Frau Amman-Volkert in a letter, undated but most likely written in December, 1922, supporting the view that Rilke had been quietly working on parts of the last elegies before announcing his calendar of Elegy-days.

13. Mason, *Lebenshaltung*, pp. 131–86 points to the host of interpretations which the symbols of this elegy have gathered.

14. Rilke ascribes to the word "smile" a mystic significance in that it "represents the consent of the Spirit to reside within us" (SW II, 455), a creation resulting from the interplay between male and female. In the elegy, the boy's smile is as hopeful as a lover's. In the draft versions, Rilke

capitalized smile, LÄCHELN, but then replaced it with the word meaning healing-herb, *Heilkraut*. In the paraphrase here, I have drawn from all versions.

15. Leishman and Spender, p. 51.

16. Letter to Countess Crouy, June 1, 1923.

17. To Countess Crouy, April 12, 1923. The difference of subtlety in poetic treatment of the anemone analogy may easily be marked between Rilke's sonnet here and the poem "Migliera," written in February, 1907: "Close, close tight your eyes / . . . And still, you know, we can then at evening close like anemones, / enclosing within the happenings of a day / . . . that is what we are here for: to learn a closing up / over infinitude." (SW II, 19) The associations are richer in the sonnet. How extremely personal and intense analogies can be for Rilke is seen in a letter to Lou, in June, 1914, in which he compares himself to an anemone he saw that had opened so wide during the day that it could not close at night. He thought the sight of the anemone's "frantically torn open calyx" to be dreadful: "I too am turned so helplessly outward, hence distraught too by everything, refusing nothing . . . if there is a noise, I give myself up and *am* that noise, and since everything once adjusted to stimulation wants to be stimulated, so at bottom I want to be disturbed . . ." Rilke calls on these feelings as the reasons "why all kindness of people and nature remains wasted" on him.

## 7—*Rose, Oh Pure Contradiction*

1. Katharina Kippenberg, *RMR*. (Leipzig, 1948), p. 329.

2. Letters, August 17 and October 21, 1924.

3. *Lettres milanaises*, p. 92. In the exchange of letters with the Duchess Aurelia Gallarati Scotti there are occasions when duchess and Rilke heatedly disagree on the merits of Mussolini during his rise to power. If Rilke is to be taken to task for alleged sympathies with fascism, as the English critic Mason has done, then such astute political luminaries as Churchill were guilty of the same shortsightedness in assessing the early Mussolini.

4. Occasionally Rilke sees a qualitative difference be-

tween life and death: "Unstable scale of life / ever swaying
. . . / Beyond the tranquil scale of death / . . ." (SW
II, 171; mid-July, 1924).

5. Valuable first-hand information about Rilke's work
habits and out-loud thinking is contained in Marga Wertheimer's recollections, *Arbeitsstunden mit RMR* (Zürich-
New York, 1940).

6. That Rilke referred to Valéry as the magician is clear
from Rilke's poem "Le Magicien" (SW II, 649).

7. The word "frühen" should be translated as "early,"
but the sense refers to Rilke's earlier and previous transition
periods. In a narrower sense, he uses this idea in describing
his joy in successfully translating Valéry, an act of art that
permitted him to bridge the contrary malaises of his body.

8. In a conversation with Gide, Rilke expressed his
dissatisfaction with the German word "Handfläche" because
it can refer either to the back or the inside of the hand;
hence, Rilke's deliberate circumlocution, "Innres der Hand,"
to approximate the grace and feeling of "palm."

9. Letter to Arthur Fischer-Colbrie, December 18, 1925.

10. *Rilke-Taxis Letters*, pp. 267–69.

# SELECTED BIBLIOGRAPHY

## MAJOR BIBLIOGRAPHY

Mason, Eudo C. *Rilke's Apotheosis: A Survey of Representative Recent Publications on the Work of RMR.* Oxford, 1938.

*RMR: Katalog der Rilke-Sammlung Richard von Mises,* ed. Paul Obermüller. Frankfurt, in press. (This represents a comprehensive updating of von Mises' *Rilke in English: A tentative bibliography,* Cambridge [Mass.], 1947.)

Ritzer, Walter. *RMR: Bibliographie.* Wien, 1951.

## WORKS AND LETTERS

*Ausgewählte Werke,* ed. Ernst Zinn. Vol. I, vol. II, Leipzig, 1948.

*Correspondence in Verse with Erika Mitterer.* Translated by N. V. Cruickshank. London, 1953.

*From the Remains of Count C. W.* Translated by J. B. Leishman, London, 1952.

*The Journal of My Other Self.* Translated by John Linton. New York, 1930.

*Letters of RMR.* Translated by Jane Bannard Greene and M. D. Herter Norton. Vol. I, 1892–1910; vol. II, 1910–1926. New York, 1945, 1947.

*The Letters of RMR and Princess Marie von Thurn und Taxis.* Translated by Nora Wydenbruck. New York, 1958.

*Letters to Frau Gudi Nölke.* Translated by Violet M. MacDonald. London, 1955.

*Letters to a Young Poet.* Translated by M. D. Herter Norton. New York, 1954.

*Letters to Merline, 1919–1922.* Translated by Violet M. MacDonald. London, 1951.

*The Life of the Virgin Mary*. Translated by Stephen Spender. New York, 1951.

*Poems from the Book of Hours*. Translated by Babette Deutsch. Norfolk: Conn., 1941.

*RMR-André Gide Briefwechsel, 1909–1926*, ed. Reneé Lang. Wiesbaden, 1957. (Translated by Wolfgang A. Peters from the French, *RMR-André Gide Correspondence*. Paris. 1952.)

*RMR, Bücher, Theater. Kunst*, ed. Richard von Mises. Vienna, 1934.

*RMR, Duino Elegies*. Translated by J. B. Leishman and Stephen Spender. New York, 1939.

*RMR: Fifty Selected Poems*. Translated by C. F. MacIntyre. (2nd edition) Berkeley, 1940.

*RMR, Lettres milanaises: 1921–1926*, ed. Reneé Lang. Paris, 1956.

*RMR: Lou Andreas-Salomé Briefwechsel*, ed. Ernst Pfeiffer. Zürich, 1952.

*RMR: Sämtliche Werke*, ed. with notes by Ernst Zinn. Vol. I, Wiesbaden, 1955; vol. II, 1957; vol. III, 1959; vol. IV, 1961. (Vol. I includes all previously published major and minor poetic works; vol. II contains Rilke's French poems and scattered as well as posthumous German poems from 1906–1926; vol. III has poems from 1884 to 1905, including first versions and previously unpublished poems; vol. IV has Rilke's short stories and sketches, several previously unpublished, and all of his dramas; vol. V is in press and is expected to appear in two books that contain Rilke's fiction, including *Malte Laurids Brigge*, essays on art, and theater and book reviews by Rilke from 1896 to 1905.)

*RMR: Selected Works*. Vol. I (Prose), translated by G. Craig Houston; vol. II (Poetry) tr. J. B. Leishman, New York, 1960.

*RMR: Tagebücher aus der Frühzeit*. Leipzig, 1942.

*Selected Letters of RMR*, ed. Harry T. Moore, New York, 1960.

*Sonnets to Orpheus*. Translated by M. D. Herter Norton. New York, 1942.

*Thirty-One Poems by Rainer Maria Rilke*. Translated by Ludwig Lewisohn. New York, 1946.

*Translations from the Poetry of Rainer Maria Rilke*, by M. D. Herter Norton. New York, 1938.

BIOGRAPHY AND CRITICISM

Albert-Lasard, Lou. *Wege mit Rilke*. Frankfurt a.M., 1952.

Andreas-Salomé, Lou. *Lebensrückblick. Grundriss einiger Lebenserinnerungen.* Zürich/Wiesbaden, 1951.

Angelloz, J. -F. *RMR: L'évolution spirituelle du poète.* Paris, 1936.

Basserman, Dieter. *Am Rande des Unsagbaren.* Berlin/ Buxtehude, 1948.

————. *Der Andere Rilke.* Bad Homburg, 1961.

Bauer, Marga. *RMR und Frankreich.* Bern, 1931.

Belmore, Herbert W. *Rilke's Craftsmanship, An Analysis of his Poetic Style.* Oxford, 1954.

Betz, Maurice. *Rilke in Paris.* Translated into German by Willi Reich. Zürich, 1948.

Bollnow, Otto Friedrich. *Rilke* (2nd edition). Stuttgart, 1956.

Buchheit, Gert (ed.). *RMR: Stimmen der Freunde.* Freiburg im Brg., 1931.

Buddeberg, Else. *RMR: Eine innere Biographie.* Stuttgart, 1955.

Butler, E. M. *RMR.* Cambridge [Eng.], 1941.

Cassirer-Solmitz, Eva. *RMR.* (Offset) Heidelberg, 1957.

Demetz, Peter. *René Rilkes Prager Jahre.* Düsseldorf, 1953.

Emde, Ursula. *Rilke und Rodin.* Marburg/Lahn, 1949.

Fülleborn, Ulrich. *Das Strukturproblem der Späten Lyrik Rilkes.* (Diss.) Heidelberg, 1960.

Fürst, Norbert. *Phases of Rilke.* Indiana, 1958.

Gebser, Hans. *Rilke und Spanien.* (2nd edition) Zürich, 1946.

Graff, W. L. *RMR: Creative Anguish of a Modern Poet.* Princeton, 1956.

Grossmann, Dietrich. *RMR und der Französische Symbolismus.* (Diss.) Jena, 1938.

Guardini, Romano. *Zu RMRs Deutung des Daseins.* (2nd edition) Bern, 1946. (Translated from the 1953 edition by K. G. Knight as *Rilke's Duino Elegies.* London, 1961.)

Hartman, Geoffrey H. *The Unmediated Vision: An Interpretation of Wordsworth, Hopkins, Rilke, and Valéry.* New Haven, 1954.

Heerikhuizen, F. W. van. *RMR: His Life and Work.* Translated from the Dutch by Fernand G. Renier and Anne Cliff. New York, 1952.

Heller, Erich, *The Disinherited Mind.* New York, 1957.

Holthusen, Hans Egon. *RMR: A Study of His Later Poetry.* Translated by J. B. Stern. New Haven, 1952.

———. *Rilkes Sonette an Orpheus.* München, 1937.

———. *RMR in Selbstzeugnissen und Bilddokumenten.* Reinbeck bei Hamburg, 1958.

Jaloux, Edmond (biographical essay contributor). *RMR: His Last Friendship.* Translated from the French by W. H. Kennedy. New York, 1952.

Kaufmann, Walter. *From Shakespeare to Existentialism.* New York, 1960.

Koenig, Hertha, *Rilkes Mutter,* Tübinger, 1963.

Kohlschmidt, Werner. *Rilke-Interpretationen.* Lahr, 1948.

Kreutz, Heinrich. *Rilkes Duineser Elegien.* München, 1950.

Mason, Eudo C. *Lebenshaltung und Symbolik bei Rainer Marie Rilke.* Weimar, 1939.

———. *Rilke, Europe, and the English-Speaking World.* Cambridge [Eng.], 1961.

Mövius, Ruth. *RMRs Stunden-Buch: Enstehung und Gehalt.* Leipzig, 1937.

Oppeln-Bronikowski, Friedrich von. *RMR.* Dortmund, 1907.

Peters, H. F. *RMR: Masks and the Man.* Seattle, 1960.

Pitrou, Robert. *RMR, Les thèmes principaux de son oeuvre.* Paris, 1938.

Rehm, Walther. *Orpheus: Der Dichter und die Toten.* Düsseldorf, 1950.

Rose, William and G. Craig Houston (eds.). *RMR: Aspects of His Mind and Poetry,* introduction by Stefan Zweig. London, 1938.

Schnack, Ingeborg (ed.). *Rilkes Leben und Werk im Bild.* With a biographical essay by J. R. von Salis. Wiesbaden, 1956.

Sewell, Elizabeth. *The Orphic Voice: Poetry and Natural History.* New Haven, 1960.

Sieber, Carl. *René Rilke: Die Jugend RMRs.* Leipzig, 1932.

Sievers, Marianne. *Die biblischen Motive in der Dichtung Rainer Maria Rilkes.* Berlin, 1938.

Simenauer, Erich. *RMR: Legende und Mythos.* Bern, 1953.

Wohltmann, Hans. *RMR in Worpswede.* Hamburg, 1949.

Wood, Frank. *RMR: The Ring of Forms.* Minnesota, 1958.

Wydenbruck, Nora. *Rilke, Man and Poet.* London, 1949.

# INDEX